Volkswagen Sport Tuning for Street and Competition

Getting the Best Performance from Your Water-Cooled Volkswagen

by Per Schroeder

RB www.BentleyPublishers.com

CONTENTS

Checking for unibody straightness, p. 6

Front spring shock installation, pp. 38–41

Brake upgrade kit, p. 76

Aftermarket chip installation, pp. 98–101

High-quality aftermarket spark plug wires, p. 120

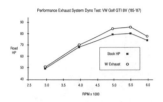

Power gain for an A2 GTI with exhaust upgrade, p. 148

Differential shim kit, p. 166

Roll cage reinforce-ments, p. 189

Copies of this book may be purchased from selected booksellers, or directly from the publisher by mail. The publisher encourages comments from the reader of this book. These communications have been and will be considered in the preparation of this and other manuals. Please write to Robert Bentley, Inc., Publishers at the address listed on the top of this page.

Since this page cannot legibly accommodate all the copyright notices, the Art Credits page at the back of this book listing the source of the photographs used constitutes an extension of the copyright page.

Library of Congress Cataloging-in-Publication Data

Schroeder, Per, 1971–.
    Volkswagen sport tuning for street and competition: getting the best performance from your water-cooled Volkswagen / Per Schroeder.
        p. cm.
    Includes index.
    ISBN 0-8376-0161-4 (alk. paper)
    1. Volkswagen automobile--Performance. 2. Volkswagen automobile--Maintenance and repair.   I. Title.
TL215.V6S3575 1997
629.28'722--dc21   97-31225
                                                   CIP

Bentley Stock No. GVHW

05 04 03 02 10 9 8 7 6 5 4

The paper used in this publication is acid free and meets the requirements of the National Standard for Information Sciences-Permanence of Paper for Printed Library Materials. ∞

Volkswagen Sport Tuning for Street and Competition, by Per Schroeder

©1997 Per Schroeder and Robert Bentley, Inc.

Manufactured in the United States of America

Front cover: Photo by Peter Wu.

Back cover: (clockwise from top right) a) Autocrossing Jetta, photo courtesy of Bob Tunnell; b) Red Cabrio, photo courtesy of New Dimensions; c) Aftermarket computer chip installation, photo courtesy of New Dimensions; d) Evil GTI, photo courtesy of Les Bidrawn; e) Autocrossing Jetta, photo courtesy of Per Schroeder; f) A3 VW 2.0-liter engine with turbocharger, photo courtesy of New Dimensions.

BENTLEY PUBLISHERS | Automotive Books & Manuals

Bentley Publishers, a division of Robert Bentley, Inc.
1734 Massachusetts Avenue
Cambridge, MA 02138 USA   *Information that makes*
800-423-4595 / 617-547-4170   *the difference®*
www.
BentleyPublishers
                    .com

Preface

Author Per Schroeder.

This book will serve as a guide to those looking to improve the performance of their water-cooled Volkswagen, both for street driving and grassroots racing. The term "grassroots" refers to racing where fun and competition are not eclipsed by the amount of money you must spend on your car. If you are looking to improve the capabilities of your street vehicle, the only limits that are imposed are those of a financial nature and federal regulations. If, however, you're looking to improve a car that is used for racing, then in addition to cost constraints, you must check with your sanctioning body for the rules concerning the class in which your car competes.

Do not be surprised if the street and racing recommendations are similar. The racing classes discussed in this book are all designed for street-legal cars; in fact most are still street-driveable. Racing and street needs are nearly the same in that the car needs to be reliable, durable, and well balanced. The only difference is that in a street car you will probably want to compromise more toward comfort than performance.

Throughout this book, there are several installation how-tos: they are meant to serve as a *general* guide to installation. More complete installation methods can be found in the Bentley service manuals. Because the torque settings for different fasteners will vary from application to application, no ft/lb figures are included for these installations: these figures can also be found in the appropriate service manual.

If you want to prepare your car for street performance or occasional autocross, you can use the sport tuning recommendations for the ultimate Volkswagen in various ways. If handling is the most important characteristic to you, a mild engine and racing specification suspension can be paired. This is probably the best way to go for someone who is first learning high-performance driving. It will teach you an important lesson in race driving: if you keep cornering speed high, you offset weak acceleration on the straights. If you want high horsepower and phenomenal handling, you can start with a full racing suspension and add a larger-displacement motor. Since the rules for racing categories are unimportant to street drivers, any combination is possible—in short, don't think that the recommendations in this book only apply to each specific racing category. There are endless combinations of modifications you can make. Think about what is most important to you in your car and what changes you are willing to make. Then go out and have fun!

A hint as to how the author spends his weekends. Autocrossing allows a street-driven car a place to race.

As you're dreaming up the perfect modification plan for your needs, do remember that one of the many keys to satisfactory high performance tuning is to balance the way you modify your car. A well-engineered car is a balance of superior handling, braking and horsepower. Don't let one area of the car become the focus of all your attention.

The high-performance goals you want to reach are not the only things to consider: sometimes, an experience you have determines how you start modifying your car. A fellow autocrosser was hit by a drunk driver, putting him in the hospital and totaling his daily driver/weekend racer. The first modification that found its way into his next car was a full rollcage and five point racing harness.

Changing your car from the original configuration is a process of individualization—what you change says a lot about who you are. People who are concerned with style and that custom "look" will have different priorities, but if you're a Volkswagen enthusiast who is genuinely concerned with performance, this book is written especially for you.

It would be impossible to thank everyone who has helped with this book along the way. Some people, however, have gone above and beyond for me on this journey. They include: Raffi Kazanjian, Jeff Moss, Tim Hildabrand, Bob Tunnell, Jimmy Hutchinson, and Jason Plummer.

Finally, this book is dedicated to the two most influential people in my life: my wife, Chris, who has been there with a helping hand always, and my dad, who gave me (or rather, infected me with) the love of cars, racing, and taking things apart (and sometimes even putting them back together. . . .)

Fig. 1. The Beetle and early enthusiasts. The 1954 on the right has a popular modification for the early days: the factory steel wheels are installed backwards, yielding a wider track for improved cornering.

In 1949, when Heinz Nordhoff and Ben Pon imported the first two Volkswagens into the country, few realized the impact that these automobiles would have on the look of American roadways. The homely little Volkswagen became widely known in the next decade, and an outright success story in the sixties.

Volkswagens had many advantages over other cars of the era, two of which were personality and a quality driving experience. Volkswagen's air-cooled Beetle was so much fun to drive that it started showing up at local automobile racing events. There, it competed against the "real" sports cars of the times such as M.G.s and Triumphs, often winning. This easy transformation from a frugal vehicle to a fun racing car spawned many enthusiasts of the marque. These early pioneers in VW modification paved the way to today's high-performance Golfs, Jettas, and Corrados.

Fig. 2. Today's Volkswagen aftermarket tuners produce cars, such as this Cabrio, with a combination of great looks, excellent handling and acceleration, and more refinement than a Beetle owner could ever believe.

Fig. 3. One reason for Volkswagen's popularity is their ease of modification. This late '80s GTI is transformed with European bumpers, grille, and an aftermarket front spoiler.

THE WATER-COOLED VOLKSWAGEN

Starting with model year 1975, Volkswagen entered a new era in automotive manufacturing with the water-cooled Rabbit and Scirocco (A1 chassis). The front-wheel-drive chassis, coupled with excellent road manners and plenty of room for both passengers and luggage, was a genuine rarity. Europe got the legendary GTI early on, but this side of the pond had to wait until model year 1983. The original "Hot Hatch" became a staple of Volkswagen performance tuning. Later, the Fox was introduced as a low-price leader. Its chassis design was unique, but the engine and fuel injection were straight out of an A1 car.

Ten years after the introduction of the first Rabbit, VW replaced the aging bunny with the Golf and Jetta 2. Slightly larger than its older brethren, the A2 cars boasted more horsepower and better handling. Its styling was evolutionary and more aerodynamic than its predecessor, while its interior swallowed five adults and mountains of luggage. The base-level Golfs and Jettas were no overstuffed cruisers; they outhandled and outran the original GTI. The revised GTI got even more horsepower, four wheel disc brakes, and an excellently balanced chassis. In model year 1990, the Corrado and Passat were introduced, creating new variables for high-performance tuning. Essentially, these cars were an evolutionary step between the A2 and the later A3 chassis.

In model year 1993, Volkswagen introduced the Golf and Jetta 3 (A3 chassis), adding improvements in sound deadening and creature comforts, which also added weight. With only ten more hp than the one it replaced, the new base Golf weighed 300 lbs. more than the old one. Clearly, this is not the best set-up for maneuverability and outright acceleration. With the introduction of the narrow angle VR6, the hp-to-weight ratio improved drastically; but the VR6 GTI, at 2700 lbs., is still heavier than most enthusiasts would like. To put this into perspective, the original GTI weighed about 700 lbs. less than the new VR6 GTI, and even the first few years of the A2 GTI weighed 550 lbs. less.

Fig. 4. The Rabbit has become a staple of aftermarket tuning because of its low price, light weight, and ease of modification.

Fig. 5. The Scirocco is very popular in grassroots racing. This E-Prepared autocrosser has been stripped of all amenities and non-essential parts, creating a lightweight racer.

Fig. 6. The A2 GTI ushered in a new era of performance; the tinkering enthusiasts were quick to modify this pocket rocket. This 1986 example shows a Vestatec aerodynamic body kit imported from Germany.

Fig. 7. The VR6 Corrado is both a luxury touring coupe and a weekend racer. SCCA has recently reclassed this car into G-stock, where it has great potential.

Fig. 8. The much awaited VR6 GTI has thrilled some and disappointed others. While offering horsepower and refinement, it has lost the raw personality of the A1 and A2 GTIs.

MODIFICATION BASICS

Your VW can be broken down into many subsystems: engine, suspension, brakes, etc. These systems are a series of compromises made by the automotive manufacturer to provide the most value and quality for the money and marketplace. These compromises are good in some ways for some people, but you are not just anybody: you are a Volkswagen aficionado, a VW nut, so to speak. This means that your VW should be different than the run-of-the-mill automobile. Luckily, you can modify the various subsystems to provide whatever mixture of comfort, acceleration, or handling that you desire.

The engine of the water-cooled VW was designed to provide good power and good fuel economy while still allowing low noise, low maintenance, and low emissions. If it seems that these requirements contradict each other, you're right. To produce power, the engine has to inhale air and fuel, ignite them, harness the released energy, and expel the burnt gases. The more fuel and air that can be ignited, the more power the engine will produce. Unfortunately, the more fuel that is burnt, the lower the gas mileage will be, and the exhaust emis-

Fig. 9. Your engine makes power by inhaling as much air and fuel as possible, igniting it and then expelling it. The turbo on this A3 engine simply tries to force more air into the combustion chamber for more power.

sions can be high. It is hard to modify one thing in this series without affecting another, so you have to be careful and not blindly rush in with a wrench.

The exhaust system is a good example of give and take. On most VWs, it was designed to be cheap to produce, long lasting, and quiet. This is both good and bad. The bad news is that your car is not producing as much power as it could be. The stock exhaust system is just too restrictive. The good news is that with a simple change of an exhaust system, your car will have more power and accelerate faster. For this reason, the exhaust system is one of the first places that you should look for more power. Be advised, however: a larger exhaust system with a less restrictive muffler leads to higher noise levels. This could be a problem for some people, and a good thing for others, depending on your perspective.

Other engine modifications will also capitalize on the fact that the engine is not much more than a large pump. Increasing intake airflow to a specific engine will increase power up to a point, as will a less restrictive exhaust. Different air filters, throttle bodies, intake manifolds, and even camshafts all will

Fig. 10. Because of restrictions in the stock exhaust system, VWs can benefit greatly from the installation of an aftermarket exhaust. The only tradeoff incurred with this stainless steel unit from New Dimensions is a slightly higher noise level.

increase airflow into the engine to create more power. The compromise here is the fact that more air usually means more intake noise or even less low-end torque if taken to an extreme.

One important point to consider when modifying a front-wheel-drive VW is how much power the chassis can actually handle. VWs do have a handicap that is next to impossible to remedy. Wheelspin will limit how fast all A1, A2, and A3 cars can accelerate from a standstill. A 130 hp and a 200 hp Rabbit with a limited slip and street tires will accelerate at nearly the same 7-second 0–60 mph time. Even equipped with racing tires, the front-wheel-drive Volkswagen has what is called in drag racing parlance "slow 80-foot times," meaning it accelerates slowly during the first 80 feet of a drag start. As the car accelerates, weight is transferred backwards, reducing traction to the front wheels; the higher horsepower will only come into play at higher speeds when the car settles down and weight transfers to the front.

A quick note on horsepower and torque. Torque is the amount of force that an engine can produce (in lb./ft.) while horsepower is the amount of force that engine can produce at a certain RPM ((lb./ft.) x RPM/5252). These forces are measured on a dynamometer, which can be either an engine dynamometer where the engine has to be out of the car, or a chassis dynamometer, which measures hp and torque available at the wheels and takes into account how much power is lost due to the drivetrain and engine accessories (about 20%).

Fig. 11. This ITB car is undergoing a chassis dynamometer run to tune the fuel injection system. A chassis dyno measures horsepower at the wheels, which is the power available after all other drivetrain losses are figured in.

Throughout this book, I will often state that a certain modification can give X amount more horsepower: keep in mind that these are average gains that depend on the individual engine and mods that have been done. There is also a limit to the absolute hp that an engine can obtain. A 1.8-liter 8-valve engine would be hard pressed to put out more than 140 hp in street trim, while a 2.0-liter 16-valve might be able to top 170, but it would be hard to get there.

It is hard to produce an engine that has both good low-end torque and lots of horsepower at high RPM. Low-end torque often relies on the high velocity of the air/fuel mixture and exhaust gas, while peak horsepower is determined by the volume of gas that is moved (within reason). While peak horsepower will sell parts, it is torque that will pull the car from a stop. For most street and Solo

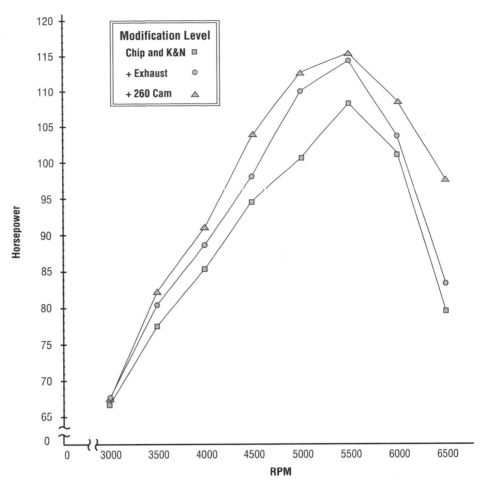

Fig. 12. Chassis dyno figures for a 2.0 liter A3 car, showing hp gains as the RPM rises. Note that these numbers are about 20% lower than numbers that are found using an engine dyno.

ll applications, stay away from any modification that will hurt low-end torque to gain peak horsepower. The car with such a modification will only perform well once the engine is turning at high RPM. Since most driving is done under 4000 RPM, the added hp is usually not useable.

The next main system that undergoes this give and take between performance, comfort, and cost is the suspension system. In order for a car to be comfortable over bumps and pot holes, it needs to have a suspension with large amounts of wheel travel, soft bushings that absorb vibrations from the road, and soft springs and shock absorbers. Unfortunately, large amounts of wheel

Fig. 13. This A3 Jetta has been fitted with shorter and stiffer springs, to lower the center of gravity and limit body roll. The tradeoff is that it is firmer over bumps and allows for less wheel travel.

travel usually mean that the car will have a higher center of gravity. Soft bushings will mean that the suspension will move more within its mounts when the car is cornered hard, making the car unsteady through the corner. Soft springs will allow large amounts of body roll, which will allow extreme suspension geometry changes and reduce the contact patch of the tires.

The happy medium will depend on your needs. For cars that primarily see track use or smooth roads, springs that lower the center of gravity, harder suspension bushings (to reduce geometry change), and stiffer spring rates (to reduce body roll) will make the car handle very well, except on roads in poor condition, which require more suspension travel and shock absorbance.

TOOLS

For the average shade-tree mechanic, there is a basic selection of tools that come in handy while working on a VW. Your selection of sockets, both deep and shallow, should range from 7 mm through 22 mm. A basic 3/8-in. drive ratchet will work fine in most instances, while stuck chassis and suspension fasteners might require a 1/2-in. drive breaker bar. The same assortment of open end/box end wrenches should be obtained. Be sure to get an extra 13-mm and 17-mm wrench and socket. You will find that Wolfsburg loves to assemble VWs with fasteners in these sizes.

The spark plugs on all 8-valve, non-crossflow-head cars require a 13/16-in. socket, while 16-valves and crossflow 8-valves use a 5/8-in. socket. Two sets of metric hex wrenches should be purchased: both the standard L-shaped and the socket type. If you are planning on changing brake lines, a metric flare nut wrench (10-mm, usually) will prevent you from stripping the fragile lines. Universal slip-joint pliers and locking pliers should only be used on stubborn bolts and nuts that will not budge with normal tools. A selection of screwdrivers, both phillips-head and flathead, will be required. Finally, for repairs needing more finesse, a hammer can be obtained.

There are some tools that are needed for fixing and modifying your VW that are not available at your local hardware store. Here are some of the most common of these tools; you can find them either at a VW tuner or through a professional tool supplier.

Fig. 14. This is the socket that is used for removing the slotted nut on an A2 or A3 strut. It is used together with a 22-mm socket or wrench.

Fig. 15. This tool is used to adjust the shift linkage on A2 and A3 4-cylinder cars. It precisely positions the shift lever and rod so that the linkages in the engine compartment can be aligned correctly.

To remove springs from your struts, you will need a coil spring compressor, which will safely compress the spring enough to remove the hardware that attaches it to your strut. To remove the entire strut and spring assembly from the front of your A2 or A3, you will need a special socket for the slotted nut on the strut bearing. To adjust the shift linkage on 4-cylinder cars, you need a shift linkage adjuster that positions your lever in the proper position while being clamped to the rest of the linkage system. To adjust your CIS fuel injection, you will need a CO (3-mm hex) wrench. Essentially, this is a 3-mm hex wrench with a long T-handle. Finally, removing the car's oxygen sensor will require an oxygen sensor socket. This tool allows you to safely remove the sensor without damaging it.

The electrical system in a VW is normally trouble free; nonetheless, a tool box should include some tools for electrical repair work. A soldering gun and rosin core solder will attach wires much more reliably than a plastic crimp-type connector. To protect the exposed wiring from shorting, use a high-quality

Fig. 16. An oxygen sensor socket has a slot in it which allows you to slide it over the wiring.

electrical tape or heat-shrink tubing. An assortment of pliers, including needle-nose, diagonal cutting, and wire stripping, are helpful with electrical repairs. Electrical diagnostics can be performed more easily with a digital multimeter with a high-input impedance. And finally, a timing light with adjustable advance will allow you to change the engine timing to factory or high-performance specifications.

Basic maintenance such as changing your oil will require an oil filter wrench, a drain pan of at least 5-quart capacity, and a funnel. The stock jack was only designed for emergency roadside repairs; a hydraulic floor jack and jackstands will lift and support your car safely during maintenance or modification. To prevent ruining all of your clothes, try to keep some clothes for repair and maintenance work only. Shop overalls are the normal choice but grungy jeans and tee-shirts work just as well. A single repair procedure involving molydisulfide wheel bearing or CV-joint grease will trash most clothing. Many professional mechanics also use latex surgical gloves to keep their hands clean and safe from toxic substances such as motor oil or CV-joint grease.

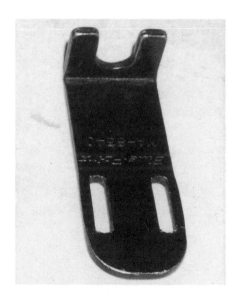

Fig. 17. An injector remover is used as a little pry bar. The rounded opening in the end fits around the injector; you pry it out using a screwdriver inserted into either of the two rectangular slots.

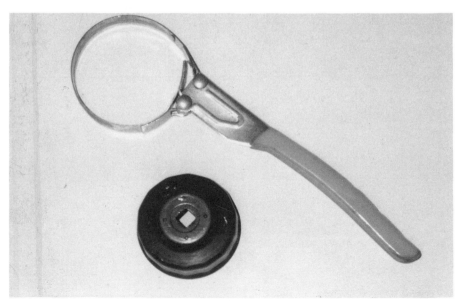

Fig. 18. The band-type oil filter wrench works well on VWs.

Fig. 19. Jack stands should always be used when working under any car.

KNOWLEDGE

The entire tool selection at Sears or the contents of a Snap-On truck will do you no good if you do not know how to use them. If you do not already have a Bentley factory repair manual for your vehicle, go out and purchase one. You will find that it is of tremendous help in working on your car. While it is not concerned with modification, its maintenance and repair procedures are explained in such great detail that they help in all areas of performance. Remember, in order to put on a high-performance part, you first have to remove the stock one. This is where the manual is priceless.

If you are changing shock absorbers on your Volkswagen, for example, all you need to do is follow the directions in the manual for the removal of the old stock units. When that is completed, simply substitute your high-performance shock for the original one during reassembly. Anybody that can read the Bentley manual and repair their VW can do almost all high-performance modifications. If you do not feel comfortable with some procedures, don't hesitate to take your car to someone who knows how. Often, by asking around, you can find out which normal VW repair shops do not mind dabbling in high-performance modifications. Since the road to high performance always leads up, your VW mechanic knows that you will be back for more.

When working on your Volkswagen, you must follow all safety guidelines. The Bentley manual and your owner's manual go over the basic guidelines to operating and repairing a Volkswagen safely. One additional safety note that must be mentioned is to limit your "racing endeavors" to the track. There are a lot of people on the road with questionable driving talents. At higher speeds it becomes increasingly difficult to avoid them.

Magazines and books are a great source of information on building Volkswagens. Two particularly helpful magazines are *european car* and *Grassroots Motorsports*, which publish many technical and racing-oriented articles. The advertisers are usually performance oriented also, making these magazines a good source of parts. The SCCA also publishes a monthly magazine, *SportsCar*, that is free with your yearly membership fee, and it, too, is an excellent source of information and race results. Other published information sources include racing and car-oriented books. The best books for novice or experienced tuners include the following: *Secrets of Solo Racing* by Henry Watts, *Engineer to Win* by Carroll Smith (also see *Prepare to Win*, *Tune to Win*, and *Drive to Win*, all by the same author), and *Performance Handling* by Don Alexander. While not written about VWs specifically, they provide excellent explanations of the basics that apply to all cars.

Another good source for VW information is the Internet. Using search programs that are available with most access providers, you can find reams of information. Simply search using the keywords "Volkswagen" or "SCCA" and you will be given many choices. Another way to find interesting stuff, if you have UseNet access, is to find the VW water-cooled newsgroup under rec.autos.makers.vw.watercooled. Finally, you can subscribe to mail servers such as Team.Net, an autocross related group, which can also be found by running a search with the keyword "Team.Net." *Keep in mind that not all of the information that you find will be accurate.* Just because it is written does not mean it is completely true. *Always* double-check any information that you find to make sure that it wasn't posted by a helpful, but ignorant, person.

Your VW knowledge should also include developing the ability to spot a good deal when you see it. If there are two racers with the same amount of money to spend, the person who finds killer deals will be faster. A lot of parts for VWs work just as well used as new. For example, you can spend fifty dollars for a used oil cooler instead of one hundred and twenty dollars for a new one. In the street market, where wheel choice is highly fad oriented, you can find examples of the "old" popular rim for very little money. The average racer usually spends too much on his or her car, but with a little common sense, you can afford to have a fast car, have a lot of fun racing, and still eat.

Fig. 20. These Ronal wheels were purchased by the author for $200 from another enthusiast who wanted to purchase a newer, more popular wheel design.

Chapter One

THE HIGH-PERFORMANCE VOLKSWAGEN

Fig. 1-1. The water-cooled Volkswagen offers enthusiasts a myriad of options for high-performance driving. Generally speaking, the A1 chassis will excel on tight courses, while the A2 and A3 will be fast on more open courses. This A2 GTI is drifting through a high-speed sweeper at an autocross in Salina, Kansas.

Many Volkswagen enthusiasts start down the high-performance path by tuning the car they already have in their driveway for street use. If, however, you are like most enthusiasts, sooner or later you will end up embarking on a search for the perfect "project car." This car may still serve as your daily driver, but your needs as a high-performance enthusiast will be different from those of the average car buyer.

BUYING YOUR WATER-COOLED VOLKSWAGEN

The first step in the decision-making process is to determine what you need. This is entirely different from the question of what you want. What you need is determined by how you plan on using your car. If it has to be a daily driver with all of the comfort amenities, you should search accordingly. If you are planning on racing the car occasionally and comfort and gadgets are only superficially needed, other choices are available. Street drivers should concentrate on finding a later model car. The combination of lower mileage and more comfort and convenience options will make commuting less of a chore. If you are only interested in racing, the choice is both easier and harder than if you need a daily driver. Figure out what class you want to be in, then pick a car that will be competitive in that class. Competitiveness can normally be determined by a combination of weight, horsepower, and handling capability.

An example of this determination is choosing a car for D Street Prepared. The choices are: A1 Rabbit, Scirocco, or Fox; A2 Golf or Jetta; A3 Golf or Jetta. The A3 cars can be ruled out for now because of their weight and the fact that they don't have the horsepower or handling to make up for it. The Fox should be ruled out as a serious Street Prepared competitor because even though it can put out the same horsepower, and is around the same weight as a Golf or Rabbit, it is more nose-heavy due to its longitudinal engine placement. This will

Fig. 1-2. The Fox is very light, and can yield good horsepower. The downside is that its engine is set forward in the engine bay, making the car nose-heavy. This makes it less nimble on the track, but it is only slightly noticeable for street drivers.

Fig. 1-3. For road racing, this Rabbit has low weight and good handling, but a small engine. Luckily, it is classed in ITC where there are other cars with similar horsepower-to-weight ratios.

tend to make it a less balanced, understeering car on an autocross course. Its low cost and ease of modification does, however, make it an excellent choice for a street enthusiast on a budget.

The choice between the A1 and A2 chassis is subject to some debate. The A1 car can put out the same horsepower, and it weighs 200 lbs less than an A2. The A2 has better structural rigidity, balance, and therefore, handling. Finally, the choice between the Golf or Rabbit and the 2-door Jetta needs to be made. The A2 Jetta weighs approximately 30–40 lbs more than the comparable hatchback. On the other hand, the Jetta will have a stiffer rear body structure with more rear weight bias due to its notchback design. This will contribute to even more balanced and predictable handling.

The second step in buying a VW for high-performance use is to determine how much you can budget for the car. Not only does this include the purchase price, it also includes any modification, maintenance, and even racing entrance fees. It wouldn't be a lot of fun to build the fastest car in the world if you couldn't afford the entrance fee for the next race, or gas to go to work the following week. To determine what the car should cost, you could consult one of the many consumer "blue books" that are available. This will give you a rough idea of how much you are going to initially spend on the car.

Fig. 1-4. Used Rabbits are good starting points for racing projects because of their low cost and lack of creature comforts. The tired 1.6-liter engine in this one was replaced with a 16-valve motor, creating a fast, if not SCCA-legal, car.

After you know how much you can spend, search for what you want in local advertisements. There are "auto trader" publications available in many areas that only advertise cars, and some have each marque in its own category. You should try to avoid buying a used car from a dealership since they have to tack on additional costs to get a profit. Also, a private party may be able to tell you the service history of the car in question. *Sportscar*, the SCCA monthly publication, has classified ads with racing cars listed that are for sale. It is often cheaper to buy a car that is already prepared than to buy a stock car and modify it yourself. For many months in *Sportscar*, there was an ad for two ITB Golf-Cup cars for sale: a package deal for six thousand dollars! You couldn't hope to build a similar car, let alone two, for that little money.

Buying a new Volkswagen as a project car is also an option. A new car does have its pros and cons as a basis for a high-performance vehicle. A new car is a good choice for the perfectionist who does not want to deal with someone else's mistakes. You can be assured that the car will be in great mechanical condition and it will have a warranty. You can also order whatever you want for options. The best bet is to limit heavy options on a car that is going to be used

Fig. 1-5. A new car, such as this H Stock Golf, will offer a warranty, which could help you make the decision between buying a new or used car. If a part on a used VW fails, and it's out of warranty, you have to figure that into your autocrossing budget, making a "cheap" car more expensive.

Fig. 1-6. These bumper rails on an A1 car, shown from above, are in good shape: watch out for buckled examples.

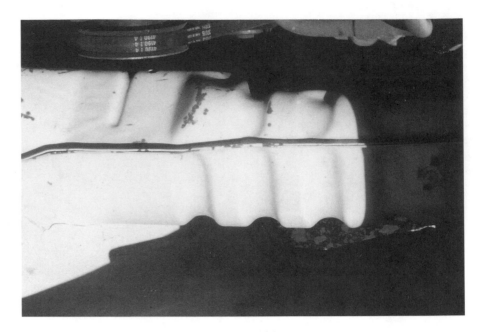

for high-performance driving. Cars with absolutely no options on them are very rare in dealer lots; they will need to be special-ordered. You can also discuss with the dealer the possibilities of deleting some "standard" options such as the glass sunroof (much heavier than the steel version in older cars) in the A3 GTIs.

The problems with a new car as a starting point are obvious. First, the new car will cost substantially more than a used one. Furthermore, you will be faced with depreciation as soon as the car leaves the dealership's lot. The new car's warranty will also frown on motorsport events. Even though autocrossing and time trialing will not adversely affect the car, you should probably not mention that this piece or that part stopped working on the way back from Solo II Nationals. Additionally, the new cars will also be substantially heavier than earlier models.

You should plan ahead to decide which modifications you would like to undertake, and what order they should come in. In considering which modifications to make, think about the cost for each part and the labor involved to install it. The cost for each change should be added to the initial cost of the car for a complete picture of your budget. When you actually start putting a price on each change, it will give you a better idea of how much performance you will be getting for your money. Smart shoppers will then want to concentrate on getting the most "bang" for their buck.

It is often easier and cheaper to do several modifications at once if they are in the same system: for example, changing the springs, shocks, and suspension bushings. A plan for future modifications also helps you keep an eye out for bargains on parts that you will want in the near future.

Another good reason for planning what modifications you want to do, and how soon you are going to do them, is that you can use that information as you shop for the car. Shock absorbers, exhaust systems, and tires are usually at the top of an enthusiast's list of things to do. You can then disregard whether or not the car you are looking at has good shocks, exhaust, or tires because you're going to replace them anyway. Cars that are going to be street driven cannot take this to the extreme, in that you need a running car to get around in. If, however, the car is not needed to run immediately, you can even look for good deals on cars that need lots of TLC. Many times you can find a car for a mere pittance and build it to a pristine state. A $200 Rabbit or a $600 Golf would take nearly the same amount of capital to rebuild to nationally competitive form as a perfect stock example. Everything that would be worn out on these bargain cars would be replaced on a competitive car anyway.

The most important part of a Volkswagen is the unibody structure itself. All of the parts that bolt onto this body are easily replaceable. For example, if the engine has low compression, it can be replaced. If, however, the entire structure is bent or rusted beyond repair, the car is a total loss except for use as a parts car. The structural integrity of the shell is very important in racing and absolutely any high-performance use. It is very difficult to properly rebuild a car that has been in a collision. There are enough good VWs for sale that it doesn't make sense to invest time and money on a marginal car.

To determine if the car you are considering buying is straight and unbent, you need to know the specifications of the new car. The factory gives this information out to various publications, both for service and autobody repair. The actual measurements of the structure are in vehicle repair guides for autobody collision repair. You should find a body shop that does work on VWs and ask to see this guide. It will give you information in terms of distances from one point on the car to another. Good examples are the distance between front strut towers and the length of the wheel base. You should copy all of this information down. Then, either measure the distances yourself or have the body shop do it. This is the only way to truly be sure that the unibody is straight.

For most people, the above procedure is a bit unrealistic. A more feasible approach is to measure a few things and then take a good overall look at the car. You should measure the height of each front strut tower from the ground. They should be at equal height. Since most cars hit things front first, here is where most of the damage usually occurs. Look at the welds and joints around the strut towers, bumper supports, and subframe on both sides of the car. Both sides should look identical. On A1 cars, you should check the accordion-shaped bumper supports. Bent and crumpled examples will indicate poorly repaired collision damage. Another clue is how pieces of metal are joined to-

Fig. 1-7. This CSP 16-valve GTI started its racing career as a wrecked daily driver. The car was repaired cheaply and a coat of green paint was applied. For racing, where looks aren't important, this is an adequate repair.

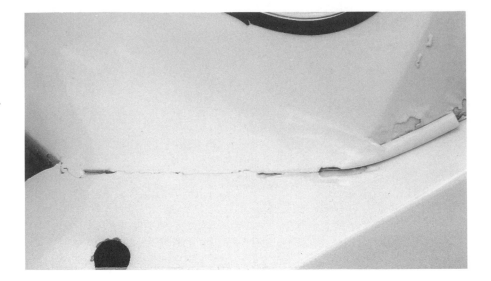

Fig. 1-8. Notice the paint cracks around the perimeter of this strut bearing. As a high-mileage U.S.-built A2 GTI, this amount of cracking is normal, but beware of A2 Jettas that have excess distortion.

gether. The factory uses spot welds to join sheet metal together. If you see welds that are long seams, either it was once a racing car (properly done, seam welds will strengthen the shell) or it has been wrecked.

The strut tower area will also tell you how much abuse the car has gotten in its life. If the paint and sealant putty that the factory applied is cracked, the suspension has been bottomed out repeatedly. This cracking was more evident on the A2 Golfs, even with normal usage, than it was on the Jettas. Cracked paint on the strut towers should then rule out a particular Jetta, but only caution you on a Golf purchase. This problem is also common with early Sciroccos, usually compounded by rust. Strut towers that are completely distorted or "ballooned" are a major red flag: chances are that the rest of the car is also bent, so avoid it.

While you are looking at the strut tower area, you can also check the color of the paint in the engine compartment. It should be the same as the exterior, provided no major fading has occurred in the exterior paint. For some people, a repainted car is undesirable. In general, the factory paint is stronger and more durable than an aftermarket finish. If the car is going to be a racing car, paint

Fig. 1-9. This is an example of checking for unibody straightness. Both sides of this Jetta have an equal hub-to-hub distance of 94.125 in., showing a potential buyer that the car has probably not been in a serious accident.

shouldn't matter. It is impossible to keep the finish of a racing car unmarred (battle scars are sometimes thought of as badges of honor). Look for further signs of non-factory paint on rubber and trim pieces. A poor masking job will make this very noticeable around the window seals.

On the exterior of the car, body joints and seams are good indications of body straightness. Look at the seam around each door. The seam should not be uneven or abnormally large. Often, you will see a car that has a door seam that gets smaller near the roof. This means that the car has been hit and the body is now banana shaped. The hood should also have evenly spaced seams around it. The height of the hood should be even in respect to the fenders and the cowl (the area between the bottom of the windshield and the hood). It is very easy to line up the hood with the fenders during a repair, but it is much harder to align it with the cowl also. Finally, watch the car from behind as it drives. Reject a car that "crabs" with the rear tracking off-center of the front.

Rust will weaken the Volkswagen's shell as effectively as chopping holes in it with a chisel. More dangerous is the fact that the rust you actually see on most cars is the veritable tip of the iceberg, with much more lurking in hidden areas. The unibody will tolerate very little rust before it becomes useless. Fortunately, Volkswagens have been galvanized since 1985 and have factory-applied undercoating and wax sealant, making them highly rust resistant. The only places you will find rust on a later car will be the following: the area around the rear quarter windows on two door cars, the bottoms of the doors, and the fuel filler pocket. If other places are rusted, this could indicate either collision damage or paint chipping due to rocks or door "dings." A3 cars have not been produced long enough to predict where they will rust. Chances are that they will be as rust resistant as the A2s.

The ease of finding a non-rusted A2 car would normally make it inadvisable to start with a rusted example. Luckily, the A2 will only suffer structural rust if it has been crashed. Proper paint preparation will cure all of the surface rust that even the worst A2 will have. The source of the rust should also be addressed when repairing the area. Often, the rust is caused by clogged drainage holes in the sheet metal. This will allow water to collect and corrode the area.

Fig. 1-10. Cheap tires, faded paint, and an uneven cowl-to-hood interface indicate that this car was not taken care of. Since there are a large number of used VWs on the market, steer clear of marginal examples like this.

Fig. 1-11. The A1 chassis seems to rust heavily at the bottom of the front fenders.

The A1 cars were not as lucky in regards to rust. Places to look for rust will include the front fenders, the inner fender wells, the bottoms of the doors, and around all of the windows. When looking at a potential project car, keep in mind that some parts such as the front fenders or the hatchback are easily replaced. Any rust that is inside of the fender wells, on the floor pan, or around the door hinge area will rule out the car as a high-performance project. If you cannot find a rust-free example in your area, look to the Southern or Western U.S. for good cars. The price premium that you will have to pay on a clean car will be made up in spades by the lack of rust repair you will have to undertake.

The mechanical condition of the car is also important. This can be checked by yourself or by a trusted mechanic. The high likelihood that a large portion of the car will be replaced makes the condition of many parts unimportant. The engine should be the last thing that you rebuild, however. To get some driving under your belt before that point, the engine should have decent compression, and no abnormal vital signs. Since the fuel injection system will be retained on most cars, check its operating condition. A simple check of the percent of carbon monoxide in the exhaust stream (%CO) can often be a good indicator of the engine's state of tune. If you are serious about buying a certain model of VW, and you do not know how to perform the above mentioned tests, you should consider having the tests performed at a qualified repair shop.

The electrical system will probably not be replaced on any car, so it should be in pristine condition. If there are poorly connected, insulated, and wrapped wiring connections, it will indicate a substandard repair. It is very frustrating to deal with electrical gremlins in a car. If there is evidence of such tampering and shoddy repair, many other electrical problems may come out of hiding once you own the car. Unless you are willing to tackle the enormous job of rewiring a car, steer clear of cars with electrical problems. This should also include cars

Fig. 1-12. Cars that have been involved in fires are very hard to repair. The utter destruction of the entire wiring harness, along with every non-metallic surface in the interior, would make the rebuild process very expensive and time-consuming.

that have fire damage. While they can be steals at insurance auctions, fire-damaged cars are very tedious to fix. What's worse is that all of the wiring color codes are useless since most of the wires will have turned black from the heat of the fire.

Both the interior and exterior can tell you what kind of owners the car has had, how many miles the car has been driven, and the quality of maintenance that the car has been given. If the car has been well cared for there will be signs of regular maintenance. This could range from a sticker from the local oil and lube shop to a clean and new-looking fuel filter. The engine should be clean, with no visible oil leaks. If the engine compartment is spotlessly clean, it may have been steam cleaned. This cleaning will erase all evidence of oil leaks, which may pop up as soon as you drive away. Spark plugs, distributor rotors, and distributor caps should all be made by Bosch. In addition, they should also be in fairly good condition. If these parts are "off-brand," it would indicate an owner who took the cheap way out on maintenance tasks.

In looking for a used car, also consider the amount of mileage. This is not as simple as peering at the odometer. On a VW, it takes about one hour to make a high-mileage car transmogrify into a low-mileage car. It is a very straightforward procedure to swap the entire instrument cluster with one that is showing lower miles. If you come across a "low-mileage" car with blown shocks, spotty tires, and a bad muffler, it's pretty likely that someone has changed the odometer. The same goes for a "low mileage" A2 or A3 which needs major maintenance such as a clutch replacement or cylinder head rebuild. These parts usually don't go bad for a long time.

The overall condition of the car should be commensurate with its mileage. High-mileage cars are not necessarily bad, they should just cost less to buy and slightly more to bring to top shape. The interior of the car will be a good indicator of overall mileage also. If the car has worn rubber on the brake and clutch pedals, worn out seat bolsters, or carpet that is worn through, the car has seen many, many miles. Keep in mind that most parts that wear out on a high mileage car are cheap and easy to replace with a trip to a salvage yard.

The mileage and quality of care is also evident on the exterior. On cars with alloy rims, check for bends and gouges from curbs, since these will indicate indifferent driving. If brake dust has been allowed to sit on the wheels for extended periods, it will pit the alloy surface. This would indicate an owner who didn't care enough to wash the car very often, which could also have lead to paint damage and fading. The tires should also be all of the same type and of decent quality. Like a non-Bosch distributor cap, cheap tires indicate a cheap previous owner.

It would be nice if all of the body panels, bumpers, and trim pieces were free from nicks and dings. In the real world, perfect body panels are next to impossible to find on a daily driven car. Because of the added aggravation of door dings and other sheet metal damage, try to avoid cars with them if at all possible. A car that has few or no door dings will indicate either an extremely lucky owner or an owner who took the extra step and parked carefully. This careful owner would also have been careful with other aspects of car care, such as maintenance.

The last thing to consider when purchasing a VW is where it was made. Some enthusiasts think that the best examples are produced in Germany, while the U.S., Mexican, and Brazilian examples are less well-built. German-built cars have a Vehicle I.D. number (VIN) that starts with the letter "W," U.S. VINs start with the number "1," Mexican VINs start with the number "3," and Brazilian VINs start with the number "9." For cars like the 2-liter 16-valve GTI, there is no choice in country of manufacture, since they were only produced in Mexico. This does not rule them out as good cars: they are truly excellent. The only time you will realistically notice a difference between countries is when you consider paint quality. The German-built cars have the best (strongest) paint of all of the VWs, while others will chip more easily.

SALVAGE YARDS

Fig. A. The salvage yard is an excellent place to find parts to update or backdate your car for the most power, lightest weight, or best handling. The rolled GTI in the foreground yielded a manual steering rack for a project car.

So, you are in need of Volkswagen parts and you can't afford to buy new? Salvage yards (also called dismantlers, junkyards, or wreckers) can be a viable alternative. The owners of the yards go to insurance auctions and buy cars that have been wrecked or dam-aged, then sell them whole or in parts to private individuals. They will make money (of course) in these transactions, but the rule of thumb is that the prices are one half (sometimes less) of what the dealer would charge. Keep in mind that some parts, like brake pads or bearings, should not be purchased at a salvage yard.

Salvage yards can be found anywhere. However, some yards are more likely to have what you are interested in. Your best bet is to look for a place that specializes in Volkswagens or import cars. In your phone book's "Yellow Pages" you will find a section called "Automotive Parts–Used." This is where most yards will advertise. Call them up, and ask for the parts you need. They should have everything inventoried to make this step painless. Alternatively, some all-VW salvage yards advertise in *european car* magazine. The number of these specialized yards has grown, and you should be able to find what you are looking for there.

Before you get in your car to go to a salvage yard, you first need to know what kind of yard it

Fig. 1-13. Brake dust and curb damage on a wheel will indicate an indifferent owner. Parking carefully and using a cleanser specifically meant for washing cars will prevent the kind of damage caused by neglect.

is. Some yards won't let you inside where the cars are actually stored, for fear of lawsuits. These places will have people who are sent to remove the part for you. Alternatively, others will have a "pick your part" policy, where the customers are allowed to go in and do the work themselves. I prefer the second type because it's A) fun to look at all of the cars, B) the prices are usually cheaper (they don't have to pay someone to do the re-moval), and C) if I remove a part from a car, I know the condition of the car it came from. I wouldn't want to buy a worn out part!

If it's a self-service yard, you will need to bring the appropriate tools. Figure out which wrenches, screwdrivers, hammers, etc., you will need to get the part off, and bring them with you (preferably in some sort of lightweight toolbox so you don't lose any). You will also need to wear the appropriate clothes. In other words, dress like a mechanic. You *will* get very dirty, greasy, and grimy on your foray.

Once you get there, and the owner lets you in, you will notice that cars are divided into two sections: Rebuildable and Salvage. Rebuildable cars are ones that have been totaled (and may or may not have "Salvage Titles") but can be fixed. The advantage of these cars is that you can usually get the car fixed and running for much less than the car is worth at a wholesale level. This is a great source for cars to be used for racing, as long as the chassis hasn't taken a major hit (e.g., if the roof is buckled, don't even consider it). Hail- or storm- damaged cars are very good candidates for a racing project. Hundreds of dimples caused by falling hail won't make the car any slower (the running joke is that it will actually make your car handle better due to a lower center of gravity) and you can concentrate on driving instead of worrying about hurting a pristine car. The drawbacks of rebuildables are: banks won't loan money on cars with salvage titles, the extent of damage is sometimes unknown until you start working on the car, and

cont'd. on next page

Grassroots Racing

Tuning your water-cooled Volkswagen for street use will undoubtably make your driving experience more fun, but if you really want to test the limits of your prized project car, the track provides a relatively safe place to do so. There are many places to race your Volkswagen today, ranging from your local chapter of the SCCA's autocrosses, to regional Time Trials, to road racing at a national level. Wherever you choose to play with your VW, you can't help but have fun. Your racing endeavors can become social as well; it's great to get together with fellow racers from all over the country, who have a wealth of tips and tales to share.

The racing classes that this book will concentrate on are the Sports Car Club of America (SCCA) Solo II categories of Stock and Street Prepared, and the SCCA road racing categories of Showroom Stock and Improved Touring. These classes represent what are thought to be the best ways to race on a limited budget. Here, the competition is fierce, with attention to detail and driver skill eclipsing the need for lots of money.

SCCA also offers classes that range from the entry level to the professional, with one class building to the next, offering competitors the chance to move up rungs of the racing ladder one step at a time. A car that is in a stock class can compete there for a while, be modified to a Street Prepared or I.T. state, and then change to Prepared or Production specs. The address and phone number of the SCCA and other sources for parts and information can be found at the rear of the book.

Salvage Yards (Cont'd.)

it's very hard to make a car perfect that has been damaged enough to be totaled by an insurance company.

Salvage cars are the ones that are cannibalized for parts. These are sometimes organized into sections of particular types; sometimes what you are looking for can be spread across acres of automotive wasteland. When you ask for the part you need at the entrance, they will usually direct you in the general location of what you are looking for. I find it interesting to walk around anyway, so it doesn't bother me if I don't find the piece I am looking for right away. A leisurely stroll will often lead you to interesting finds; this is how I noticed that you could use Audi 4000 marker lamps as cheap European side indicators.

Once you find the particular type of car that you need parts from, look for an example that is in reasonable shape. The price of your part will be the same no matter what car you take it off of, so pick the best example. Find the car with the least damage in the area that your part comes

from, then look for the car with the lowest mileage (assuming they all still have their odometers). Don't take electrical parts from cars that have flood damage (mud in the instrument cluster, dashboard, or headliner is a good hint). If cars have been in fires, they sometimes will have usable parts, but only in areas that were unaffected by heat. Cars that have been rear-ended or side-swiped will probably have good engine compartments, although when the wrecking yard sells an engine, a lot of the ancillary parts get lost.

A lot of damage will happen to parts merely by sitting in the yard. If hoods have been left up, the engine compartment will deteriorate very quickly. Look for engine compartments that look like they could actually "work" (not covered in mud). Of course, common decency would indicate that you should close any hoods that you open in your quest. Interior parts should be removed from cars that have all of their windows intact. This will insure that no rain/snow/mud/wildlife has gotten in and dam-

Fig. 1-14. IMSA focuses exclusively on professional-level road racing events. Here, a Touring class GTI follows a Honda CRX at Watkins Glen in New York.

The International Motorsports Association (IMSA) also hosts racing that VWs can compete in here in the U.S. The IMSA classes are somewhat similar to SCCA's, but the actual mods are more unrestricted. IMSA races tend to be more of the professional variety. The high cost of entrance fees and lack of entry-level racing rule out IMSA as a grassroots racing organization.

aged anything. Please close the car doors afterwards so that the rest of the interior isn't damaged from the elements.

Some cars are considerably harder to find with the good stuff intact: these include GTIs, GLIs, and Corrados. Volkswagen's sport seats, alloy wheels, rear disc brakes, and high-performance engines are quick to be sold. Passats can be good sources for Corrado bits, however, and many of the base Golf/Jetta parts will be interchangeable with GTI/GLI parts. Ask the owner when they expect to get a car, and be prepared to come back the day it comes in.

Once you have the part you need, take it to the owner, and if they haven't already given you a price, ask for one now. Some owners respond well to haggling, and others won't. Don't try to get something for nothing, but you can usually talk the owner down some. One psychological tip: the nicer you are dressed, the more money they will charge you for a part. Electrical parts will not come with any sort of warranty, but you can usually return parts within one week if they

don't work; check to make sure!

Salvage yards are fun places for most car enthusiasts. They can be a treasure trove of interesting parts to make your VW go faster. Keep your eye out for parts that you would like on cars that aren't wrecked, and remember the type of car for the next time you go to a yard. The owner might remember you and give you better deals the more times you come in.

Fig. B. Salvage yards can offer economical performance choices, but I don't know the mileage of the car that they came out of.

GRASSROOTS RACING CATEGORIES

Autocrossing

Stock Class
Allows alternate D.O.T. legal tires, front anti-roll bar, sport shocks, exhaust from cat-back.

Class	General Description	Sample Cars
SS	over 250 hp, excellent handling	Mazda RX-7 Twin Turbo, Chevrolet Corvette
AS	200-250 hp, excellent handling	BMW M3, Porsche 944S2
BS	low-hp, good handling sports cars	Mazda Miata, BMW Z3
CS	older sports cars	Toyota MR-2, Porsche 924s, Datsun 240z
DS	under 150 hp, 4-cylinder compact cars, can have limited-slip differentials	Dodge Neon, BMW 318i, **VW Corrado G60**
ES	'sporty' 4-cylinder compact cars (generally under 135 hp)	**VW GTI**, Toyota Celica GT, Saturn SC2
FS	V8 RWD pony cars	Chevrolet Camaro, Ford Mustang
GS	V6 'sporty' cars	Mazda MX-6, **VW VR6**
HS	low-hp, small cars	Toyota Celica ST, **VW Golf 3**

Street Prepared
Stock mods plus unlimited wheels and D.O.T. legal tires, intake and exhaust systems, stiffer springs.

Class	General Description	Sample Cars
ASP	high-hp, low-weight cars (excellent hp/weight ratio)	RX-7 Twin Turbo, Porsche 911
BSP	heavier performance cars (o.k. hp/weight ratio)	Chevrolet Corvette, Datsun 240z
CSP	small performance cars (good hp/weight ratio)	Honda CRX, **VW VR6**
DSP	low-hp, low-weight small cars	Fiat X1-9, **VW 4-cylinder**
ESP	V8 pony cars	Chevrolet Camaro, Ford Mustang

Prepared
Racing slicks, stripped interiors, camshafts.

Class		Sample Cars
AP		Lotus Elan, **VW VR6**, Datsun 240z
BP		Chevrolet Corvette, **VW G60**
CP		Camaros and Mustangs
DP		Austin Healey Sprite, Honda CRX
EP		Honda Civic, **VW 4-cylinders**

Modified

Class		
AM	cars built specifically for autocross	
BM	road-racing-based 'sport s racers' (e.g. Sports2000)	
CM	low-hp road-racing cars (e.g. Formula Fords)	
DM	small-displacement production-based cars (e.g. Lotus Elan)	
EM	large-displacement production-based cars (e.g. V8-powered Fieros)	
FM	Formula 440 or Formula Vee	
F125	125-cc Shifter Karts	

Road Racing

Showroom Stock
Showroom Stock is being replaced with new designation called 'Touring', with Solo Stock-type modifications allowed.

Improved Touring
Tires, suspension, intake, exhaust (somewhat similar to Street Prepared with more strict wheel and intake allowances). Cars must be 5 years old, non-turbo.

Class	General Description	Sample Cars
ITS	7-inch wheels, over 150 hp	**VW 2.0-liter 16-valve**, Datsun 240z, Mazda RX-7
ITA	7-inch wheels, usually less than 150 hp	**VW 1.8-liter 16-valve**, Honda CRX
ITB	6-inch wheels, less than 120 hp	**VW 1.8-liter 8-valve**, BMW 2002
ITC	6-inch wheels, less than 100 hp	**VW 1.7-liter 8-valve**, Honda Civic 1300

Fig. 1-15. SCCA allows racers on any budget a place to race, from local events to the more professional ProSolo2, which is shown here. Here drivers are gathering for a meeting to discuss safety issues.

Autocrossing

If you have ever seen large groups of people gathered in parking lots or airstrips amidst a sea of pylons, don't be alarmed. These people are "autocrossing" (Solo II), also called "slalom" or "sprinting." This is one of the most grassroots forms of motorsport events. A very tight course is laid out with pylons, then competitors run one at a time for the lowest time through the gates. The pylons are soft and flexible, and will not harm your paint if you hit one. Autocrossing is considered a low-speed type of event, with speeds rarely exceeding fifty or sixty miles per hour. Do not let the low speed fool you: it is very challenging and exciting to negotiate an autocross course at this speed.

Safety requirements are: helmets with a Snell rating (usually Snell 90 or higher), operating seat belts, and a car in safe operating condition. Autocrossing is very popular because it allows you to use your daily driver as a race car. Although it is not risk-free, there have been few accidents on these courses.

Autocrossing is a nationwide sport. Every SCCA region hosts its own Solo II events under the direction of that region's Solo II committee. The season will last from January to December in some warmer climates, and March to October in the colder areas. The end of SCCA's official season is marked in September by the Solo II Nationals in Topeka, Kansas. This week-long affair attracts nearly eight hundred competitors each year. A trophy earned at Nationals is truly something to be proud of.

SCCA also sponsors the ProSolo2 Championship series. The difference between the normal Solo II event and a ProSolo2 event is that in the latter, there are two separate mirror image courses laid out. The cars on each side will start from a drag-racing style "Christmas tree" set of starting lights and race each other back to the finish. The ProSolo2 events are, as the name implies, professional. The drivers and sponsors are highly motivated by fun, sponsorship, and for the winners, prize money! You are required to purchase a ProSolo2 license for entry into two or more events in a season. The final race for this pro season is the ProSolo2 Finale. It is staged the week before the normal Solo II Nationals at the same site in Topeka, Kansas.

One class of cars in autocross events is the Stock class. Here, the cars must be fairly unmodified, but this does not mean slow. SCCA allows certain normally expendable pieces to be replaced with those of a higher performance nature. Shock absorbers, exhaust systems from the catalytic converter back, air cleaners, and tires can all be replaced. The tires must be Department of Transportation (DOT)-approved, but this allows "R" compound tires such as the BF-Goodrich Comp T/A R1 or the Yokohama A008R. Other tricks of the trade will

Fig. 1-16. ProSolo2 uses a "Christmas tree" light to start racers. The author's car, shown here, is leaving on the green at the Jacksonville Florida Pro event in 1995.

Fig. 1-17. Keli Cadenhead on her way to the finish at the ProSolo2 Finale in 1991. This car was later sold as a complete package for under $4000, with extra rims/tires/etc., showing how low the cost for national competitiveness can be.

be discussed in subsequent chapters.

In Solo II Stock, most Volkswagens run in E Stock, the hot models being the 2 liter GTI and some of the 100 hp 2-door Jettas. In H Stock, the heavier Golf and Jetta 3 should perform adequately. Depending on the weight of the individual car and how many heavy options it has, these could do quite well at a national level. The VR6 cars have been classed in G stock where they would be well matched against the competition.

Street Prepared is another popular class of autocrossing. Here, suspensions, wheels, and tires are fairly unrestricted as long as the tires are DOT-approved. Intake and exhaust systems can be modified. Seats can be replaced with any fully upholstered racing seat. The class also allows updating and backdating of parts within the same chassis production run. This seems to be a class of easy bolt-on parts, allowing the average VW that has been fiddled with to have a place to race. In Street Prepared, the most competitive cars are early Sciroccos and Rabbits (with engines updated to '83-'84 GTI specs), and some of the 2-door Golfs and Jettas. The 8-valve cars are all classed in D Street Prepared, while 16-valves all end up in C Street Prepared.

Fig. 1-18. The Stock class racer, utilizing lightweight wheels and R-compound tires. This A2 Jetta was campaigned in Stock for just a few months before the owner switched to Street Prepared.

Fig. 1-19. Classed in H stock, the four cylinder A3s are very capable performers on fast courses because of their good hp and transitional handling.

Time Trials

One step up from the autocross is the time trial (or Solo I). Here, the course is usually a normal road racing circuit where cars run at higher speeds. What differentiates this from road racing is that passing is limited to certain straightaways, and the cars used can still be daily drivers. Most groups require roll bars if not roll cages, racing harnesses, Snell SA90 helmets, and full fire retardant clothing. In Solo I events, the classes of cars are a mixture of Solo II and road racing. Solo I includes both a Street Prepared and an Improved Touring class, with different safety requirements for each.

In addition to SCCA, the Porsche Club of America also holds time trials, often with more actual time on the track for competitors. The PCA allows non-Porsche cars to compete, but be forewarned: they get testy when a lowly VW outguns them. Other marque clubs also sponsor events, and there are some non-national sports car clubs that sponsor time trials at local tracks. This is a great chance to run your VW at a big name racetrack, including the oval type. It is thrilling to drive on the high banks of a NASCAR superspeedway.

Fig. 1-20. The '91-92 16-valve GTI is an excellent choice for Stock class use. Features include 15 x 6.5 in. wheels, 134+ horsepower, and excellent brakes.

Road Racing

The final type of racing that this book covers is road racing. This is the real Mc-Coy of racing, with bunches of cars racing wheel to wheel for the checkered flag. Risks of contact with other cars preclude using daily drivers in this group. In road racing, safety requirements are strictly enforced and driver licensing is required. Drivers must complete two driving schools in order to get a competition license, and then must compete in a certain number of races a year to remain licensed. The cost of racing is substantially higher than autocrossing or time trials.

There are, however, certain classes where modifications are limited, and costs are, therefore, reduced. One such class is SCCA's Improved Touring, or I.T., where the cars are prepared about the same as a Solo II Street Prepared with some differences. Intake systems must be of the same type as stock, wheel rim widths are restricted, interiors may be gutted, and rollcages can be welded instead of bolted in. Tires are unrestricted as long as they are DOT-approved. For I.T., the 2-liter GTI (ITS) and the 1.8-liter (ITA) are good cars, but outclassed. ITB, on the other hand, is the playground of the 8-valve GTI (A1 and A2), while ITC gives the Rabbits and Sciroccos with small engines a category to run in. The cars in the I.T. class can not be from the current model year or the four previous model years.

Another grassroots road racing class is Showroom Stock. The "stock" here has a more strict definition than in Solo II stock. Cars can be from the last four

Fig. 1-21. The A1 Scirocco is by far the most popular VW in Street Prepared competition. Its light weight and good power helped Eric Strelneiks drive this car to a ProSolo class championship in 1991.

Fig. 1-22. Time trials offer higher speeds than autocrosses, often on road racing tracks. This 8-valve Golf (now in ITB) can be raced at time trials, road races, and autocrosses—lots of seat time!

Fig. 1-23. Road racing involves both greater excitement and greater risk. All three of these VWs are cornering at their limits in close proximity to one another.

model years or the current model year for national level competition and an additional two model years old for regional level competition. Cars must have bolt-in rollcages, window nets, fire extinguishers, and racing seat harnesses. The only allowable modifications are tires and driver's seats. Tires can be anything DOT-legal and can be up to 20 mm larger than stock. Driver's seats can be replaced with any one of the racing varieties. Golfs, Sciroccos, and Corrados have all run in Showroom Stock, sometimes competitively, sometimes not. This year, with the introduction of the V6 cars in Showroom Stock A, the prospects for VW in this type of racing are looking up. On a road racing circuit, the added weight of these newer cars is less of an impediment that on an autocross course, allowing VW to once again be in the running for national standing.

Nationals for Showroom Stock and all other SCCA road racing classes (except Improved Touring) are held each year in October at the Mid-Ohio track in Ohio. This venue was changed from the Road Atlanta track in Georgia to Ohio in 1994. The Improved Touring Nationals are held as the American Road Racing Championships at Road Atlanta in October. The I.T. Nationals are a new phenomenon; this class is officially a regional-only class with no national standing in the eyes of SCCA. This might change as the class is currently one of SCCA's most popular types.

Fig. 1-24. Rabbits are popular in Improved Touring because of their low cost and ease of replacement. This ITB 1.6-liter Rabbit has since been reclassed to ITC along with the 1.7-liter cars.

RULES

For exact rules and regulations, contact the SCCA and get the applicable rule book for your type of racing. If you want to race, these rule books are the first high-performance option you can buy for your car. They will teach you what you can do and what you can't do if you want to remain in a competitive class. The thing to remember about SCCA racing is that some seemingly insignificant changes in a car can move you up into a class where your car will not be competitive. It is still fun to autocross even if you are stuck in a class with purpose-built race cars. If your car is strictly a street car or is rarely autocrossed, then the rules will not matter to you.

Since the different classes of racing in Solo II and road racing build on each other, the more modified classes can use all of the tips in this book. For Prepared and Modified, which are steps above Street Prepared, and Production, which is one step above Improved Touring, just consult the SCCA rule books and change what needs to be changed. You can also call SCCA headquarters for rule interpretation, assuring you that your car is completely legal.

CROSS-POLLINATION

SCCA allows cars that are legal in Showroom Stock to compete in their respective Solo Stock classes, with no interchange of rules. Improved Touring competitors can compete in Solo Street Prepared, also with no interchange of rules ("interchange of rules" means mixing and matching the rules to get the fastest car possible, which is not allowed; your car has to follow the rules for one class or the other). While a dedicated road racing car will probably not be competitive at a national Solo level, local and regional Solo events give you additional time in your road racing car. This added seat time can be used to sort out the handling or drivetrain. It is also nice for the host Solo event as it can boost attendance and let competitors and spectators know about other types of racing.

CHEAP FUN?

If you want to start racing, even at the grassroots level, the unavoidable truth is that you have to spend money to be competitive. The least expensive racing type is autocrossing in a stock category with whatever you are currently driving in. Here, besides entry fees (normally $10-$20), you will have few other ex-

Fig. 1-25. The largest expense in most types of racing is tires. The DOT-legal BFGoodrich Comp TA R-1 offers a soft compound and low tread depth for maximum cornering. A nationally competitive racer will go through at least eight of these in a typical Solo II season.

penditures; the biggest expense will be your tires and brake pads, which will wear faster than normal. Some drivers find that they can do quite well at a local club level in a bone-stock car. Certain regions of the SCCA have realized the potential for this competition, adding classes more restrictive than "Stock" that prohibit R-compound tires (DOT-legal racing tires made with a supersoft rubber compound and a stiff carcass/sidewall) or aftermarket shock absorbers.

To be nationally competitive (versus regionally competitive) in Solo Stock, you will have to find a car that performs well in its class and then do some modification. You will want to change shocks, get a performance alignment, install a low restriction exhaust, and get a good racing-type harness. These modifications will cost less than seven hundred dollars, but they will improve performance and safety substantially. Furthermore, you should get an extra set of rims and mount R-compound tires. If you scour salvage yards and classifieds, you can usually find good deals on factory alloys, maybe as low as $150 for a set of four. R-compound tires cost anywhere from $80 to $120 and up, each, for most VWs, which is comparable to most high-performance street tires. These sticky

Fig. 1-26. Kim Stewart, whose SSC Golf is shown here, also competes at a local level in H Stock, which allows a lot of seat time in the car. This is actually the only SSC VW being campaigned as of this writing.

Fig. 1-27. The days of driving a car to a road racing track, racing, and then driving home are nearly over. Plan on spending at least a thousand dollars on a used open trailer. Don't forget that you will also need a separate tow vehicle to haul the car to and from the track.

Fig. 1-28. Sponsorship can help fiscal difficulties in many types of racing. Bob and Patty Tunnell are sponsored by Dr. Boltz, a repair shop that helped them rebuild this nationally competitive Jetta after it had been stolen from the Tunnells and then recovered.

tires should last an entire season with moderate autocross participation. If you are planning to hit every race you can possibly go to, budget for two sets during the year. The first full season for a nationally competitive Solo Stock Volkswagen will require a minimum of $1200; subsequent racing seasons will be substantially less.

Showroom Stock cars are expensive to race for a number of reasons. First, they must be nearly new. Second, they must remain absolutely stock even when parts get broken or wear out. This means that if a catalytic converter melts down, you need to run to the dealer and fork out $600 for a new one. Finally, to get any performance advantage over your competitors, the entire chassis and driveline needs to be torn down and rebuilt for maximum "stock" performance and reliability. To offset the high cost of this class, most competitors will solicit sponsorship from a VW dealer, repair, or tire shop.

One way to look at Street Prepared and Improved Touring is that for the same price as an average econobox you can have a real racing car. Used Rabbits, Sciroccos, and Golfs are easy to find and fix up. In addition to getting a quick and lively car, you also get the satisfaction of rebuilding to your personal tastes. Street Prepared is a cheaper class than I.T. in that you can still drive the car every day. Daily drivers in the I.T. arena are few and far between, making the cost of another car to drive to work a part of the price of racing.

Chapter Two
SUSPENSIONS

Fig. 2-1. A VW's typical cornering attitude is with the inside rear wheel off of the ground, caused by the torsion beam rear suspension and its lack of droop travel. This attitude does not hurt performance.

The suspension of your VW was designed to produce a comfortable, controlled ride over a wide variation in road surfaces. It is an excellent base with which to build a more performance-oriented handling machine. Many enthusiasts will desire a lower, more aggressive look and better handling. As with many things it is easy to get caught up in the quest for the lowest car or the stiffest suspension. If these changes alone provided the best handling, many automotive engineers would be out of work. Handling is a combination of many things, allowing the car to have the most traction and keeping it at that level, while retaining directional stability over bumps and dips.

HANDLING BASICS

When talking about suspensions and their optimal settings, a few definitions are in order. *Camber* is the angle of a wheel's inward or outward tilt from vertical. If the top of the tire is tilted toward the center of the vehicle, then the car has negative camber; if the opposite is true, then there is positive camber. *Toe* is the measure of where the front of the tires point. If they point towards each other, this is called *toe-in*. If they point away from each other, this is called *toe-out*.

Volkswagens that are used for street performance and racing use perform better with a certain amount of negative camber and some toe-out. The negative camber is used to counteract the effects of body roll on suspension geometry and therefore on tire loading and traction. When the car rolls, its wheels roll as well, increasing their positive camber: in other words, only the outer portion of the tire is touching the road, leading to decreased traction. Static negative camber will insure that the dynamic camber (i.e., the camber of the wheel in the middle of a corner) is zero for the largest contact patch and best traction (any dynamic camber, positive or negative, will decrease the amount of the tire in contact with the pavement as the car moves through a corner).

Fig. 2-2. Camber.

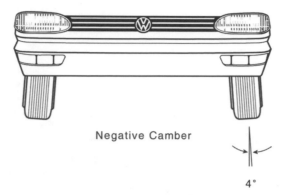

Negative Camber

4°

CAUTION —
Wheel alignment should be checked by an authorized Volkswagen dealer or qualified repair shop. Performance settings should not be used on a daily-driven street car.

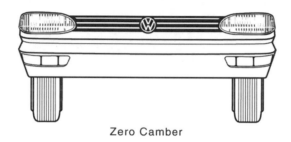

Zero Camber

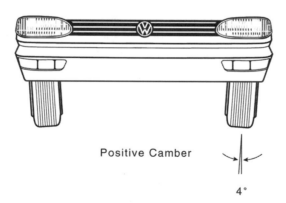

Positive Camber

4°

Where the stock toe setting is slightly toe-in for stability and safety, a toe-out setting helps turn-in and turning responsiveness , which can help toward quicker lap times. These performance settings do create some increased sensitivity at higher speeds and can be squirrelly in the rain. Another downside is that both the added toe-out and increased negative camber will increase tire wear on the street, but the track performance can be outstanding.

Fig. 2-3. Toe.

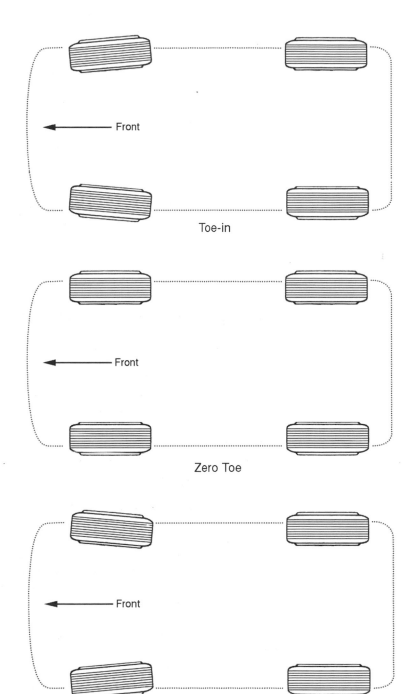

Toe-in

Zero Toe

Toe-out

CAUTION —
Wheel alignment should be checked by an authorized Volkswagen dealer or qualified repair shop. Performance settings should not be used on a daily-driven street car.

The handling balance of the car is either described as understeering or oversteering. In an understeering car, the front loses traction first, causing the car to push off the course front first. In an oversteering car, the rear loses traction first, causing the car to spin. The roll-couple distribution plays a big part in determining whether your car will oversteer or understeer. Briefly stated, the roll-couple distribution is how much roll stiffness each end of the car has. If you have a stiff front end, the car will tend to understeer. If you have a stiff rear, the car will tend to oversteer.

Fig. 2-4. This autocrossing Jetta has enough negative camber to allow the outside front tire to remain perpendicular to the ground in the middle of this sharp turn.

ANATOMY OF A VOLKSWAGEN SUSPENSION

Your Volkswagen suspension consists of several main components: the suspension arms, anti-roll bars, springs, and shock absorbers. Additionally, the suspension pieces themselves are mounted to the body structure via rubber bushings. Even the body shell itself can be considered a portion of the suspension. Indeed, when your car encounters a bump or other force, the unibody itself will flex. This will change how the suspension reacts, leading many people to call the unibody the "fifth spring."

The suspension arm is the physical structure that pivots when the car encounters a bump or has body roll. The suspension arms on a VW are quite simple. In the front there are two arms, each shaped like the letter "A," on either side of the front suspension. These arms are completely independent of each other. In the rear, the water-cooled VW has what is called a trailing arm or torsion beam suspension. The torsion beam is shaped like the letter "U," where each arm of the "U" is bent upwards when the suspension is compressed. In this design the two rear wheels are not completely independent of each other. When one side is compressed, the beam is twisted, causing the other wheel to rise also. This characteristic is similar to an anti-roll bar.

The anti-roll bar is a part of the suspension that will limit the body roll of the vehicle and usually improve traction on the end of the car opposite where the bar is. An anti-roll bar will not improve the net traction of the axle it is installed on. Instead, it will transfer weight from the inside wheel to the outside. A good way to check out this principal in action is to watch a Street Prepared VW with too much anti-roll bar stiffness on the front. In the process of increasing roll stiffness on the outside front wheel, it will completely lift the inside front wheel off the ground during a hard turn. Anti-roll bars are a good way to easily vary the roll-couple distribution of the car; and they come in a wide variety of flavors for both ends of your Volkswagen. They can be either hollow (lighter) or solid (stiffer roll resistance); some are also adjustable.

Here's a tip on installation and set-up of the front anti-roll bar: avoid having pre-load or binding in the end linkages. It is very easy to simply bolt on the unit and tighten the end linkages as tight as you can; but if you do this, you will bind the anti-roll bar so that it will not be free to move, causing the car to understeer excessively. For Neuspeed units, this means that after you install the bar, take

Fig. 2-5. The Autotech
hollow anti roll-bars have
the advantage of being
lightweight. They do not,
however, have the same
stiffness as a solid unit.

the car off the jacks and roll the car back and forth to allow the suspension to
settle. Then loosen the nylon locking nut that secures the ends of the anti-roll
bar to the lower control arm until you can just turn (not spin) the bottom-most
washer on the assembly. Do this for both sides and try to make them as even as
possible. If you're used to a too-tight unit, the difference will amaze you.

The springs are the devices that actually absorb the shock of road irregularities. The springs also keep the wheel in contact with the ground as the body
rolls due to weight transfer. If there are no springs whatsoever, or if an abnormally stiff spring is installed on your car, the wheels skip over bumps and lose
traction. If the spring is too soft, there will be too much body roll, causing the
body to lean over; the suspension and tires will also have to lean with it, reducing the contact patch of the tire. A properly designed and rated spring will prevent body roll, front-end dive during braking, and rear-end squat during

Fig. 2-6. The Neuspeed
rear anti-roll bar is adjustable by changing the end
links position between
these three holes. Using
the most forward hole will
create the most stiffness,
while the rearmost hole
will make the anti-roll bar
softer.

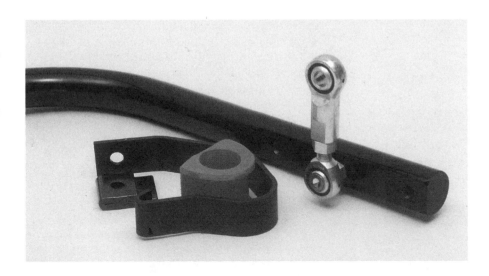

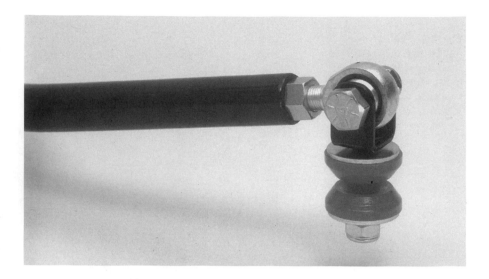

Fig. 2-7. When you install the anti-roll bar's end links to the A-arm, make sure that the bottom washer and bushing are not too tight. Overtightening this link will cause binding in the front suspension.

acceleration without allowing the wheel to lose traction over bumps. In conjunction with the anti-roll bar, spring rates determine the roll stiffness of the car.

Adjusting Roll Resistance for Performance

The spring rate will only partially determine the resistance of the car to roll during cornering, squat during acceleration, and dive during braking. The real factor in reducing these motions is the overall wheel rate. To explain this will require some definitions more technical in nature.

Spring rate, measured in pounds per inch of deflection, is defined as the amount of force it takes to compress the spring a specified distance. *Wheel rate*, which does not equal spring rate, is the amount of force it takes to move the wheel (or hub) upwards. The suspension geometry acts as a mechanical lever to either raise the rate or decrease it. The effectiveness of this "lever" can be expressed as a wheel rate multiplication factor which can be multiplied by the actual spring rate. The wheel rate multiplication factor for most VWs will hover around .90 for the front suspension; so if you have a 400 lb./in. front spring, the overall wheel rate will be 360 lb./in. The torsion beam rear suspension has a wheel rate multiplication factor of about 1, making the spring rate equal to the wheel rate in the rear.

The wheel rate of the anti-roll bar can then be added to the wheel rate of the suspension. Anti-roll bar rate is determined by the length of its lever arm, the overall length of the bar, and the diameter (actually, radius to the fourth power) of the bar. In calculating bar rate, the diameter of the bar makes a huge impact, while the lengths of the bar can be used for fine tuning. The front anti-roll bar's rate is very hard to calculate due to its complex shape. The following numbers were calculated, but a more accurate method would be to design a test jig to manually test the rate of each bar. Most 22-mm bars will have a wheel rate of approximately 300 lb./in., while a 25-mm bar will have a wheel rate of 500 lb./in. A hollow 25-mm bar will have a wheel rate of about 400 lb./in.

Rear anti-roll bar rates are easier to calculate. A rear 25-mm bar will have a wheel rate of around 450-500 lb./in., while a 28-mm bar will have a rate of around 750 lb./in. Tubular torsion bars (such as those used by OPM, Shine Racing Services, and H&H) have rates available from 700 lb./in. up to 1200 lb./in.

In addition to anti-roll bar rates, the rear suspension has its own torsion beam rate. This will range from 120 lb./in. on the base model cars to 180 lb./in. on cars with an integral rear 20-mm hollow anti-roll bar welded into the rear torsion beam. This extra rate that is built into every water-cooled VW partially explains the car's willingness to lift its inside rear wheel under hard cornering. This is due to a combination of high roll stiffness in comparison to the front and lack of droop suspension travel (how far the wheel will travel downward when the car is raised).

After all of these rates and values are added or multiplied, you can get a complete wheel rate. The optimal values for this all-inclusive rate for the front or rear will depend on what kind of driving you do, whether you like oversteer or understeer, and what kind of tracks and conditions your car will be driven on. If you like an oversteering car, you'll want to increase the rear wheel rate and lower the front. Understeering cars are set up in the opposite way, with a stiff front. An alternative idea is to put a stiffer front anti-roll bar on a car with soft (less than 300 lb./in.) springs. The front anti-roll bar in this case will prevent the front from rolling, eliminating camber change at the wheels. This will allow the front to retain traction, reducing understeer.

Performance Springs

There are two types of performance spring systems available for the performance VW. The first is the conventional spring that fits on the stock spring seats and strut bearings. The second type is the coilover unit. This is where you use spring seats that are adjustable for ride height and corner weight. Both are used in Volkswagens, with the former being much more common.

Good sources for the coilover units and other VW racing products are shops that specialize in VW racing exclusively. Coilover producers are also sometimes helpful with your I.T. or autocross needs. One advantage to going with an I.T. tuning firm is that they can often develop a complete suspension package geared to your specific needs. They'll ask you for the car's weight, where it races, what kind of roll cage it has, and what kind of tires it runs on; using computer programs, they can input all your operating parameters and tell you the spring rates, shock damping, and anti-roll bars that would be most beneficial for your car. If you have a home computer and you can find out the suspension geometry of your car, you can buy your own software to assess your needs.

Fig. 2-8. This spring is progressive, with some coils being spaced closer than others. This will cause the rate of the spring to rise as it is compressed. The advantage of this design is that it will allow comfort over sharp bumps, while preventing larger motions such as body roll.

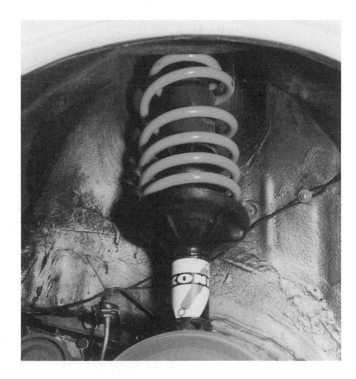

Fig. 2-9. Lowering the ride height makes your VW faster, but like anything, moderation is key; you don't want to lower it so much that you bottom out with every little bump in the road. The car should not be lowered past the point where the A-arms are parallel to the road surface.

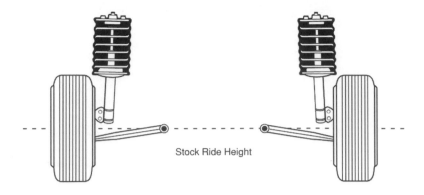

Stock Ride Height

CAUTION —

If you lack the tools or experience necessary to adjust ride height, this work should be left to an authorized Volkswagen dealer or qualified repair shop. Attempts to adjust the ride height without the proper tools are likely to cause serious injury.

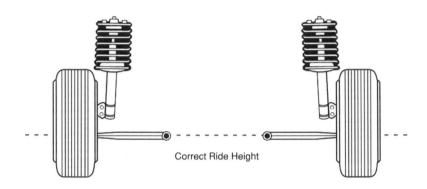

Correct Ride Height

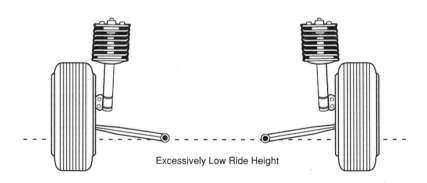

Excessively Low Ride Height

Performance springs allow faster cornering speeds by lowering the car's center of gravity and increasing roll resistance. These effects will keep the tire's contact patch firmly planted, giving optimal traction. Volkswagens, which are not mushy cruisers to begin with, become graced with slot-car-like handling. Most performance springs will lower the car around one inch; more than this causes it to bottom out too easily. Lowering the VW suspension too much will also cause unwanted suspension geometry changes, such as increased bump steer or increased wear on your constant velocity joints. Do not try to hide lack of roll stiffness with excessive suspension lowering—the car will handle worse than with the stock ride height and optimal roll stiffness. The best amount to lower the car without hurting handling is to the point where the A-arms are parallel to the road surface: usually only 1 or 1.5 in. lower than factory stock.

Fig. 2-10. This GTI has been lowered approximately 1.5 in. from the stock height. Lowering the car any more than this will cause unwanted suspension problems such as bump steer.

Performance Shocks

The shock absorber is poorly named. It is actually a damper that slows down the movement of the suspension. By slowing down the suspension, the shocks will control the oscillations of the spring, the suspension arms, and the wheels. This will allow the suspension to be compressed and rebound without continuing to oscillate back and forth. The shock will also control the oscillation of the entire car. When the car encounters a dip, the body will travel downward and then upward as the suspension is compressed and allowed to rebound. If the shocks are bad or too soft for the springs, the car will continue to go up and down, or "porpoise." A well-engineered shock absorber should control all movements of the suspension to keep them at manageable levels. Ideally, the shock should not be used to prevent suspension movement such as body roll.

Stock Volkswagens are horribly underdamped even for everyday street driving. A good set of performance shock absorbers will remedy this problem. The racing shocks are all excellent for track use, but might be overkill if your a car that sees no racing. Instead, use any of the following shock absorbers: Boge Gas, Sachs Gas, Bilstein or specially valved Neuspeed-Bilstein, or Koni heavy duty. These units can work with either the stock springs or sport springs (not race) to improve handling.

High-performance street, Street Prepared, and most other cars with performance-tuned suspensions are infamous for being extremely unforgiving on the street. This is largely due to shock absorber damping, not spring or anti-roll bar rate. When you increase the wheel rates of a VW with stiffer springs and/or anti-roll bars, you do not need high compression damping, in contrast to Solo II Stock classes, where you try to use huge front anti-roll bars and stiff shock settings to limit the body's propensity to roll quickly and compensate for wimpy springs. With higher spring rates, you can use the Koni sport shock absorbers, set between soft and medium. The spring will give the car enough roll resistance that the Koni's firm settings are not needed for stiff compression damping. Another good sport shock is the Bilstein. These nearly indestructible shock absorbers have speed-sensitive, pre-set damping: that is, the faster the piston inside moves, the stiffer it becomes. While not adjustable to affect the handling balance, these are still excellent shocks.

There are several manufacturers of adjustable shock absorbers that make applications for VW high-performance use: the two most common are Koni and Tokico. While some prefer the Tokico's design, I recommend the Koni be-

Fig. 2-11. Konis are adjusted using this supplied knob. The range from full soft to full stiff is 2.25 turns.

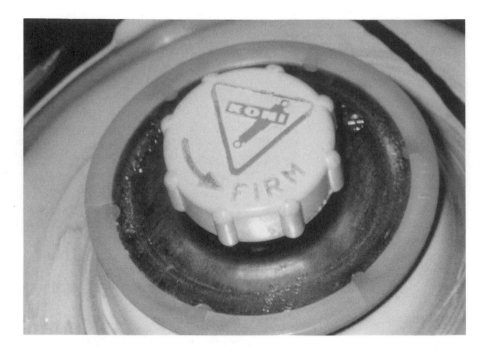

cause they can adjust to a stiffer setting than their competitor (when you buy the "sport" and not the "heavy duty") and their life expectancy is usually higher. While all reputable sport shock absorbers have a lifetime warranty, it is nice when the units last a good long time, saving installation and maintenance time.

Since the shock absorbers are adjustable, the balance of the handling can be changed to suit course or driver considerations. You can stiffen the rear and soften the front for more oversteer, or vice versa for more understeer. For a water-cooled VW, a good starting point is one-half stiff on the front and full stiff on the rear. The idea here is to just dampen movement of the spring and limit the speed of the body roll (but not the total amount) without making the car bounce over surface irregularities. Up until just a few years ago this Koni was only available with external adjustments on the front units. Now, because of Neuspeed's efforts, they are available with external adjustments on the rear also, making them easier to use. You can adjust them to be soft or medium for street use, and then quickly change them to a higher setting at the track.

Bushings and Strut Bearings

The suspension of your VW is mounted to the bodyshell with bushings and strut bearings. The stock suspension bushings do a good job of isolating the cockpit from road noise and vibrations. The compliance necessary to do this makes the stock bushings not quite stiff enough for high-performance use. Since the top of a McPherson strut suspension has to turn as the wheels turn, there must be a bearing that makes this possible. In all VWs this is accomplished by a strut bearing that rides inside a large rubber bushing which helps to dampen road noise. For high-performance and racing purposes, the stock units are too soft, allowing the tops of the struts to move within their mounts. This movement causes unwanted camber change, reducing cornering power. The trade-off for improved cornering ability with stiffer bushings and strut bearings is that both suspension noise and harshness will increase.

Fig. 2-12. This polyure-thane lower control arm bushing will firmly locate the suspension to the chassis. This will prevent camber and other suspension geometry changes for precise handling.

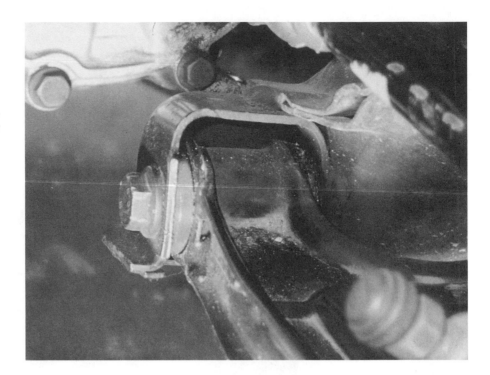

The Unibody

The final portion of the suspension, the unibody, can be stiffened by either using roll bars and roll cages (discussed in the chapter on safety) or by bolting on a "stressbar." These braces are simply metal tubing bolted from one side of the suspension mount to the other. For A1 cars, there is one for connecting the lower control arm mounts, the upper strut towers, and the rear shock towers. While the upper front stress bar is the more attractive of the bunch and is highly noticeable, the lower front stress bar is more important. In fact, for the A2 chassis, VW redesigned the front suspension to stiffen this area, negating the need for a lower brace on the later cars. For A2 and A3 cars there is just the upper strut tower brace and the rear shock tower brace.

THE BEST SET-UP FOR YOU

As far as suspension set-ups go, every one has an opinion as to what they personally like on their car. If you poll ten different race shops as to the best suspension set up for a given car, you will get ten different answers. Some will feel that body roll should be reduced with anti-roll bars, while others will feel that high-rate springs should be used to control body roll exclusively. Many shops say that you can counteract a front wheel drive's propensity to understeer by increasing rear wheel rate substantially, while others say that you need wheel rates that are proportional to the amount of weight supported by the wheel. Each of these ideas is valid and will work for some people. If what you are currently doing is not giving you the handling you desire, try a different theory.

Final adjustments of the car's cornering attitude can be made by adjusting both the camber and tire pressure. Camber settings and tire pressures should be determined by the heat of the tire after a track session. You can check these settings with a tire pyrometer, a great tool for properly setting up a race car. This device, available through most racing supply houses (along with camber gauges), measures the temperature of the surface of the tire.

Fig. 2-13. This upper stress bar will prevent the upper strut towers from flexing during cornering or over bumps for A1, A2, and A3 cars.

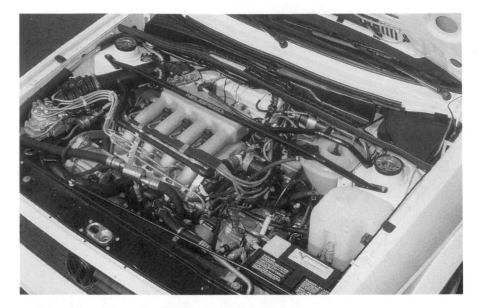

Fig. 2-14. Imported from Germany, the D&W lower stress bar improves the A2 subframe slightly.

Fig. 2-15. An infrared tire pyrometer being used to check tire temperatures.

The proper amount of camber and tire pressure will yield temperatures that are even across the face of the tire. Even temperatures signal that all portions of the tread surface are working similarly. If the outside portion of the tread is hotter than the rest, there is not enough negative camber. If the inside is too hot, then there is too much negative camber. If the tread is cooler in the center compared to the outside, then there isn't enough tire pressure. If the center is too hot, there is too much tire pressure.

On very tight autocross courses, it might be advantageous to increase the negative camber and cause the inside edge of the tire to heat up more quickly. This change will allow the tires to warm up quicker at the start of the autocross run. Remember to adjust tire pressure after each autocross run or each track session. As the air inside the tire warms up, the pressure rises, changing how your car handles.

Generally speaking, optimal camber settings depend on the amount of body roll the car has. If the car has large amounts of body roll, more camber will be

Fig. 2-16. It's a good idea to keep track of the modifications you make to each element of your suspension by recording them in an organized fashion.

CAUTION —
If you lack the tools or experience necessary to modify your suspension, this work should be left to an authorized Volkswagen dealer or qualified repair shop. Attempts to modify the suspension without the proper tools are likely to cause serious injury.

Chassis Set-Up Log

Date _____

LF & RR Cross		Front Weight		RF & LF Cross	
lbs	%	lbs	%	lbs	%
		TOE: IN OUT			

Left Front | **Right Front**

Left Front				Right Front	
lbs	%	WEIGHT		lbs	%
		PRESSURE			
		CAMBER			
		SHOCK or SETTING			
		SWAY BAR			
		SPRING RATE			
		RIDE HEIGHT			
		TIRE SIZE / BRAND / COMPOUND			
		WHEEL SIZE / OFFSET			

Rear Weight

lbs	%
TOE: IN OUT	

Left Rear				Right Rear	
lbs	%	WEIGHT		lbs	%
		PRESSURE			
		CAMBER			
		SHOCK or SETTING			
		SWAY BAR			
		SPRING RATE			
		RIDE HEIGHT			
		TIRE SIZE / BRAND / COMPOUND			
		WHEEL SIZE / OFFSET			

Left Side		Total Weight	Right Side	
lbs	%	lbs	lbs	%

necessary to keep the tire perpendicular to the ground in a dynamic cornering state. Camber settings also depend on the tire brand used: for example, if the car uses BFGoodrich tires, less camber will be needed than if it uses Yokohamas, because of the former's asymmetric sidewall construction. The only true way to determine what your car needs for alignment or tire pressure is to check tire temperatures with a tire pyrometer.

With these guidelines, you can determine the proper settings for your car, driving style, track conditions, etc. The optimal settings that are given in this chapter are rough guidelines or starting points so that you don't waste time barking up the wrong trees. The best way to find your ideal settings is to map everything out on your chassis set-up log (see Fig. 2-16), and just keep tweaking each category until you get the performance you're looking for.

Fig. 2-17. Checking camber with a Smartcamber gauge.

STREET AND STREET PREPARED MODIFICATIONS

The SCCA calls its high-performance street-driven class *Street Prepared*, or *SP*. That's exactly what it is too: preparing a car that can be used on the street and for racing. The intent of Street Prepared rules are to allow the fastest street-able car on DOT-legal tires. SP rules allow most common bolt-ons and modifications, making many of the commercially available suspension pieces that are used on the street quite acceptable.

SP suspensions are equivalent to high-performance street settings, but there is a range of suspension spring rates and alignments that can be used. While the extreme suspensions can get very stiff and unforgiving on rough roads, many cars are still daily drivers (entertaining ones at that). One very nice thing about owning a Volkswagen is that, even prepared to the limits, the cars can still be driven and relied on. Most of the other nationally competitive cars are trailered to events rather than driven.

Since you can run higher spring rates on the street and in SP, the high amounts of negative camber used in stock class racing are not necessary. Depending on exact tire type and size, the optimal settings should be around 2 degrees negative camber in the front, with 1/8- to 1/4-in. toe-out. Cars that are driven primarily on the street might want to reduce these camber and toe-out settings somewhat. One and a quarter degrees negative camber and 1/16-inch toe-out will improve handling immensely over stock settings with little increased tire wear. The guidelines for building a Street Prepared car would produce a very fast street car, rivaling almost any Porsche on a twisty road.

Springs

The spring rates for a stock VW are in the range of 110 lb./in. in the front and 80 lb/in in the rear. Performance street spring systems are in the range of 190 lb./in. for the front and 140 lb./in. in the rear. All-out race springs are in the neighborhood of 400-550 front and 325-375 rear (350-450 front and 275-325 rear for A1 cars). Proper spring rates are very important for whatever you use your VW for. Do not trust cheap springs, as the rates will usually not match each other, and will change with use. Invest in springs once and go with the best that you can.

The conventional type of stock diameter springs are the most common because, for the most part, they are the most cost-effective. These can be anything from stock springs with one or two coils cut off (not recommended) to custom-wound racing springs. The most common type of spring that you see on an autocrossing VW is the sport/street lowering springs. These are available from many aftermarket firms and improve handling immensely over stock. Sport/street springs should be coupled with mild front and rear anti-roll bars. While not being as stiff as a full race set-up, they are still comfortable on the street. With all of the big name tuning firms in the VW aftermarket, there is no one best sport/street lowering spring, so you can shop by "name" preference.

By lowering the car, the sport springs also improve the looks of your VW. Good street sport springs can have progressive rates, giving you a smooth cruising ride with excellent handling. As the car leans into a turn, the soft portion of the spring will be "used up" and the stiffer rates will come into play, limiting further body roll.

If you want to improve handling but do not want to lower the car, you can use Neuspeed's SoftSport™ springs, which are stiffer than stock but retain ground clearance and wheel travel. Another way to accomplish the same task

Fig. 2-18. These Neuspeed SoftSport™ springs are designed with a higher rate than the factory units, but they will only lower the car around a half an inch. This will improve handling on rough roads.

Fig. 2-19. Neuspeed Race springs offer high rates, with the ability to work with the stock perches with no other modification.

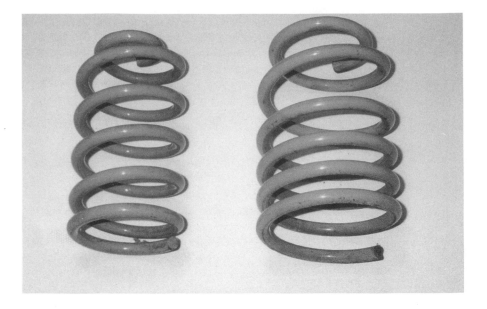

on a lightweight early car is to specify sport springs for 16-valves or A3s instead of the normal sport springs for your 8-valve. The only real difference between any of the springs for the different year and make cars is the weight of the car in question. The heavier the car is, the taller the spring is, thus raising ground clearance when the springs are installed on a lighter car. The exceptions to this

FRONT SPRING/SHOCK INSTALLATION

Fig. A. While the car is still on the ground, loosen the top nut securing the strut top to the shock shaft. This will require either an impact wrench or holding the strut top to keep it from turning. If your shock shaft has an allen wrench hole, insert the wrench into the shock shaft to keep it steady.

CAUTION —

If you lack the tools or experience necessary to disassemble the front suspension struts, this work should be left to an authorized Volkswagen dealer or qualified repair shop. Disassembling the struts without the proper tools may cause serious injury.

Fig. B. After the strut top is removed, loosen the slotted nut (using the proper tool) while the car is still on the ground. This will usually apply enough pressure to allow for easy removal without making the shock shaft spin.

WARNING —

Loosen nuts securing the strut top to the shock shaft only while the car is on the ground. The leverage required to do this could topple the car from a lift or jack stand.

rule are the Rabbit's rear springs and both front and rear springs for the Fox. These are slightly different designs with different spring diameters which would prevent them from working with other perch designs.

For a race spring that fits the stock spring perches, you must look at the Neuspeed Race Springs. Their rates, at 400 lb./in. front and 340 lb./in. rear (300/275 for the A1 chassis), are quite stiff, and with the proper anti-roll bars, can be used very effectively. Generally, they are half the price of coilover units. These springs work best with a small or no anti-roll bar in the front and a medium anti-roll bar in the rear. When coupled with Koni Sport adjustable shocks, these springs are tolerable on the street. Another race spring (front only) that works with stock perches is put out by Carrera (part no. 8MB500P); it offers a rate of 500 lb./in. and will lower a 2200-lb. car around 1 in.

For the all-out racing VW, the set-up of choice includes the coilover spring units, which have the advantage of infinite ride-height adjustability. You can swap the spring itself in ten minutes with one of another rate. These units consist of a collar that welds onto the strut (SCCA rules require that it be welded) and then an aluminum threaded spacer which rests on top of the collar. A large nut that threads onto this spacer acts as the spring perch. Thus, if you turn the nut one way, height goes up, and if you turn it the other way, ride height goes down. This comes in handy in the process of corner-weighting the car. If a corner of the car is low in weight, you raise its ride height, causing a weight gain there and in the diagonally opposite corner, with a corresponding drop in the other two corners. If the weight on that corner is too high, you lower its ride

Fig. C. Loosen the lower shock mounting bolts. To help maintain wheel alignment, mark the bolts and the strut so that it can be installed in the same position; it is, however, best to get an alignment done after this procedure.

Fig. D. Using a spring compressor (purchase or rent from a supply house), remove tension from the upper strut bearing. When compressing the spring, point the assembly away from your body in case the stored energy of the spring is released suddenly.

cont'd. on next page

height. In this way you can achieve an optimally balanced car with equal diagonal weight figures (RF+LR=LF+RR).

Since tracks and surface conditions change, the quick change capability of the coilover unit is appreciated. As a general rule of thumb, the A1 chassis should start at 350 lb./in. front and 300 lb./in. rear. GTIs from '83-'84 should start at 400 in the front and 300 in the rear. A2 cars should be around 450-550 in the front and 325-375 in the rear. The A3 chassis should require rates of around 500 in the front, and 400 in the rear to compensate for the extra weight. These rates are for a car with little or no front anti-roll bar and a medium rear anti-roll bar. If you want to run a large (huge) rear anti-roll bar with correspondingly less spring rate, start with a 200-250 lb./in. rear spring rate. This set-up would be more suited to an Improved Touring car, as the soft rear spring rates would hurt off-the-line launches in a Street Prepared autocrossing car. Cars that are tuned for no anti-roll bars (not even the factory integral piece in the rear) will need close to 600 lb./in. rear springs to counteract body roll and squat.

Some teams have tried controlling all roll resistance through springs with no anti-roll bars front or back. This will not work easily on most Volkswagens or other front drive cars without exceptionally high rear spring rates, since some additional roll resistance is required in the rear to keep the front of the car from picking up the inside wheel. This is because if the car is accelerating out of a turn, all of the weight will be transferred off of the inside front to the outside rear. This will allow wheelspin to occur when you least want it as that inside front wheel is up in the air. A rear anti-roll bar will prevent this more effectively than running high spring rates in the rear. Keep in mind that high rear spring rates may make the car very sensitive to any surface irregularities.

FRONT SPRING/SHOCK INSTALLATION CONT'D.

Fig. E. Due to rust, some cars, such as the Rabbit, require the use of an impact wrench to remove the shock shaft nuts.

Fig. F. With the spring compressed, finish loosening the slotted nut on the shock shaft, and remove the strut bearing, bump stop, and spring from the shock. Replace any worn parts now.

CAUTION —
Do not re-use self-locking nuts or bolts. They are designed to be used only once and may fail when used a second time. Always replace self-locking nuts or bolts with new parts.

Fig. 2-20. This is a typical coilover package with a threaded collar, spring, and upper perch. The C-shaped piece of steel is welded to your stock strut and the threaded tube rests on top of that.

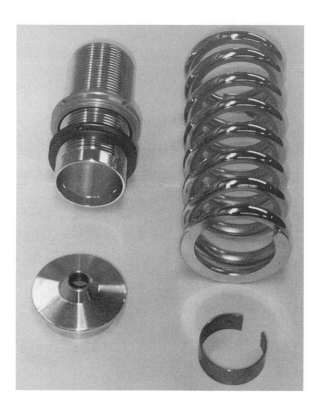

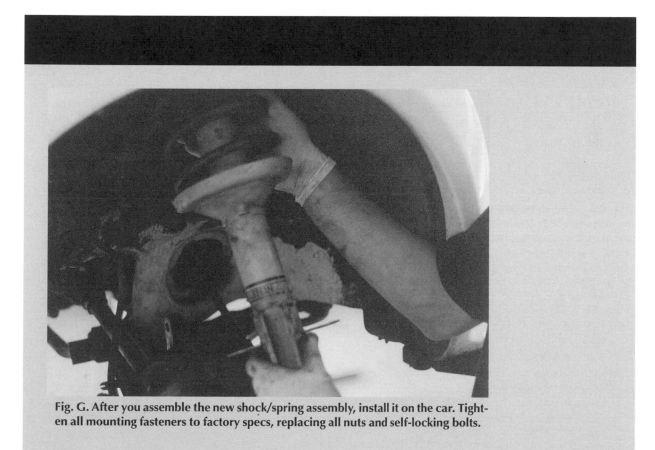

Fig. G. After you assemble the new shock/spring assembly, install it on the car. Tighten all mounting fasteners to factory specs, replacing all nuts and self-locking bolts.

Fig. 2-21. An installed coilover spring system. The bottom collar is welded to the strut, while the threaded sleeve just rests on the collar.

Anti-Roll Bars

For good handling when running stock or street sport springs, you should keep the 22-mm (A1) or 25-mm (A2, A3) front bar for stock class and add a rear anti-roll bar. A1 bars for the rear are usually 25 mm (28 mm hollow). On the later A2 and A3 chassis, some cars came with an integral 20-mm bar. If that is the case, you can add either a 25-mm adjustable or a 28-mm hollow bar. If the car did not come with this integral anti-roll bar, then the best choice is the 28-mm adjustable unit. The pairing of the factory integral bar and a large 28-mm rear anti-roll bar will make the car overly tail-happy.

Fig. 2-22. The Shine Racing Services rear anti-roll bar uses the stock trailing arms to provide the lever arm. The design is similar to the factory's own rear anti-roll bar design.

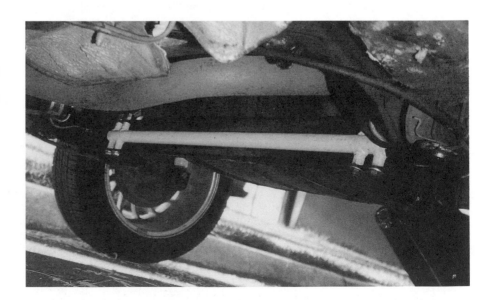

Anti-roll bars are also an excellent idea on any street-driven car. They will improve handling without vastly degrading ride comfort. The smaller bar sizes are best for street use (19 mm on the front and 25 mm rear for A1, 22 mm and 25 mm for A2 and A3); anything larger would be overkill. Keep in mind that the stiffness provided by heavier anti-roll bars will also have the effect of reducing traction on slippery roads. If you live in the snow belt, you should stay away from large anti-roll bars and try to limit body roll with slightly stiffer springs.

For cars running either the Neuspeed race springs or the stiff coilover spring units, the game plan changes. Because of the usually stiff springs, less anti-roll bar stiffness is desired. The best bet on the front would be either no front anti-roll bar or the stock 15- or 18-mm piece. For the most part, the rear anti-roll bar should be of a medium rate (such as 25 mm) with racing springs. This will give you more than enough roll resistance, while boosting the car's responsiveness to turning.

OPM Motorsports, H&H Specialties, and Shine Racing Services have an anti-roll bar design for the rear of a VW that has proven its worth in many I.T. races. This design would work equally well on a street or autocross Volkswagen. The interesting part of the design is that it uses the stock rear trailing arms as the arms of the anti-roll bar, reducing unsprung weight. In fact, the design is similar to the stock integral 20-mm bar found on some A2 and all A3 cars. This design also eliminates all binding that is present in more traditional types of anti-roll bars. There are several different roll-resistance levels available with these units to fine-tune the handling for your individual needs. In particular, H&H and Shine Racing Services each make gigantic rear anti-roll bars to be coupled with relatively soft rear springs (250–300 lb./in.).

Suspension Bushings

Polyurethane, Delrin, or stiffer rubber bushings will prevent excess suspension movements that cause toe and camber changes during hard cornering. This

Fig. 2-23. The A2 and A3 rear trailing beam pivot bushing will create a passive steering action as the suspension is deflected upwards; this helps stability on the highway and on a race course.

Fig. 2-24. A1 vs. A2 strut bearings. Often, your stock bearings are worn out. Replacing them will rejuvenate a tired car.

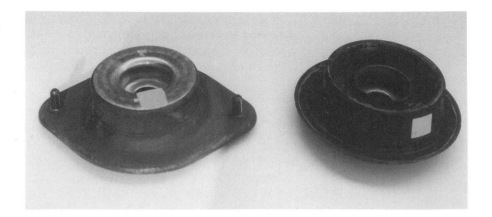

will make the car handle better while only a small increase in suspension harshness will be felt. The limiting of unsprung suspension movement will effectively raise the spring rates of the car, increasing roll resistance. Available at all VW high performance shops, polyurethane bushings are also relatively inexpensive at around $100 for a complete set. They are time-intensive to install though, requiring a bearing or gear press to remove and install them. Be sure to properly grease each unit so that it will not squeak once it is installed. A good, sticky grease for this purpose is waterproof molybdenum disulfide grease, which is available at any local automotive supply store.

For Street Prepared you can change the suspension bushing as long as the amount of metal vs. non metal in the bushing is not changed. In other words, you cannot replace the entire assembly with a metal bearing. What you can do is to change the soft rubber to a higher durometer rubber or polyurethane.

There is one bushing on the A2 and A3 chassis that should *not* be changed to polyurethane for street: the rear trailing arm pivot bushing. The A2 and A3 both have a passive rear steering system in which, as the rear suspension is deflected sideways, the toe-in effectively increases on one side (decreasing, of course, on the other side). This movement is determined by the stock pivot bushing; poly bushings have no provision for this passive rear steer. The rear steer is beneficial in inclement weather and should not be eliminated.

Strut Bearings

Strut bearings are considered high-wear items. That said, a good first step in high-performance suspensions is to just see if your strut bearings are worn out. If they are, they will clunk over low-speed bumps. Another test is to jack the car up, and shake the top of the strut back and forth; if it moves up and down or side to side, the strut bearings are probably bad. Just replacing them with high-quality factory replacement parts will firm up a car's tired handling.

For the early A1 Rabbits and Sciroccos there is a polyurethane unit available that greatly improves handling. It is a direct replacement for the stock unit and increases suspension harshness somewhat. It also has the side benefit of lasting longer than the stock unit, making it a cost-effective upgrade at around $100.

For A2 and A3 cars there are two high-performance options. The first is to use the stock strut bearing from a G60 Corrado or Passat. These units look identical to the others but are slightly reinforced. The second option is to use the stronger, longer lasting strut bearing from a VR6 car. Most shops sell them for around $90 and supply adapters so that they can be used with any shock absorber. One neat feature of the VR6 bearing is that it increases the caster of the car, causing it to require less static camber. With increased caster, negative camber becomes more pronounced as the steering wheel is turned off-center.

Fig. 2-25. A typical camber plate that offers high strength and adjustability.

Fig. 2-26. Installing these OPM Motorsport spacers under your camber plate will increase suspension travel by one inch.

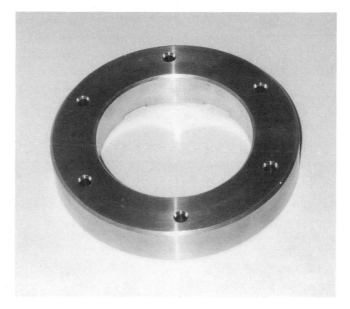

The ultimate strut bearing for an A1, A2, or A3 on the track is the camber plate, available from Euro Sport, OPM Motorsports, Havoc, and Shine Racing Services, among others; they are typically priced at $170 for the pair. These replace all of the stock rubber and bearing unit with a metal spherical joint mounted on an aluminum plate with slotted adjustments. This unit will allow camber to be adjusted quite easily at the top of the strut without necessitating removal of the wheel and tire. The camber plate design will also give greater negative camber capabilities, although this is not necessary on most VWs, as they can get enough negative camber by using the small camber bolts on the bottom of the strut. Because of its metal-on-metal contact, the camber plate will increase noise, vibration, and harshness from the front suspension.

The reason most VW racers use these units is not for camber capabilities. Rather, the camber plate will remove all of the compliance that the stock rub-

Fig. 2-27. If you rotate a camber plate 90 degrees, you get a caster plate. This will increase negative camber as the steering wheel is turned, requiring less camber when the wheels are pointed straight; it will also increase steering effort and improve high-speed stability.

ber strut bearing causes, yielding much more precise handling. The camber plate will also allow greater suspension travel, allowing the racer to lower the car and its center of gravity, while not increasing its propensity to bottom out. Since the camber of the front wheels can be adjusted from the top, the slotted adjustment holes on the McPherson strut are not needed. Some I.T. racers have found it beneficial to weld material into these holes, changing them from oval to round. This will strengthen the joint in case of racing accidents or abuse.

STRESS BAR INSTALLATION

Fig. A. Trial-fit the stress bar on the car, aligning it from side to side. Make sure that it will clear the throttle cable, coolant reservoir, etc. Once you are certain of its position, use a punch and mark where the strut towers need to be drilled.

Fig. B. Drill the strut towers where they have been marked. Use a small drill bit first as a pilot, and then use a larger one to prevent the drill from walking.

Stress Bars

The stress bar or strut brace is one suspension part where simpler is better. The one piece tubular steel front and rear stress bars are probably the best on the market for a racer and street enthusiast. They are simple, strong, and they are also the least expensive. Almost every other VW aftermarket business has its own brand of stress bar on the market, some built from tubular steel, and others from aluminum. For the money, stress bars are one of the most cost-effective ways to improve the handling of any VW; the improvements in structural rigidity and steering responsiveness are amazing. The stress bars also act to preserve the structural integrity of the chassis, reducing its chances of getting flimsy after many thousands of miles.

Fig. 2-28. A simple tubular front stress bar, light and strong.

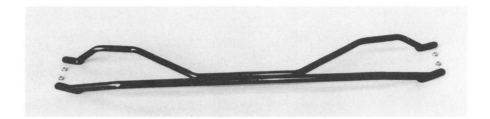

The popular triangulated rear stress bar from Neuspeed is illegal in both Street Prepared and I.T. racing, but it is a possible choice for a street car. The only downside to the triangulated rear stress bar on a street car is the fact that it does cut into trunk space.

Fig. C. Push the nutsert into the drilled hole and tighten, using the supplied nutsert tool.

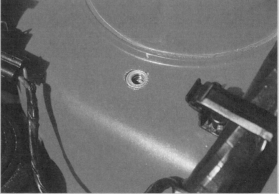

Fig. D. A properly-installed nutsert. These work very well and can withstand serious punishment. Some racers have removed the nutserts and simply use a nut and bolt through the unibody (necessary only for road racing).

cont'd. on next page

Fig. 2-29. The triangulated rear stress bar installed on a Prepared class car, which would be illegal in Street Prepared.

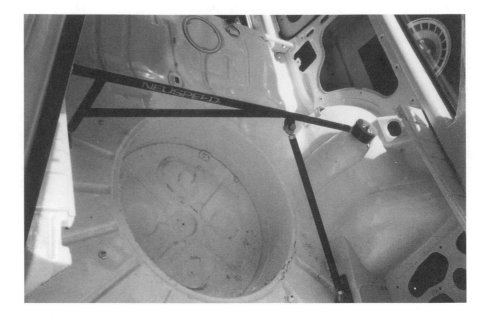

Bump Stops

The bump stops on your VW do more than limit extreme movement of the shock absorber. The rear bump stop on the A2 and A3 chassis actually acts as a progressive-rate helper spring. If you lower one of these cars with the bump stops unmodified, you will actually be riding on the stops after about an inch of wheel deflection. This is not a bad thing. The long foam bump stops will progressively add resistance as they are compressed, up to 150 lb./in. when they are nearly squished. After the long, soft portion of the bump stop is compressed, the more conventional action of the bump stop will be addressed. It

STRESS BAR INSTALLATION CONT'D.

Fig. E. Bolt the stress bar on and enjoy!

Fig. 2-30. The A2 and A3 rear bump stop, in conjunction with the linear rate coil spring, creates a progressive spring system. Additional spring rate can be gained by adding spacers onto the shock shaft to allow the system's rate to rise faster.

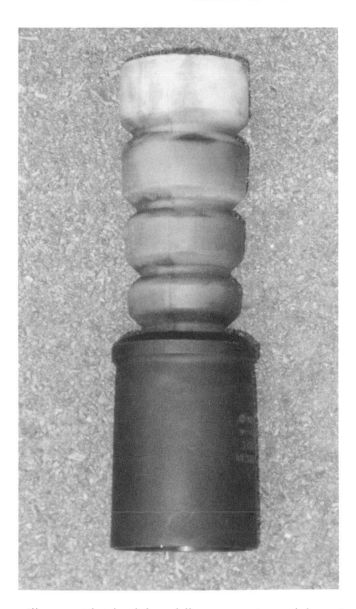

will prevent the shock from fully compressing and damaging itself on a large bump (the bump stop's "spring" rate will rise to infinity).

It could be useful to put spacers (soft rubber or more sections of other soft bump stops) on the shock absorber shaft to allow the long-soft portion of the bump stop to be used sooner. The more spacers you put in, the higher the overall spring rate will be. This can be an easy, cheap way to add spring rate to the rear of the VW. This idea would work on the A1, A2, and A3 chassis and could possibly be adaptable to all the front shocks.

SHOWROOM STOCK MODIFICATIONS

In Showroom Stock, the modifications are quite limited. All pieces must be as they came from the factory. The adjustments of the stock pieces must also be within stock specification as specified in the factory workshop manual. There are some tricks, though, to greatly improve performance. Showroom Stock racers are for the most part experts at bending rules. For this reason it is difficult to find out all of the possible tweaks a person can make; people tend to guard their racing secrets well.

Fig. 2-31. Make sure that strut-tower-to-strut-tower distance is equal to factory specs. If these values are larger than the factory specified amount, you may have less negative camber (unless you get an alignment done).

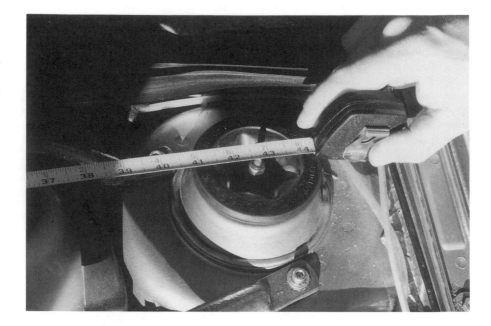

With such limited modifications, a successful racer will make sure that the car is operating at the optimal factory specifications. This does not mean that it will be as it left the dealership. Production variances are such that no two cars are the same. Therefore, some end up faster than others. Since all of the physical specifications of a car are listed in body shop repair manuals, you can see to it that the entire structure matches this blueprint. By measuring track widths, strut-tower-to-strut-tower distances, and wheel base from side to side, you can tell how true to the factory specifications the car is. If it is out of spec, you can have the whole car put on a professional body shop's frame machine to be pulled back into shape. A blueprinted chassis will handle better than a "normal" chassis, as the alignment and suspension settings will not have to take into account variances in the entire body shell. The actual alignment settings that should be used are the maximum factory negative camber and toe-out values. These are published each year in the Showroom Stock rule book.

Showroom Stock racers must also make sure that all suspension (and all other parts for that matter) are in new condition. Some parts such as strut bear-

Fig. 2-32. This lower control arm bushing, shown in the stock position, can be rotated 90 degrees to prevent unwanted suspension movement. Aftermarket bushings for this joint are often simply pieces of polyurethane that fit into the holes in the factory bushings.

ings and shock absorbers will have to be replaced at least once or twice a season to retain optimal handling. Parts will need to be removed and replaced as they wear, not when they wear out.

Some racers try to firm up the handling of the car by playing with the suspension bushings. These locate the suspension in the chassis and allow it to move and flex around for ride comfort. The extra play and flex is not good for predictable handling, however, so firmer bushings are desired. Since it is illegal to change bushing type, some racers make them harder by leaving them outside in the elements for a while (sometimes a year or more). Yet another way to harden these bushings is to bake them in the oven at around 200 degrees for a little while. Take them out, check them, and put them back in for a while more until they are more to your liking. Be careful not to let them burn, because they sure do stink! One note on these tricks is that most technical inspectors for racing events have specifications for almost any vehicle. If your car is protested for illegal suspension bushings or any other part for that matter, SCCA technical inspectors will procure the correct factory piece for comparison purposes. If the durometer (hardness) of your bushings falls out of the range that is given, you will be disqualified.

One additional trick for the A2 and A3 chassis cars is to rotate the rearmost front control arm bushing 90 degrees. The factory bushing has an air gap in one side that helps ride comfort, but it allows too much flex in that plane. By rotating the bushing, the whole control arm becomes better located within its mounts. This trick was used almost universally in the Bilstein Golf-cup series in the mid-eighties, and no one was protested for this modification. This change might not be looked upon kindly by tech inspectors nowadays.

Fig. 2-33. These bolts have a smaller shank that allows more camber adjustment.

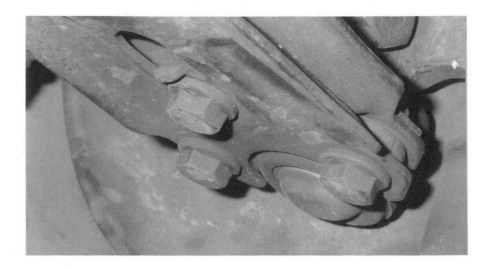

Fig. 2-34. More negative camber can be gained by loosening these bolts and taking advantage of the control arm's slotted holes. Some earlier cars will have rivets that need to be drilled out.

SOLO II STOCK MODIFICATIONS

SCCA Solo II Stock allows some very limited modifications that make the car quicker on the autocross course. The rules were formed with the intent of allowing daily driven cars a place to race. Due to the limited allowed modifications, simple things like alignment become very important. For street driving, the radical camber and toe settings may not be desired. Since these are easily adjusted with a camber gauge (available from many racing supply shops) and measuring tape, one can think of these as just another thing you need to do to prepare your car the day before or morning of an autocross.

Stock class autocross cars tend to prefer high amounts of negative camber (as much as 4 degrees). By loosening the lower strut mounting bolts on the hub and pushing the top of the hub/brake rotor in towards the center of the car, then tightening the bolts, you can get approximately 1.5 degrees of negative camber. If you replace one of the bolts at the bottom of the strut on an A2 car (VW part # N 100 766 01), you can get as much as 2.0 degrees negative camber. If you replace both, around 2.5 degrees negative is possible. These figures are approximate values. Due to production variances, the actual camber you get might be different.

A3 cars all come with the smaller shanked bolts; additionally, their bottom strut mounting hole is also elongated. This can allow up to 3.5 degrees of negative camber, which can be useful considering how much body roll the A3s have with stock class suspensions. This can hamper traction in the exit of a turn. I would suggest experimenting with the camber values to determine what is fastest for your driving style.

Another area that can be adjusted to gain negative camber is the lower control arm/ball joint assembly. If you loosen the bolts (some VWs came with rivets that must be drilled out and replaced with factory VW bolts) that connect the ball joint to the control arm, you can see that there are slotted adjustment holes in the actual control arm. Simply pull on the bottom of the tire (or brake rotor if the wheels are removed) to slide the ball joint mounting flange out. The further out you pull it, the more negative camber you can get. Keep in mind that you can't pull it out all the way; you just want to use all of the adjustment capabilities of the slotted holes. Don't try to make the adjustment holes any larger than they already are. This will result in damage to the CV joint and axle assembly. Tighten the mounting bolts and check the toe of the car. A toe alignment is necessary after anything has been done to increase camber, since the toe will change also. Toe settings should be between 1/16 and 1/8 inches toe-out. Just by setting the camber and toe of a Solo II Stock car you can bestow it with responsive and lively handling.

The rear camber and toe settings are non-adjustable. While some dealers and alignment shops offer special shims that install between the stub axle and the axle beam, these are not legal for most classes as they are not factory specified. Generally speaking, the rear alignment does not make a whole lot of difference in performance if it is near stock specifications. Some A2 cars did suffer from misalignment of the rear axle from the factory. In these cases, the factory decided to install different rear stub axles to prevent excess rear tire wear.

Solo rules permit shock absorber changes as long as the shock length and spring perch placement are identical to stock equipment. While there are many sport shock absorbers on the market, the adjustable types are the best idea. Since shock absorbers are one of the few places where a person can tune the car, the adjustability comes in handy. The exception to that rule is the Bilstein sport valved shock, which has the advantage that you can install it and forget about it (one less thing to be stressed about at a race).

The last suspension modification allowed in the Stock category of Solo II is to the front anti-roll bar. You can remove or replace this with any type of anti-roll bar as long as it serves no other purpose (such as suspension reinforcement). With the stock bars being either 15 or 18 millimeters, the best replacements would be a 22 mm for the A1 chassis, and the 25 mm for all the others. Those are the largest sizes possible for those chassis and go a long way toward improving handling.

Looking at the VW suspension design, one would think that going to a tremendous front anti-roll bar would make an inherently understeering car understeer worse. This is not the case in Solo Stock. The large diameter anti-roll bar prevents understeering, as discussed earlier, by limiting body roll and therefore camber change at the wheels. This will give the front of the car better bite. It will mask the problem of overly soft stock spring rates. Coupled with the large amounts of negative camber, the front anti-roll bar makes the car both quicker and more balanced.

Fig. 2-35. A large front anti-roll bar, such as this Neuspeed 25-mm, will actually help a Stock class VW get more front traction.

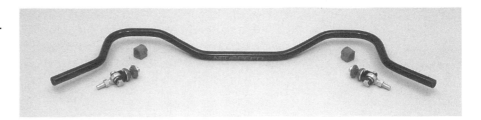

IMPROVED TOURING MODIFICATIONS

Improved Touring rules are very similar to the Street Prepared Solo II rules. This means that, for the most part, so are the best modifications. The two major exceptions are alignment specs and shock absorber choices. To win races in I.T., a car needs to be prepared to the best specifications. In this competitive class, coilover spring units and camber plates are what the front-running cars are using, with no exceptions. You can start at a lower preparation level and finish a race, but you'll be at the back of the pack.

Alignment specifications for Improved Touring are different than Street Prepared due to the higher speeds attained while road racing and the different tire types and compounds. Camber values by and large will be greater in an I.T. car, often reaching four degrees negative. Camber values (and possibly wheel rates) in an I.T. car will also be asymmetric depending on the course. If the track is

Fig. 2-36. Carrera offers shocks that can be tuned to your track's surface; with the addition of the threaded spring perch, the suspension can be set up to any configuration.

counterclockwise, camber will be more negative on the right side, while a clockwise track like Lime Rock in Connecticut or Willow Springs in California will require more negative camber on the left.

Improved Touring racers also do not exclusively use Koni shocks. Both Bilstein and Carrera make excellent shocks that can be purchased with the shock valving set for your individual car. Both types also come in forms that already have threaded portions for coilover height adjustment. Autocrossing and road racing have different shock absorber needs. The average autocrosser will compete on 20 different "tracks" each year, making adjustability a deciding factor. A road racer will rarely see more than four or five tracks a year, allowing the racer to tune the car to a specific track.

In Improved Touring you can only install one stress bar. This bar can be either between the two strut towers or between the lower suspension pick-up points. For the A2 and A3 chassis cars the choice is simple. Since a lower brace is not beneficial, a good upper stressbar is all you need. For the A1 cars it is not quite as simple; for maximum handling it would be good to have both upper and lower braces. The lower stress bar is more important for racing use and this should be the bar that you use. It is against the rules to use a rear stress bar on all cars; however, as mentioned in the safety chapter, a welded in brace in the rollcage can negate the need for one.

One additional allowance for Improved Touring is that suspension bushings are completely unrestricted. You can use all-metal bearings in place of the stock bushings, removing absolutely all play from each suspension joint, thus making the car handle better. An all-metal bearing would perform better than a polyurethane bushing because the latter can still allow some unwanted suspension geometry changes under high stress. The downside of this is that the bearings will not last as long as polyurethane or stock bushings, especially if they are not properly lubricated. The bearings will need to be thoroughly cleaned and reoiled every time the car is run to avoid the dirt that is attracted to the lubrication, which will destroy the bearing. These metal bearings are obviously a great choice for a racing team with a high budget. Some spherical bearings that are available have teflon linings. These are considered to be "prelubricated," reducing a large portion of the maintenance and wear associated with most bearings. Shine Racing Services sells teflon-lined suspension bearings for both A1 and A2 chassis.

Fig. 2-37. The lower stress bar for the A1 chassis is the best bet for IT racing.

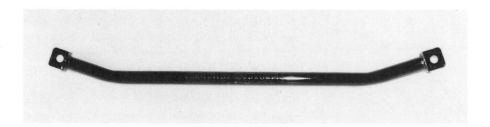

Chapter Three
WHEELS AND TIRES

Fig. 3-1. These 17-inch wheels can use tires up to 215/40/17, which is the optimal size for these wheels, offering excellent traction and transient response. The downside is that ride harshness will increase and they provide less protection for the rim when encountering potholes.

Besides keeping the car from riding on its brake rotors, wheels and tires can be either true performance modifications or mere jewelry for your Volkswagen. If you are interested in performance handling, look at the size and specifications of a wheel or tire before you consider its looks. Luckily, most performance rims look as good as they perform, making your choices easier.

On the side of any tire that is DOT-legal, you will see a number combination that tells you the dimensions of the tire. Examples are 195/50/15 or 185/60/14. The first number is the tread width of the tire in millimeters. The second number is the percent of the tread width that the side wall height is. The third number is the diameter of the rim it attaches to, in inches.

TIRE CHARACTERISTICS

Tires are designed as a tradeoff between a myriad of characteristics. The tires can ride soft or firm. However, the softer the ride is, the more the tire's sidewall will flex. This causes imprecise handling and low grip. The tire can be good in dry weather with high grip and low tread depth, but it will be treacherous in the rain. A tire that has a rubber compound with good high-heat characteristics will become slippery when the weather turns cold. Finally, a tire's rubber compound can be soft or hard. The softer the compound is, the quicker it will be on the track, but in general it will wear out much faster. Tires are another area where you need to decide what kinds of sacrifices you can make.

One of the most talked-about characteristics in a performance wheel/tire combination is the width of the footprint. Generally speaking, the wider the footprint, the better the handling, no matter what the diameter of the tire is. For example, a 15 x 7 wheel will not handle better than a 14 x7 because the footprint is not any larger, using a tire size of 225/50/14 or 15. I mention the rim diameter because the street VW performance crowd has been edging towards

55

larger and larger diameter rims, some as large as seventeen inches. Larger rims will require tires with shorter sidewalls to keep the overall diameter (and hence, gearing) the same. These combinations look good, but do not handle better than a smaller-diameter rim with the same width, except for a slight improvement in transient response. In other words, when you turn the steering wheel, the direction change is transferred quicker to the contact patch (where the tire meets the road) because there is less tire sidewall to flex. The downside to large rims with low profile tires is that the sidewall flex is reduced, decreasing ride comfort; and you're more likely to bend the rim, as it would have less protection from potholes.

Another important consideration with wheels and tires is how much they weigh. The unsprung weight of a car will determine how well the car will handle in bumps and transient maneuvers. The lighter the suspension/wheel is, the quicker it can react because it has less momentum. Instead of skipping over a bump and losing traction, a light suspension/wheel will follow the contour of the irregularity with the tire always in contact with the road. For this reason, alloy rims, although fragile, will improve handling over steel rims.

Fig. 3-2. These forged factory rims from the Passat or Jetta Carat are both lightweight and strong. They are made by Fuchs, a manufacturer of Porsche wheels.

All of the racing classes discussed in this book require DOT-legal tires. Several manufacturers have responded to this requirement and have built DOT tires that for all intents and purposes are true racing tires. They have extremely shallow tread depths and very soft rubber compounds, helping them to stick to pavement very well. These are for racing use only, as their life expectancy and wet-weather traction both leave a lot to be desired for street use. Some manufacturers have different autocross and road race compounds, with the autocross compound being stickier and not lasting as long. The companies that make these tires are: BFGoodrich, Yokohama, Hoosier, Goodyear, Kumho, and Toyo. Several other manufacturers produce R-compound tires (soft-compound racing tires), but are not competitive at this time.

Choosing the right R-compound tire for you and your driving style is like choosing a mate. There are many differences in transient response and how the tire performs at the absolute limit of adhesion, sometimes making the choice one of personal preference. I do not pretend to be the "Dating Game" and I will not say what you should run on your car. I will, however, tell you what the top drivers are running and what sizes they use. This will change as soon as it is

Fig. 3-3. The Yokohama A008R series was the originator of the asymmetric tread block design. This A008RS-2 is the latest iteration. Its popularity has waned in the past few years because of the influx of new and more competitive rubber from other manufacturers.

written, as the tire companies try to gain larger segments of market share with new tire designs. The best up-to-the-minute information source for tire brands and their competitiveness is the magazine *Grassroots Motorsports*. Every time a new tire design comes out, they test it against the others of its type. The editors are not paid by any tire manufacturer and have great unbiased reviews of the tire's performance.

One interesting tidbit of information about DOT racing tires is that the weight of the actual brand tire is very important. While the BFGoodrich Comp T/A R-1 has the ultimate in outright grip at the moment, it is also extremely heavy. A 215/50/13 R-1 weighs 20 lbs., an amazing amount considering that the typical rim that this tire will mount on weighs 12 lbs. The 225/45/13 Hoosier Autocrosser, on the other hand, weighs only 10 pounds. This light weight can be attributed to its bias-ply construction without any steel radial belts. This light weight will reduce the aforementioned unsprung weight and total vehicle weight. A Hoosier(again, bias ply)-equipped car will weigh 40 lbs. less than one equipped with BFGs!

The only downside to this revelation is that the Hoosier Bias Ply does not have the sensitivity to steering input or overall grip that the BFGoodrich has. Some people hate them and some love them. I have found that on a tight autocross course, it is very hard to feel what the bias-ply tires are doing when I turn the wheel. Decreased steering feel is a significant downside on a front-wheel-drive car. The new Hoosier Radial has a good feel and is comparable to the sticky BFG R1; it weighs about 2 lbs. less per tire.

The R-compound tires can be made even faster by shaving off a portion of the tread. This will prevent excess heat from building up in the tire's carcass, making the tire remain sticky through more heat cycles. The shaving will also prevent the tread portion of the tire from squirming under high cornering loads. The wet-weather traction with shaved tires will be even worse than with normal R-compound tires. Many racers will have several sets of both unshaved and shaved tires. The unshaved tires can be used in rainy conditions, while the shaved will work best in the dry.

Fig. 3-4. The Hoosier Autocrosser offers high traction and low weight. It does not, however, give very good steering response on account of its bias-ply construction.

Fig. 3-5. The Hoosier Radial has two deep circumferential grooves and then "holographic" diagonal grooves. The near-slick tread design eliminates the need for shaving. A disadvantage of the Hoosier radial is that it requires a lot of negative camber or else the outside edge will wear out quickly.

The newer a tire is in terms of how many races it has been run in, the faster it is. As a tire warms up to racing temperature and then cools off, it becomes slightly harder. Over one or two heat cycles, this does not matter. Over ten or more cycles, however, the tire will become so hard that the traction will be measurably less than with a new tire. This heat cycling will cause many tires to become useless before they are completely worn out. Well-funded racers can simply use new tires for every one or two races. The budget enthusiast is not so lucky. At the very least, you should replace your R-compound tires once a year, since, after a year, the heat cycling and the hardening of the rubber due to age and ozone exposure will reduce the tire's stickiness to the point where your once-competitive car is bringing up the rear of the pack.

Fig. 3-6. These BFG R-1 tires have been shaved to a 4/32-in. tread depth. This will prevent the tread blocks from overheating and "chunking."

Fig. 3-7. These BFG tires have not been shaved: notice that the outer tread blocks have additional lateral grooves that have been removed on the shaved tire.

Fig. 3-8. Competitive autocrossing will require a second set of wheels and tires. Instead of trailering the car to and from events, you can haul extra tires, wheels, jack, air tank, etc., in the trunk. Believe it or not, this will all fit in the trunk of a Jetta. Golf owners will probably have to flip down their rear seats.

Fig. 3-9. A portable air tank, besides being a cool place to put extra event decals, will be helpful when adjusting your pressures at the track. It will be faster than an electric air pump and is easily refillable at a local gas station.

For autocrossing competitors who do not want to trailer their cars to events, the best way to be competitive on the track and safe on the street is to have two sets of wheels and tires. Street wheels can be anything you want, aesthetically pleasing or not, while your racing tires can be "no compromise" killers. Your racing tires will fit in your trunk area and can be installed at the site; that way, you can have the best of both worlds. Changing to your racing wheels will become a ritual, and with practice, take little time. Do not continue to use the stock jack; a hydraulic floor type is much safer and easier to use.

Fig. 3-10. Air pressure is an excellent tuning tool. In this instance, the author is adjusting the pressure upwards in the rear tires to promote oversteer.

Fig. 3-11. White shoe polish can tell you how much tire rollover you are getting, a gross test to determine the correct pressure.

Tire pressure checks are free in all types of racing and are a great tuning aid. For stock type cars, tire pressure is one of the few tools available for adjusting handling balance. Most Showroom Stock and Solo Stock racers have good luck running higher than average pressures in the front. As the body of the car rolls, the tires have a tendency to tuck in and roll over onto their sidewalls: a change most apparent in the front of a VW, due to its forward weight bias. Adjusting the front tire pressure upwards will alleviate this tendency; some people go as high as 50 psi. The rear tire pressures are subject to some debate: some people will say that you should reduce tire pressure in the rear to induce oversteer, while others say that you should increase rear pressure to induce oversteer, the advantage being that the tire is more predictable at higher pressure. I agree with the latter as a last resort. Remember that by inducing oversteer in this fashion, you are killing the end of the car that is actually sticking. If you get the front to stick to the ground, you do not need to prevent the rear from sticking.

Tire pressures are also a good first-performance modification for a beginning autocrosser or street driver. The only tools you require are a tire pressure gauge, an air source, and some white shoe polish. The shoe polish is to determine how much tire rollover you are getting. By putting a line on the tire from the tread to a few inches down the sidewall, you can see how much is scrubbed off with each run or track session. Most tires handle best with enough tire pressure to prevent more than a half an inch of the shoe polish from being scrubbed off from the sidewall. If there is any one else running a similar car in your class, don't hesitate to ask them their tire pressures. It is rare to find a competitor who won't help a novice. As discussed in the suspension tuning section of this book, final and more exact adjustments of tire pressure or camber can be done with a tire pyrometer.

Fig. 3-12. VR-6 cars require 5-lug wheels, the advantage being that the added lug will increase strength to prevent shearing due to high horsepower.

STREET WHEELS

For street use on the water-cooled Volkswagens, the best compromise of fit versus performance is a 7-in. wide wheel. The wheel diameter that you choose is a matter of taste, although as your tire diameter increases, so does the price. On A1 and A2 cars I would stick with 13-, 14-, or 15-in. wheels and on A3 cars you could run 14-, 15-, or 16-in. wheels with no problems. Some people do run larger rim sizes than these, but there is no clear performance advantage. Keep in mind that as the rim diameter increases, so does the ride harshness and likelihood that you will bend your rims on a less-than-perfect road. For people who live in the snow belt where roads are often atrocious at best, you should definitely stay away from the 16- and 17-in. wheels.

My only other recommendation for street wheel rims is to buy something you personally like the looks of. Wheels can be very fad oriented. In the mid-80s, the most common wheel type was the mesh spoke, with many copies of the excellent BBS available, some good, some bad. In the early 90s, the five-spoked star became popular, with hundreds of variations. Now it seems the soft, rounded outer rim is the style of the moment. They might be what everyone likes, but you are the one who has to live with them until you can afford to buy another set.

Wheel strength is also very important for street use. Many 16-valve 2.0 GTI owners discovered quickly that those beautiful three-piece BBS wheels that came factory standard are very easily bent. This is very typical of modular wheels, since the thin outer lips are quite weak compared to one-piece wheels. Cast-alloy one-piece wheels are recommended for any street use. They will last longer and stay in balance longer than the three-piece modular type. Ronal, MSW, TSW, and Fittipaldi make strong and attractive wheels for your Volkswagen that are reasonably priced.

Wheel finish is another important factor in deciding on a rim for your car. There are three finishes commonly seen today. The strongest and most long lasting is the powdercoated clear or colored finish. This baked-on finish requires no special care, except for cleaning with a damp, soft sponge. Like any other painted or coated surface, you should avoid harsh chemicals when cleaning. Stick with a high-quality wheel cleaner such as P21S® that will not harm the finish.

The second type is a polished finish. If a polished finish is not protected with a good painted/powdercoated clear layer, it will require constant diligence to stay attractive. Bare aluminum corrodes as quickly as bare steel. The white oxides that form on the aluminum's surface are just the tip of the iceberg, as the underlying corrosion will quickly form pits that will weaken the wheel. The best bet for this type of finish is to polish and wax the wheel after each car wash, to insure long-term beauty and strength.

The third type is a chromed finish. Outside of sun-baked California, this is probably the worst idea for anything but a show car. The chrome outer layer (actually a sandwich of copper, nickel, and chromium) is very brittle, while the underlying aluminum is very soft. It can be compared to trying to spray-paint Jello. If it is subjected to any bumps or scrapes, the surface coating will come off in huge flakes. Besides maniacal avoidance of any curbs or potholes, the chromed wheel will also require a layer of wax each time you wash the car.

The street tires that you buy for your car should be appropriate for the type of driving that you do. This simply means that if you need good wet-weather traction, you might want to stick with an all-season design. If you live in Southern California, except for the occasional monsoons, you could probably make do with ultra-high-performance dry-weather tires. As mentioned earlier, if you do any weekend racing, you should invest in another set of rims and tires that are strictly meant for racing. You will be quicker on the track, and your street

Fig. 3-13. These BBS-clones offered by MSW in the eighties were both stronger and cheaper than the real thing. This GTI uses 14-inch wheels to keep some ride comfort on the rough roads of Vermont.

tires will thank you with increased mileage that will offset the cost of the extra racing tires.

For a great selection of both wheels and tires for the street crowd, try calling a mail-order wheel and tire distributor. They have almost any wheel you can think of and offer specials with tire and rim packages for the budget conscious. They can also be a great source for tires alone, with prices far less than a local tire dealer, with no sales tax. The downside is that you would have to pay for shipping (about $6 per tire) and mounting and balancing in your home town.

Fig. 3-14. The modular BBS wheels fitted to the 16-valve GTIs are very fragile. The owner of this '91 GTI replaced his with copies that are much stronger, and yet nearly identical.

Fig. 3-15. The much-copied BBS wheel. High price doesn't always guarantee lasting strength.

Fig. 3-16. These three piece aluminum wheels, made by Keizer, only weigh 9 pounds!

STREET PREPARED WHEELS AND TIRES

The regulations for Street Prepared wheels and tires are especially liberal. The wheel can be any size or offset and the tire can be anything DOT-approved. A competitive autocrosser will take advantage of this rule and go as wide as possible. For a while the hot set-up was a 13 x 7 wheel with a 205/60/13 Yokohama or 225/45/13 Hoosier. Now people are running wider rims than that with nearly the same size tires. A good set-up is a 13 x 8 with the BFGoodrich R-1 in a 215/50/13 size or Hoosier Radial in a 225/50/13. Some people have even been seen running 9-in.-wide rims, which is beyond the recommended rim width for the BFGs.

The reasons for running 13-in. rims are plenty. You have a greater selection of R-compound tires, in wider sizes. You can run tire sizes that are smaller in diameter than stock, which lowers your final drive ratio, making the car quicker. The smaller diameter also will limit the amount of rubbing and scraping of the wide tires on the fender wells. A 13-in. combination also weighs less than the large rim sizes. The only disadvantage is the limitation that it imposes on brakes. You are limited to 9.4-in. brake rotors, which actually work adequately on an autocross course. One thing to think about is that most formula-type cars run 13-in. wheels, illustrating that it is truly possible to be quick on small-diameter rims.

For the best fit on a VW, the wheel that you are considering should have a backspacing of 4.5 to 4.75 in. This offset will allow the largest widths possible. An 8-in. wide rim will rub in the rear of some cars. This is remedied by rolling over the inside fender well with a hammer (gently).

There are several manufacturers of 13-in. racing wheels that will fit a Volkswagen. The ever popular Revolution racing wheel is available in a 13 x 6, 7, and 8. The 13 x 8 is a modular unit costing upwards of $250 whereas the smaller one-piece casts are around $185. Revolution makes an excellent racing wheel that is both strong and light (around 10 or 11 lbs.). They also have several offsets so you can stick on the widest rim possible without rubbing too much. Racing Wheel Services also imports the Alleycat, available in a 13 x 7, which looks like a Minilite, Superlite, or Panasport-type wheel and costs about $125.

Keizer and Duralight both make modular 13-in. aluminum rims that are extremely light (9 lbs.) and are available in any width or offset. These rims are moderately priced at around $150 a piece and are quite popular. Made of lightweight spun aluminum, they will bend easily and are good for racing use only where they won't hit potholes. They are actually meant for circle track racers and sprint cars but will work great on an autocross car.

Another circle track wheel manufacturer, Diamond Racing Wheels, makes lightweight spun-steel wheels. No, that wasn't a misprint: they are light and steel (around 12.5 lbs.). While not being much stronger than the spun-aluminum rims, they are especially cheap, running around $60. These wheels can be any offset and any width in the 13-in. diameter and are available in a silver powdercoat finish that looks exactly like polished aluminum.

Panasport, a long-time favorite, has no 8-in.-wide rim for the VW Street Prepared competitor. For the same classic good looks, however, you can look at Performance Industries Superlite brand of wheels. These are available in a 13 x 8-in. size with the correct offset for upwards of $115 each. Superlites are available in a 13 x 7 but have the wrong offset and actually rub more than the 13 x 8. They are a strong, lightweight alloy construction (11 lbs.) and look great on any VW. Performance Industries now has a modular rim that looks nearly the same but offers a wider variety of sizes. Unfortunately, the modular wheel costs much more. One tip on the Superlite wheels is to purchase a set of hubcentric rings for Fittipaldi brand wheels that are used on VW-size hubs. These are available from most any mail-order tire company and press-fit into the Superlite wheels, eliminating vibrations.

The fastest tires you could put on any of these rims would be the BFG 215/50/13 Comp T/A R1 or the Hoosier Radial in a 225/50/13. Although Hoosier does make a 225/45/13 Bias Ply Autocrosser, it is not as quick as the other two. As in Solo Stock, if you are having problems with tire wear and cannot afford to replace tires as often, try the Toyo or Kumho in a 205/60/13. These would also be good tires for Street Prepared Time Trial cars.

Tire pressures for a Street Prepared VW will be much lower than for a stock-type class. The higher pressure is not needed as the rims are much wider, and

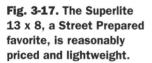
Fig. 3-17. The Superlite 13 x 8, a Street Prepared favorite, is reasonably priced and lightweight.

Fig. 3-18. These BFG 215/50/13 tires have about 9 in. of footprint, highly necessary in fast Street Prepared competition.

the body roll is greatly reduced, making the tire less likely to roll over onto its sidewall. For a Street Prepared car running 13 x 8 wheels with 215/50/13 BFGoodrich tires, the best starting point would be 24 psi front and 24 psi rear. Using a tire pyrometer, you can get the exact pressure you need from there.

SHOWROOM STOCK WHEELS AND TIRES

The rules for Showroom Stock wheels and tires are simple: SCCA rules limit wheel rims to the exact type that came on the car for that year and model, no exceptions. Tires can be 20 mm larger than stock, and aspect ratio can be reduced by five percent. If your car came with 185/60/14 tires, you can go to a 205/55/14, which will be faster.

The top-ranked people in this class run either the BFGoodrich Comp T/A R1, Goodyear GSC-CS, or Hoosier Radial. Other competitors are running the Toyo Proxes RA1 or the new R-compound from Kumho; their popularity is increasing as more people discover them. Yokohama's A032-R would be an excellent wet-weather racing tire.

SOLO II STOCK WHEELS AND TIRES

SCCA requires cars in this class to have the same width and diameter wheel as stock with up to a 1/4-inch offset change (6 mm). The offset change will allow you to increase the track of your car to reduce weight transfer and improve handling. Wheels can be lighter than stock so aftermarket alloys can be used. As a reference point, most stock alloys (14 x 6) weigh 17 lbs., and stock steel wheels weigh 24 lbs. Tires can be anything DOT-approved that fits on those rims and does not stick out of the fenderwell.

Most competitors in this class will run the stock factory alloy wheels or lighter weight aftermarket alloys. The most popular of the latter are Revolution racing wheels (imported by Racing Wheel Services). These very lightweight wheels are available in nearly any width or offset, allowing you to maximize performance while still staying within the rules. Revolutions are much lighter than a stock-type alloy wheel (14 x 6) at 14 lbs., but it would be much more

Fig. 3-19. Manufacturers such as BFGoodrich and Hoosier offer free on-track support, as well as free mounting with your tire purchase.

Fig. 3-20. The Revolution RFX is a lightweight wheel that is very popular in grassroots racing.

cost effective to stick with factory alloys. Stock alloys are fairly easy to come by and do not cost nearly $200 a copy as do the Revolutions.

The fastest people in this class either run Hoosier Radials (road race or autocross compound) or BFGoodrich COMP T/A R1s; and, as in Showroom Stock, look for newcomer Kumho to gain in popularity. In some cases the fastest tire would be a harder road-race compound, especially on longer courses or hot days, as the softer compounds can overheat.

IMPROVED TOURING WHEELS AND TIRES

The I.T. regulations limit the diameter of the wheel to what it came with from the factory. All non-GTI Rabbits and Sciroccos run 13-in. wheels while everything else (Rabbit GTI, Golf 8-valve) runs 14-in. wheels, except the 2-liter, 16-valve GTI, which has 15-in. wheels. ITA and ITS, which include the 16-valve cars, allow 7-in. wide wheels. ITB and ITC, which constitutes everything else in Improved Touring, only allow 6-in.-wide wheels. A wheel that is used in Improved Touring has a much harder life than one in Solo II, making expensive wheels a costlier proposition if you bend or break one. This fact should also rule out the lightweight spun-aluminum variety: one good bump and they are history.

Tire allowances are similar to Street Prepared in that anything DOT-legal is fine. For the most part, Toyo seems to be the most popular tire type. Its high levels of grip and durability make it the best choice for many racers. BFGoodrich, Goodyear, Yokohama, and Hoosier are also used in Improved Touring. BFGoodrich and Goodyear are used by some of the better-funded racers because of their slightly better grip, but with a cost of shorter tread life. Hoosier "Dirt Stocker" tires are used in the rain by many teams. These DOT-legal dirt-track tires offer phenomenal wet-weather traction.

For the ITS competitor who runs a 2-liter GTI, there are many choices. The 15 x 7 wheel size is very common on the street market. O.Z. Wheels, MSW, Borbet, and Ronal all make high-quality wheels that will not break the bank. Since there is such a plethora of high-quality, lightweight 15 x 7 wheels on the market, it does not make sense to look for the more expensive Revolutions or Panasports. The good tire size for this rim is the 205/50/15 or sometimes the 225/50/15.

Fig. 3-21. These five-spoke stars are available cheaply (less than $100) at nearly any wheel/tire supplier. These Fittipaldi Monolithics were purchased during a close-out sale, yet they are light and perfect for an ITS car.

Fig. 3-22. 14 x 6 rims, such as this Borbet Type C, are very common in the aftermarket.

Fig. 3-23. Another good choice is a factory alloy rim; they are available at nearly any salvage yard and they will always fit.

ITA racers with the 1.8-liter, 16-valve engines can run a wheel size of 14 x 7. Here, the choices are quite limited. Revolution has a rim in this size that works but is expensive at over $185. Panasport just released their lightweight wheel series ("Lights") in 14 x 7 and they're a good choice at around $165. For the budget minded, TSW makes a 14 x 7 wheel called the "Stealth." Albeit slightly heavier than the others, it retails at around $135. The 225/50/14 is the fastest tire size for this rim size.

If you have a car in ITB that uses 14 x 6 wheels, your options are legion. Factory and lower-cost aftermarket alloys are very popular in this group. If you can afford them, Revolution and Panasport have lighter wheels for the well-heeled racer. The most popular tire size is the 205/55/14, which all of the manufacturers make. Some competitors do run the larger 225/50/14, but realize that it does require higher tire pressures to prevent the sidewall from buckling on a narrow rim.

The 13 x 6 wheel size that Rabbits and Sciroccos require used to be the staple of high-performance wheels. Nowadays, it is very hard to find good examples of this size wheel. Panasport and Revolution both make this size, and are expensive. Superlites do come in this size and are extremely cost-effective at around $94 a piece! Borbet's type C is also available in a 13 x 6 and costs less than $100. The tire size 205/60/13 seems to be the most common here and it is offered by all of the R-compound manufacturers.

Chapter Four
BRAKES

Fig. 4-1. The first step in brake upgrades: vented rotors. The vents allow air circulation to prevent heat build-up.

Now that your Volkswagen handles and sticks to the track, you have to prepare it to stop equally as well. The brake system consists of the pedal; the master cylinder, which converts your foot pressure to the movement of hydraulic fluid; and calipers, which convert the movement of the brake fluid into pressure, forcing the brake pad against the brake rotor. This system is responsible for slowing your car down: not a light task, considering that most VWs weigh over 2000 lbs.

When a braking system overheats and stops working, it is said to "fade." Fade is caused by overheating of either the brake fluid or the brake pad. When the brake fluid overheats, it starts to boil; as this fluid turns to gas, the gas can exert less pressure on the pads to slow the car. The brake pads will overheat when the material the pad is made of (a mixture of metallic compounds and binding agents) gets hot enough that the binding agents start to boil. This boiling will cause gaseous compounds to be released from the pad. This gas has nowhere to go, because it is trapped between the pad and the rotor. Thus the pad cannot fully press against the rotor to stop the car.

To help prevent this occurrence under racing or panic situations, you can upgrade your VW's brakes. The first step is to go to high-performance brake pads, which will still operate at higher working temperatures than the stock or bargain brand types. Second, you can change your brake fluid to one of a higher boiling point. Solid brake rotors can be swapped with ventilated ones from a

GTI for longer lasting brakes. Rotors can even be cross-drilled to allow the gas that builds up under the brake pads to escape.

Whatever modification or maintenance you do on your brakes, remember this: brakes are vital for safe motoring, more than any other operating system on a car. Do not take short cuts and don't fail to recheck all fittings and lines that you have worked on. If, after reading your Bentley repair manual, you are unsure as to what needs to be done on a brake system, take your car to a reputable automotive repair shop. The money the mechanic charges you will be far less than what it could cost you if something you did causes an accident.

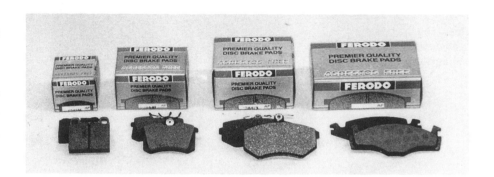

Fig. 4-2. Ferodo pads are a popular choice for street and autocross because they provide good high-temperature performance. They are available for many different applications, both front and rear, for VWs and other cars.

Brake Pads

Stock brake pads do an adequate job of slowing your car down. Unfortunately, certain aspects of their design are less than desirable: for example, the stock pad will start to fade after several hard stops, limiting the amount of performance driving you can do in one session. Stock pads also emit a large amount of black, sticky dust that is hard to clean off wheels. Thankfully, there are many direct-fit replacements available.

The old standby for high-performance brake pads, the Repco Metal Master, is being eclipsed by new products on the market. The Metal Master is a good pad for most applications and is readily available, but it has high brake pedal effort and is very hard on brake rotors. A similar type pad, the Mintex Silverline, is a good pad but has the same deficiencies as the Repco type. Ferodo has a good street and autocross compound, which has a high coefficient of friction for less pedal effort and good high-temperature performance. Its only downside is that it emits more brake dust than the Repco as the pad is used.

Carbon metallic pads are becoming *de riguer* in road racing applications. Their high-heat capabilities and great stopping power make them excellent choices for I.T. racing. The pad itself is made up of carbon fibers and metallic particles held together with high-temperature binding agents. The carbon fibers give the pad its high heat resistance and some racing pads are completely made of carbon fiber filaments.

Performance Friction, a maker of carbon brake pads, has a good street and autocross pad called the HP. Priced slightly more than the Repco, this pad warms up much quicker than racing carbon pads and still has good heat-resistant properties, making it an excellent choice for the autocrossing car. Hawk, in addition to making many racing compound pads (such as their "blue" pads), makes a pad designated Y5, which is very popular with autocrossers and street enthusiasts. A newcomer in the VW brake pad arena is the Carbomet brand pad. Like the Performance Friction HP, the Carbomet is a carbon metallic pad with quick warm-up capabilities. It also has the advantage of being the same price as the normal semi-metallic pads. Carbomet claims that their pad lasts two to three times longer than the semi-metallic pads. If this claim is true, you will probably need to replace rotors long before the pads wear out. These pads are available through Euro Sport.

In all cars that have rear drums, both Ferodo and Repco make good replacement shoes. These brake drums can be used in any class you run in or on the street and are more than adequate at slowing down the lighter end of the car. For rear disc set-ups, all of the manufacturers who make front pads also make rear pads.

Fig. 4-3. Be sure to turn your rotors between pad changes. This allows the pad's surface to align closely with the rotor's face.

When replacing brake pads or shoes, the rotors (or drums) should be either new or freshly turned to remove any grooves. Most of the ventilated rotors can only be turned once, and sometimes not even that if the brake pads are particularly hard on them.

Brake pads are not something that you can just install and immediately expect improvements of stopping ability. Brake pads need to be properly bedded in, such that the pad surface exactly matches the surface of the rotor. Additionally, there are excess binding agents in pads that need to be fully cured before they can withstand high heat.

Some pad makers will include instructions on brake bedding. If not, it is easily accomplished in the following way: Find a lonely stretch of straight road. Accelerate up to about 60 or 70 and then slow very hard down to about 10 (don't come to a stop), then accelerate back to 60. Repeat this until you start to feel the pads fade. Then let the brakes cool off (a couple of miles should do it) and repeat the process twice. This should allow the pads to mate with the rotors and allow the binding agents to cure.

BRAKE FLUID

Brake fluid changes are allowed in all of the discussed classes and would be a great idea for any street car. The main reason for changing brake fluid is that it attracts and absorbs water from the atmosphere. Over extended periods of time this water will diminish braking efficiency and corrode the braking system.

To determine a brake fluid's resistance to water affecting its performance, there are two types of brake fluid boiling points. First is dry boiling point; the higher it is the better the brakes will be when the fluid is fresh. The second boiling point is wet; this is measured after the fluid has absorbed a substantial amount of water from the atmosphere. Good dual-duty brake fluids would have high wet and dry boiling points while a race-only brake fluid would have an extremely high dry boiling point and a low wet boiling point. Low wet boiling point racing fluids need to be changed very often (once every other race). Good dual-duty brake fluids should be changed at least every two years, or even every year for maximum performance.

I recommend several different types of brake fluid for street, autocrossing, and road racing. A good brake fluid for most cars is Pentosin Super DOT 4. This brake fluid has both high wet and dry boiling point levels and works well in any car. If Pentosin cannot be found, another good brake fluid is Castrol GT LMA.

BRAKE PAD/ROTOR CHANGE

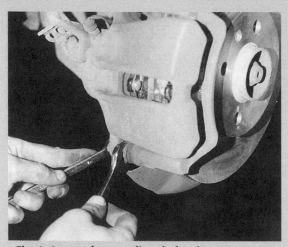

Fig. A. Loosen lower caliper bolt using two open-ended wrenches.

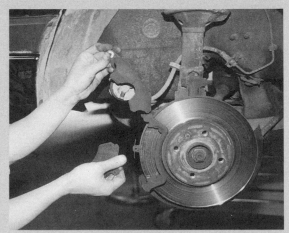

Fig. B. Pivot caliper up, and remove old brake pads.

CAUTION —
If you lack the tools or experience necessary to modify your brakes, leave this work to an authorized Volkswagen dealer or qualified repair shop. Attempts to modify brakes without the proper tools and experience are likely to impair the efficacy and safety of your brake system.

LMA stands for low moisture absorption, making it a good choice for a street or race car where brake fluid is not changed often. Its dry boiling point levels are not as high as the Pentosin, but it is readily available at any automotive parts store. ATE Super Blue, a new brand of fluid on the market, offers higher wet and dry boiling points than even the Pentosin! For the all-out racing car, AP 550 is an excellent brake fluid with an exceptionally high dry boiling point. It will need to be changed often as its wet boiling point is rather low, but it is the best for a no-compromise racer.

STREET BRAKES

Braking systems are more important on a street car than on a racing car. I say this because on an autocross course there's really nothing to hit. On a road racing circuit there is just the track and other racers who are equal or better drivers than you are. On the street you need to contend with other cars, people of differing abilities behind the wheel, varying road conditions, pedestrians, wildlife and other unforeseeable events that could lead to a collision. Street brakes need to work the first time you use them on a cold morning with little or no warm up and continue working no matter where you drive.

Most automotive manufacturers do a tolerable job at designing street braking systems; VWs are usually better than the norm. For additional safety and performance capabilities there are many improvements that can be made. A good template for these performance upgrades is to follow the example that Porsche sets in all of its modern production cars. All have exceptional four-

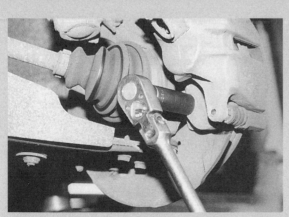

Fig. C. Loosen bolts that secure the caliper carrier to the hub.

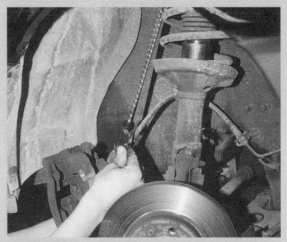

Fig. D. Support the caliper and bracket assembly with a bungee cord so that you don't damage the brake line.

cont'd. on next page

Fig. 4-4. This is everything that is required to upgrade your brakes from 9.4 in. to 11 in. Notice that the bearing housings, bearings and calipers need to be replaced as part of this upgrade.

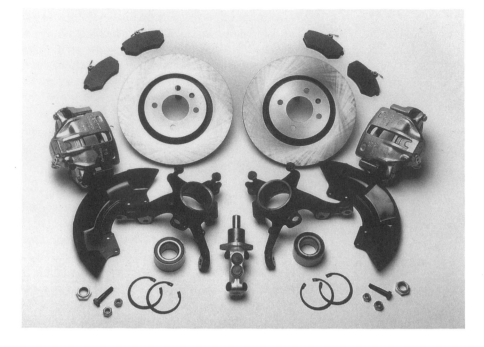

wheel cross-drilled rotors that never fade or fail to stop the car. Porsche's brakes are also easy to modulate, with pedal effort proportional to brake force.

BRAKE PAD/ROTOR CHANGE CONT'D.

Fig. E. Clean off the new rotors with a brake cleaning spray.

Fig. F. Install the new rotor using a new phillips-head screw.

CAUTION —
If you lack the tools or experience necessary to modify your brakes, leave this work to an authorized Volkswagen dealer or qualified repair shop. Attempts to modify brakes without the proper tools and experience are likely to impair the efficacy and safety of your brake system.

The first upgrade in a street car's braking system should be the replacement of both the brake pads and the brake fluid. Pentosin or Castrol LMA are good choices for brake fluid. The Performance Friction HP, Ferodo Street/Autocross, or Carbomet pads for the discs and Repco and Ferodo shoes for the drums would be excellent on the street. These pads and fluid changes, along with double-checking the integrity of the stock system, are a good first step for a street car.

If you are running 14-in. wheels, you can upgrade your discs to the 10.1-in. rotor units from the Scirocco 16-valve or A3 chassis. If you have gone to 15-in. wheels, you can upgrade to the Corrado 11-in. rotors, vastly improving braking power. (Some 15-in. wheels don't fit with 11-in. brakes; check with the manufacturer.) By increasing the diameter of the brake rotor, you increase the swept area of the brake system, thus applying more braking force to the wheel, while being more resistant to heat-induced fade.

The braking system can also be improved by installing cross-drilled rotors. These rotors are available from many companies in any of the rotor diameters and make good brakes simply outstanding. Cross-drilled rotors are drilled with a computer-controlled mill and then balanced to prevent vibrations. If you cannot upgrade brake diameter, the cross-drilled 9.4-in. rotors are still an excellent choice and perform quite well.

An alternative to cross-drilled rotors is the slotted rotor, which utilizes grooves that are machined into the face of the rotor to channel gases away from the hot brake pads. Like the cross-drilled type, slotted rotors are hard on brake

Fig. G. Install the caliper bracket and caliper assembly to the hub and rotor.

Fig. H. Apply a brake pad paste (available at most automotive stores) that prevents the pads from shimmying (squealing) in the caliper.

cont'd. on next page

WARNING —
Tighten all fasteners to the specified tightening torque as listed in the manufacturer's repair manual. Make sure that the caliper mounting bolts, sleeves, bushings and spacers are clean and free of corrosion.

Fig. 4-5. Cross-drilled rotors allow heated gas to escape from beneath the pads.

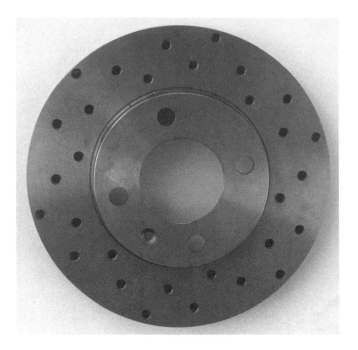

pads. The advantage over cross-drilling is that the rotors will be less prone to cracking under high-heat conditions.

BRAKE PAD/ROTOR CHANGE CONT'D.

Fig. I. You will need to push the caliper piston back into the caliper before you can install the new pads; this can be done with a caliper retractor (available at most automotive stores) or it can be done carefully with a pair of large channel-lock-type pliers.Install the new brake pads, and pivot the caliper down; tighten caliper bolts.

WARNING —
Brake fluid is poisonous. Wear protective glasses when working with brake fluid, and wear gloves to prevent fluid from contacting the skin. Do not siphon brake fluid by mouth.

NOTE —
To prevent brake fluid from overflowing the master cylinder fluid reservoir when you push in the caliper pistons, use a clean syringe to remove some fluid from the reservoir.

Fig. 4-6. Slotted rotors act similarly to cross-drilled rotors; while less prone to brake fade, they do have a tendency to wear pads quickly.

The rubber brake lines should be replaced with teflon-lined, braided stainless lines. The stainless line will not expand under the 300 psi pressure that brake lines are subject to. All of the energy of your foot on the pedal is transformed into brake pad pressure against the rotor, with minimal loss. With stock rubber lines the brake pedal is mushy to the touch, with little feel as to how the brakes are actually working. When you upgrade to stainless the pedal becomes firm and easy to modulate.

Fig. 4-7. Stainless braided brake lines will improve pedal feel and braking force because they expand less under pressure, unlike stock rubber lines.

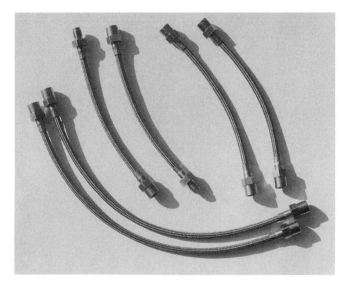

On Volkswagens with rear drum brakes, you can upgrade from the drums to the discs. If you have upgraded the rear drum shoes to Repco or Ferodo, you will rarely notice a difference between the drums and discs. People who do need the added capabilities of the rear discs can change all of the appropriate parts. The parts you need include the discs, hub carrier, stub axle, and brake lines. These will be available at any salvage yard and can range from $50 to $300, depending on demand in your area.

Fig. 4-8. To change to rear discs, you can either purchase an entire rear axle beam from a salvage yard or you can replace the individual stub axles, rotors, calipers, lines, etc.

On some Volkswagens there is a stock, adjustable brake-proportioning valve that is ride-height sensitive. The thinking is that if you have a large load in the trunk, the rear of the car will be lower. A lever attached to the trailing arm changes the brake-proportioning valve to allow more rear braking force in a heavily loaded car. If you lower one of these cars, you fool the system into thinking that it has a lot of weight, making the rear brakes lock up too soon. To get rid of this problem, most companies offer the small clip that attaches the trailing arm to the valve in different dimensions than the stock unit. You can also adjust the valve by turning the center allen head bolt to fine-tune the brake balance (clockwise gives more rear brakes). On cars that do not have this valve, an aftermarket brake-proportioning valve can be used to limit the brake pressure to the rear lines.

Brake-proportioning valves should be adjusted so that the front brakes will lock up before the rears for street use. To test this, find a *deserted* parking lot (*do not* test around other cars or obstacles or on the street!) and brake very hard. If the fronts lock up first, you will feel a difference in the steering wheel (it will become "light"). If the rears lock up, the rear of the car will move to one side or the other. Adjust the bias with either the factory A2 unit or an aftermarket unit so that the fronts lock up first in a straight line but you can get the rear inside wheel to lock up in a sharp turn (it will be unloaded because it will more than likely be off of the ground). A logical way to do this is to adjust the brakes so that the rears lock up first; then start backing off the valve, testing and repeating until the fronts just start to lock up before the rears. Keep in mind that the re-peated stops will start to fade the front brakes, affecting the balance. *For safety purposes, make sure the fronts lock up before the rears: otherwise the car could*

Fig. 4-9. The A2 and A3 factory brake-proportioning valve. To adjust, loosen the 17-mm nut and then turn the allen bolt.

WARNING —

This is a delicate adjustment that affects the safety of your car, and should not be made unless you can test in a track situation away from other cars and obstacles. Make sure the fronts lock up before the rears—otherwise the car could be unstable during braking.

be very unstable during braking. For racing, you can tune the car's balance under braking using this method.

Brake ducting will also keep the brakes cooler and help prevent fade during high-speed driving. As in Improved Touring and other types of racing, you can either choose the factory route with the 16-valve ducting or you can find what you need at any racing supplier. Of course, brake ducting would only be helpful and feasible at the front of the car.

Most of these modifications will also work on cars equipped with anti-lock brakes. Stainless braided lines, high-performance pads, and brake ducting will all help your braking systems. Brake-proportioning valves and brake fluid should be left as they came from the factory. While ABS brakes are a worthwhile option when buying a new car, they would be a major hassle to retrofit into an earlier car.

STREET PREPARED MODIFICATIONS

Fluid and pad changes can be made in Street Prepared cars; a good dual-purpose DOT 4 brake fluid such as Pentosin, ATE Super Blue, or Castrol LMA and pads such as the Ferodo Street/Autocross, Hawk Y5, or Performance Friction HP will do the trick for this class. In addition, all Street Prepared cars can change brake lines to braided stainless types, and brake master cylinders and boosters can be changed. Brake-proportioning valves are allowable additions but are seldom necessary.

Since Street Prepared rules allow updating and backdating of any cars listed on the same line of the Solo II index, you can change all solid rotor cars to the vented rotor type. You cannot update to a larger brake rotor diameter, as these are only available on certain cars that aren't listed on the same line of the SCCA rule book as cars with smaller rotors. This is of little consequence for two reasons: braking is excellent with the smaller vented rotors and the large rotors will not fit inside the recommended 13-in. wheel. You can update the Golf and Jetta II to rear disc brakes. However, this would only be a good idea if you found a great deal on the disc brake package. With uprated rear brake shoes, the stock drums do a good job. Adding a brake-proportioning valve might also

Fig. 4-10. 10.1-in. rotors vs. 9.4-in. rotors. For Street Prepared racing, stick with the smaller ones as the 10.1-in. rotors will not fit within 13-in. wheels.

be more trouble than it is worth for an autocross car, but if you are having brake bias problems, this is a good way to remedy them.

SHOWROOM STOCK AND SOLO II STOCK MODIFICATIONS

In the racing classes we have been discussing, braking modifications are very limited, so everything allowable must be done to gain advantage. From an overheating point of view, autocrossing is easier on a braking system than road racing. However, the braking force (dependent on coefficient of friction of pads against rotors) must be the same as or greater than in road racing with quicker warm-up times. These differences necessitate different compound brake pads which would be either road racing or autocross types. Luckily, the manufacturers of road-racing brake pads make high-performance street pads of the same quality. Street brake pads make excellent pads for an autocross car as they warm up quickly and have a high coefficient of friction for stopping power.

Brake fluid and pads are all that can be changed on a Showroom Stock car, while Solo II Stock allows these mods plus the replacement of the factory rubber brake lines with stainless lines on 1992 or older cars. Showroom Stock cars should use a fluid such as the ATE Super Blue or AP550 with a road-racing specification carbon fiber pad (such as a Hawk Blue). Solo II Stock cars would benefit most with a good dual-purpose brake fluid such as the Pentosin, ATE Super Blue, or Castrol LMA. Good brake pads for a Solo II Stock car would be the Ferodo Street/Autocross, Hawk Y5, or the Performance Friction HP.

IMPROVED TOURING MODIFICATIONS

The regulations for Improved Touring are similar to Street Prepared except that the needs are different. The only difference in the rules is the ability to add brake cooling ducts. These can extend from the front spoiler or airdam area back to near the brake rotors, feeding fresh cool air to the braking surfaces. Holes can be cut in an aftermarket or factory front airdam to accommodate the ducting. For A2 cars, you can use the factory 16-valve ducting system or you can make your own as you have to on the A1 chassis.

Improved Touring brake pads need to be able to survive much higher temperatures than the autocross or street type, and it matters less if it takes a while

WARNING —
Some brake pad compounds, such as carbon fiber, require that the pads be warmed up before they become effective. Do not use race compound pads on street cars.

Fig. 4-11. This Tilton brake-proportioning valve allows you to adjust front-to-rear brake bias. Pushing the lever forward increases front brake pressure and pulling it back increases rear pressure.

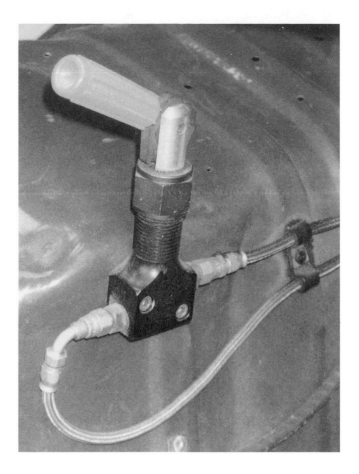

for them to warm up. One long-time favorite brake pad brand was the Ferodo DS11. For more high-tech brake pads, Performance Friction makes three different race compound pads for your racing VW. These three race pads are designated 80, 83, or 93. The 80 compound has a medium friction level and medium level of pedal effort. The 83 compound has the least amount of pedal effort and has a high coefficient of friction for maximum stopping power. The 93 compound is a new formulation that resists premature wheel locking while assuring faster stops. All of these pads have operating temperature ranges in excess of 1200°F, far hotter than other brake pads. The Hawk Blue compound pad is also a good bet for I.T. fitments.

Since the temperature of the braking system gets far hotter on a road-racing car, the recommended brake fluid is AP 550. It can handle the added temperature well and its extra maintenance levels should not be a problem for a dedicated I.T. team.

Brake-proportioning valves are also allowed in I.T. competition and are an excellent idea because of the higher speeds and the need to slow down from them. At higher speeds, brake proportioning becomes more crucial as the recovery time in case of error is much smaller. If the front-to-rear proportioning is not right, the car will be unstable during hard braking. The most common brake-proportioning valve used is a Tilton unit.

Brake lines are unrestricted in Improved Touring. All rubber lines should be replaced with teflon-lined, braided stainless to improve braking. Additionally, the hard steel lines can be replaced. You can reroute the steel lines into the cockpit to put a brake-proportioning valve within reach of the driver. This would be exceptionally helpful under changing track conditions.

Fig. 5-1. An exhaust gas analyzer, using a probe inserted in your car's tailpipe, can tell you what the ratio of air to fuel is in your intake system by measuring %CO and exhaust gas particulates. Several U.S. states have rigorous smog inspections to prevent pollution.

It has often been said that an internal combustion engine is not much more than a pump. It relies on the pumping of air and fuel into the combustion chamber to be ignited, then pumped out to allow room for new air and fuel. The engine relies on the intake system to move all of the ingredients into the engine. This intake can be split into two parts. The first is everything prior to intake manifold/cylinder head interface, while the second, the cylinder head, intake valves, and camshaft, also play a role in the movement of air and fuel. These two sections are easily adjusted and modified, but the actual cylinder block, pistons, and crank are still in the car, making modifications to those parts a little more difficult.

For an engine to make horsepower and torque it has to be able to take in the fuel and air it needs in the proper mixture and, at this mixture, needs to be moving at the proper velocity. The mixture then needs to be ignited completely and without pre-ignition. The spent gases are required to exit as quickly as possible and in sufficient volume. This section is concerned with the first of these needs: the intake of air and fuel.

The Environmental Protection Agency considers the intake system a pollution control device, making nearly any changes illegal. Switching fuel-injection types, richening the mixture, and removing vacuum lines are all taboo. Even replacing the horrible stock carburetor with a twin sidedraft design is not approved. This makes most modifications fall under the category of "proceed at your own risk." While this is a mild inconvenience for a racer, it is a serious complication for a street enthusiast. To tell if something is legal or not, a good rule of thumb is that if it increases fuel flow for a given airflow into the cylinder, it is illegal. If the modification improves airflow, it is usually EPA-legal, because the system automatically compensates with more fuel to keep the ratio correct.

The most basic adjustment of an intake system is the air/fuel mixture. As in all chemical reactions, the amount of each combustible is highly important. The stoichiometric ratio (the ratio of ingredients in any chemical reaction) of air to fuel in the fuel-injection system is set to about 14 to 1—14 parts air to 1 part fuel. This is also called *lambda*, the point at which combustion is most efficient. This 14:1 ratio is a compromise for your Volkswagen's intake system. For maximum power the ratio needs to be 13.2:1–13.6:1 (more fuel) and for best fuel economy the ratio needs to be at least 16:1 (less fuel). There are other points to consider in these equations. The greater the stoichiometric ratio is, the hotter the engine will run. This will cause the engine to knock or ping as the air/fuel mixture is ignited prematurely. If the stoichiometric ratio is too low, not only will the fuel economy suffer, but the car will pollute more and the increase in heat can damage the converter. Too much fuel will also not be burned properly, and will actually wash the walls of the cylinder, reducing its lubrication.

TUNING YOUR INTAKE SYSTEM

When you start tuning your intake system, whether you have a carburetor or a fuel-injection system, you'll need to check your air/fuel mixture. You only need to do this, however, if you don't have an oxygen sensor or if you bypass your car's existing oxygen sensor (which is, of course, illegal for road use).

To measure your mixture, you can use a system with an oxygen sensor or you can measure the percent of carbon monoxide in your exhaust stream. This is best measured with a %CO meter. For maximum performance, a substantially higher than stock %CO is not really required; you just have to make sure that the %CO does not decrease as the RPM rises. Most stock systems will have %CO of 1.0 or less. For the best performance, and in any racing class that allows mixture change, you should set it at around 2 %CO. A fuel injection system with an oxygen sensor will adjust itself to compensate. However, the oxygen sensors are not used by the injection system at wide-open throttle, allowing the increased mixture to help horsepower.

Another way to measure the air/fuel mixture is to install an aftermarket gauge that uses an oxygen sensor to measure oxygen content in the exhaust. These air/fuel monitors are available from K&N and TWM Inductions and are extremely user-friendly, telling you if your engine is running rich (too much fuel) or lean (too little fuel).

If your car already has an oxygen sensor, you have to splice into its wiring and no additional sensor is needed. According to TWM, for one-wire oxygen sensors, this means connecting the lead wire from the gauge to the wire that leads out of the sensor. For three-wire oxygen sensors, there will be two wires (+ and –) that supply power to the sensor's integral heating coil. The third wire will be the actual wire that sends the signal to your car's brain or to the gauge you are installing (the color of that wire will vary with the car model: check a wiring diagram found in a service manual). If you don't have an oxygen sensor, you need to drill and weld a fitting (an 18 x 1.5 nut) into your exhaust manifold's downpipe or your header.

A final way to determine your air/fuel mixture is to measure the temperature of your exhaust. An engine where the air/fuel mixture is set correctly will have an exhaust gas temperature of between 1300 and 1400 degrees Fahrenheit. Hotter temperatures indicate lean burning and cooler temperatures indicate rich conditions. There are gauges and sensors available for this temperature reading. The most popular type is produced by VDO, and can be fitted to any car.

Fig. 5-2. Sidedraft carburetors, on account of their large, direct air flow design, offer good high-RPM horsepower. Unfortunately, the amount of fuel they deliver is usually imprecise, leading to low fuel mileage and high emissions.

CARBURETION

There are two main designs for getting the air and fuel into the combustion chamber: carburetion and fuel injection. Carburetion is a passive intake system: fuel and intake air is sucked into the combustion chamber via reduced pressure of the downward-moving piston. Since the system is passive, it cannot adapt to changes in air quality related to temperature, humidity, or elevation. This makes it very hard to tune for a compromise of fuel efficiency, emissions, and good power; settings end up being on the rich side. Manufacturers have all but stopped producing cars with carburetors for U.S. consumption because these systems can't easily meet current emissions laws while giving car owners the driveability they expect. This passive system also makes it difficult for manufacturers to compensate for intake manifold variations.

Carburetion was used on some Volkswagens until 1984. The stock carburetor on all of these cars is not a high-performance unit and should be replaced if you want any horsepower gains. Usually the stock unit is replaced with either a good downdraft type such as in I.T. racing or a pair of sidedraft carburetors.

Street and Street Prepared Carburetors

For Street Prepared and high-performance street driving, you can install dual sidedraft carburetors with between 40 and 45 millimeter venturis. The most readily available brands are Weber, Dellorto, SK, Solex, and Mikuni. It is not recommended to change the fuel injection system on your engine to carburetion, both for legality and performance sake.

The main advantage of dual sidedraft carburetors is a slight increase in high-RPM horsepower. This equates to about one or two hp more on a Street Prepared car with dual sidedrafts when compared to a well-tuned fuel injection system. That increase comes at the expense of increased maintenance and lower fuel mileage. Often the car will not accelerate any quicker than a lower horsepower fuel-injected car. This is because the high-RPM horsepower gain of the carbs took away the low-end torque. As the saying goes: horsepower sells parts, torque wins races.

Improved Touring Carburetors

For Improved Touring use there are certain specified carburetors (single downdraft type) that can be used. While the optional units must not be modified, the jets, needles, and metering rods may be replaced. Proper set-up and tuning is a black art that has all but vanished in today's world. If you are unsure about what does what in a carburetor or you would like advice on optimal performance, consult an I.T. shop on how to set one up. Improved Touring shops are one of the last places that still tune carburetors for Volkswagens. Some I.T./high-performance shops will even sell I.T. competitors "spec" carburetors that have been optimized for racing. The optimal spec carburetor is a Holley/Weber 5200. This can be tuned quite readily, yielding nearly the horsepower of a fuel-injected car. This specific carburetor is also commonly used in SCCA's Formula Ford category, making high-performance tuners plentiful.

One thing to think about is that a VW that is used in I.T. racing will perform better with the stock fuel injection system than one of the specified carbs. After the initial outlay of funds to switch from carbs to fuel injection, the car will be cheaper to maintain and will require less fiddling during the season. If your car came equipped from the factory with the option of either carburetors or fuel injection, update to fuel injection.

FUEL INJECTION

In a fuel-injected car, the process of getting air and fuel to the combustion chamber is different than with carburetors. As the piston moves in its downward stroke, the vacuum pulls fresh air into the chamber past a device that is called an airflow meter. The meter tells the system how much fuel is needed for combustion. The necessary fuel is then sprayed onto the intake valve where it mixes with the incoming air, and is then drawn into the combustion chamber. The basic air/fuel mixture is set at the airflow meter; other systems (the cold start valve, the frequency valve, the differential pressure regulator, etc.) adjust the mixture for particular operating conditions. Additionally, all fuel injection systems since 1981 (1980 in California) have oxygen sensors mounted in the exhaust stream to provide feedback on combustion efficiency so the system can vary the mixture accordingly.

The most basic type of fuel injection found on water-cooled Volkswagens is the Bosch CIS system. This is an almost completely mechanical fuel injection system with most of the basic air/fuel adjustment done via the airflow sensor plate. As the engine sucks more air, the sensor plate rises and physically moves a valve system (fuel distributor) to give more fuel. The CIS "basic" system was used from model years 1976 to 1980.

In model year 1981 (model year 1980 in California), the CIS with Lambda was introduced. This added an oxygen sensor feedback loop to the basic system that kept the air/fuel mixture at lambda, giving better fuel mileage and emission quality. In model year 1984, GTI and GLI models got a full-throttle enrichment switch to give more fuel for maximum power. This system was used from its introduction until model year 1987, with the A2 chassis cars using it only on the base models.

Fig. 5-3. This Scirocco uses an A2 Digifant manifold and fuel injector rail in conjunction with a Haltech fuel-injection system. This is a cheap way to get complete tuneability of the intake system. Note that Haltech does not use an airflow sensor, just an intake temperature sensor and a throttle potentiometer.

In model year 1985, VW introduced the CIS-E system on the GTI and GLI models. The CIS-E system came with full-throttle enrichment switches and an actual "brain" with fuel delivery maps that varied mixture according to load and RPM. In addition, the frequency valve of the earlier cars was replaced with a differential pressure regulator, giving more precise mixture variation. The CIS-E fuel injection system was used until model year 1990. The CIS systems are highly tuneable and there are a plethora of high-performance parts available.

With ever-tightening emission control laws, VW decided that it needed to vary ignition timing as well as fuel mixture to meet the tightening specifications. VW also decided that it could make a good injection system itself, without paying Bosch to design it. From model years 1988 through 1992, the Digifant system was used on all of the 8-valve cars. This system is geared primarily for good fuel mileage and low emissions, not performance. While some Stock class racers have had good luck with this system, it is not a good idea for performance use, as it can't provide enough fuel at high RPM, due to its airflow sensor and fuel injector design, if airflow is increased substantially. Additionally, the entire system is adaptable, which is normally a good thing. Unfortunately, the Digifant system seems to learn bad habits from a performance standpoint. For example, it reduces the timing of the car when the coolant sensor senses above average coolant temperatures. This would be bad in a racing situation as the engine needs to continue to put out maximum horsepower even under high temperatures There are few high-performance parts available to increase horsepower either. For cars that are running in Street Prepared, I recommend changing this system to either a CIS (basic) or an aftermarket programmable fuel injection system. For highly modified street cars, I recommend changing to the CIS-E system.

Changing the Digifant system is a fairly straightforward, however lengthy, procedure requiring the replacement of the entire intake system, from the air filter housing to the intake manifold. The intake manifold and throttle body will need to be swapped with one from a CIS 8-valve car. Changing the systems also requires swapping the fuel pump, fuel lines, injectors, and fuel pump relay to the specific type for the system you are changing to. Additionally, the entire ignition system needs to be replaced with a donor car's, including distributor, coil, and ignition module. Street-driven cars should swap to

Fig. 5-4. Here is a close-up of a Haltech throttle potentiometer. This piece is actually a General Motors part. It just bolts to the top of the throttle body and connects to the throttle cable linkage assembly.

the CIS-E, making the knock sensor, throttle position switch, and related paraphernalia necessary. You shouldn't have any legal problems resulting from this changeover as long as you make the swap using an intake system from a car of the same model year as yours or later. That's the only way you can be sure that the system meets the emissions performance standards in effect during your car's model year.

The 16-valve cars in 1990 received a much better system than the Digifant. The CIS-Motronic system, like the Digifant, varied ignition timing with the fuel mixture. However, it was biased towards performance and is conducive to high-performance tuning. In addition, there are many high-performance replacement computer chips available that custom tune the engine for even more power. Motronic systems are used today in all of the A3s as well.

As in carburetion, there are aftermarket units available for increased power. Haltech and Electromotive both have programmable fuel injection systems for VWs. These systems can look similar to a dual sidedraft system, where the intake air goes through one of four throttle butterfly plates, or they can use a manifold and throttle body from a factory injection system. The advantage of these is the user programmability. The entire fuel delivery map can be custom-tailored to your engine's need. With the increasing popularity of laptop computers, the ability to tune a VW exactly to a particular track, in the paddock, is here. This is where the extra performance comes from, not an increase in fuel or air flow. These are possible alternatives to factory-type systems in Street Prepared competition, if you can afford $1500 for a basic set-up. You will also need to rent a chassis dyno to properly tune this injection system. Shop around your area to find the best/most affordable dyno you can rent.

Electromotive produces one of the better aftermarket systems for your VW. A complete system will cost nearly two thousand dollars, but includes many interesting designs. The Electromotive system has an integrated crank-triggered ignition system that utilizes two coils, each firing two cylinders (creating a distributorless ignition). A crankshaft-mounted toothed wheel and block-mounted sensor tell the computer the timing position of the engine. (Alternatively, you can mount the toothed wheel to the now-unused distributor shaft.) The proper spark is then delivered to the twin coils, and therefore, the spark plugs. To determine how much fuel the engine needs, the injection system uses a throttle position sensor that is easily mounted to the factory throttle body or to throttle bodies similar to dual sidedraft carburetors. The Electromotive system will then open the injectors as needed for maximum power.

Fig. 5-5. K&N air filters come in many shapes and sizes, they are re-useable, and they can improve air-flow over the stock paper element.

Air Filters

A good substitute for the factory paper element is the K&N air filter. This washable unit consists of a fabric medium surrounded by a metal screen, all formed into pleats. The benefits are increased airflow and no diminishment of the airflow as the filter becomes dirty, unlike the original paper type. Since it is washable, it never needs to be replaced. K&N air filters should be washed every fifty thousand miles with K&N's cleaner and then re-oiled with their filter oil. This makes it a very cost-effective upgrade at $40.

Fig. 5-6. Cutting holes in the fender side of the air box can improve throttle response and high RPM horsepower. Intake noise will increase with this modification. In some instances, this modification will cost power if the engine is inhaling warm air.

Airboxes

In addition to fitting a K&N air filter, you can also modify the box that the filter is housed in. This would include removing the preheating system and cutting holes in the box to improve airflow. Additional holes should be cut in the front of the box near the headlight and the side that faces the fender well to allow cold, dense air to enter the engine. No additional holes should be cut in the engine side to prevent hot air from entering the intake stream. The colder the intake air is, the more horsepower an engine can put out, and pre-ignition of the fuel air mixture (knocking or pinging) will be reduced. To insure that only cold air is inhaled in the intake stream, you could use flexible tubing to duct air from in front of the radiator or inside the fender well. Make sure the tubing is not routed low to the ground, as you can accidentally have your engine ingest water from a puddle; this will destroy the engine.

All of the non-CIS cars can replace the entire air cleaner housing with an aftermarket part that allows you to mount a cone shaped K&N air cleaner. Modification of the air box will improve power between 3 and 5 hp. The downside to this power gain is that the stock air box muffles the intake air. Modifications such as these will cause the car to be louder at full throttle.

Airflow Sensors

A1 cars that came with a 60-mm air flow sensor plate can gain about 6 to 8 hp if they go to a larger unit (80 mm). The 1.7 liter cars are usually equipped with the small type; the GTI's and many of the other cars have the larger version. This part is expensive if purchased from the dealership. You should be able to find a reasonably priced one at a salvage yard. A used airflow sensor will need to be cleaned before it is installed (using a carburetor cleaning spray). The air/fuel mixture will also need to be adjusted after installation.

Fig. 5-7. The A1 intake manifold suffers from a small throttle-body flange and restrictive runners. It can be improved with porting to the runners and matching the flange opening to a larger throttle body.

Fig. 5-8. The A2 8-valve manifold can flow as well as any ported A1 unit, with more torque due to its long runners. This piece can be adapted to the A1 engine by relocating the rest of the fuel injection system to the passenger side. While not quick and easy, it can offer some horsepower and torque gains.

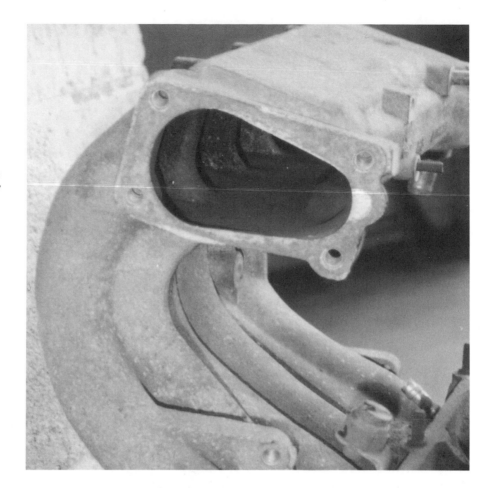

Throttle Bodies/Intake Manifolds

Rabbits and Foxes came with very small throttle bodies. Aftermarket throttle bodies are available to swap. Some of these aftermarket units come with adapter plates to adapt a large throttle body to a small opening in the intake manifold. Unfortunately, the throttle body will do little good in this configuration. It would be better to match the opening in the manifold to the throttle bodies outlet. Many aftermarket firms can supply you with a ported and matched intake manifold for this swap.

Another way to increase horsepower is to install the intake manifold and throttle body from the A2 CIS cars. This will place the airflow sensor and fuel distributor on the passenger side of the car. It will also necessitate the air cleaner housing from a A2 chassis car. This will be cheaper than the aforementioned modifications; according to Techtonics's dyno tests, there is a loss of 2 peak hp, but others have found that this modification will gain you both more horsepower and more torque at lower RPM. The standard A2 throttle body is the same as the aftermarket throttle body and can be adapted to the earlier cars. An unmodified intake manifold from the A2 chassis will allow more airflow than most ported and polished earlier units, while mild porting will increase airflow (and hp) even further. Additionally, the later manifold has longer intake runners, enhancing torque. These parts are available at any salvage yard that has Volkswagens and will be very cost-effective.

Fig. 5-9. Velocity Tuning offers oversized throttle bodies for even more airflow. The throttle body with the darker butterfly plate has a diameter 4 mm larger than the smaller unit, which is a stock A2 throttle body.

Fig. 5-10. A Rabbit (A1) throttle body vs. an A2 or Neuspeed throttle body. Notice how much larger the butterfly plates are. This should only be used if you also machine the intake manifold to match; don't use an adapter plate.

For very large engines (larger than 2.0 liters for 4-cylinder or turbo, larger than 2.8 for 6-cylinder), it is sometimes beneficial to upgrade the factory throttle bodies such as are used on the A2 and A3 cars. The European Corrado VR6 comes with a larger 2.9-liter engine; it also has a larger throttle body that can be fitted if you increase the displacement of your VR6 engine. For turbocharged and large displacement A2 and A3 4-cylinders, Velocity Tuning sells throttle bodies that have been bored out with larger butterflies fitted, increasing the amount of air that can be sucked into the combustion chamber.

To increase airflow into the cylinder head, you can port match the intake manifold to head surface within one inch of the gasket on either the manifold or cylinder head. You can grind out portions of either the manifold or the cylinder head that do not perfectly match up with the other part, using the gasket as a template and grinding the manifold or head to match it. The most precise gaskets for this purpose are the factory stock units. They have more precise positioning of the ports and their holes are usually larger than non-factory parts.

Fig. 5-11. A U.S. VR6 throttle body vs. a European 2.9 liter Corrado unit; the gains from this piece will only be noticeable at higher RPM, and in conjunction with other modifications such as performance camshafts. This should not be your VR6's first modification.

There are two methods to port pieces like the intake manifold, exhaust manifold, or cylinder head. The traditional approach is to attach an abrasive wheel to a die-grinder or good power drill and slowly smooth and polish the necessary parts. This is very time-consuming. The modern way is to send the piece to Extrude Hone. This company will mount your part in a fixture that pumps an abrasive compound. As this abrasive compound flows through the intake manifold, or anything else, it will grind away anything that restricts its movement. Since intake air will find the same such places restrictive, this type of machining can create the best possible airflow through the passages.

Competitors who race other makes of cars often replace the stock intake manifold with custom-made units. These are constructed from scratch from lengths of aluminum tubing that are larger in diameter than some stock manifolds. These are not an advantage for Volkswagens with the A2 manifold. The A2 manifold was designed with large enough runners to feed the engine properly with air. Also, the individual runners taper as they feed into the cylinder head. This tapering will increase velocity of the intake air charge, increasing torque and responsiveness. Euro Sport has dyno-tested a custom-made intake manifold on a Street Prepared Rabbit. The custom piece gained one horsepower at 6500 RPM with a huge loss in torque at lower engine speeds. Since acceleration depends on torque at the low and mid range, a custom manifold such as this is usually not a good idea.

Sixteen-valve owners can upgrade to the European intake manifold. This factory part has larger runners (50 mm) for increased high-RPM horsepower. It will cause a corresponding drop in low-end horsepower and torque. For this reason, this manifold is only recommended for the 2-liter engines as they have adequate torque to compensate for this drop.

Fig. 5-12. The ported A1 manifold on the right has larger and rounder ports. In addition, you can see where the runners have been cut open to port through the entire length of the manifold.

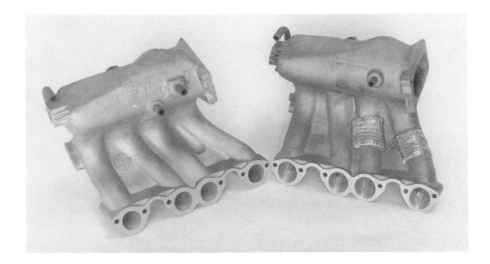

Fig. 5-13. Shrick VR6 manifold dual runners provide for good torque and horsepower.

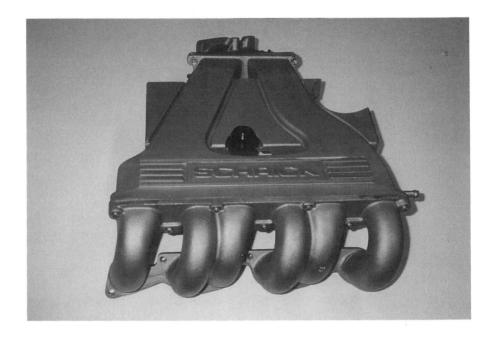

Fuel Delivery

One good piece to try from the Volkswagen parts bin for CIS cars is a warm-up regulator from the Audi 5000 (part no. 0438-140-034). A normal warm-up regulator is a part of the cold temperature mixture richening system, and functions only as such. The Audi regulator performs this function and has a vacuum assembly that senses the change in vacuum that occurs under heavy load conditions. When this happens the regulator will add more fuel to the mixture by lowering control pressure and preventing detonation under high-load conditions. Like the European fuel distributor, the Audi regulator is a last-ditch effort to wring more horsepower out of a CIS system when other, simpler options are not legal.

Fig. 5-14. This custom-made manifold will increase high-end horsepower by a little bit over a well-ported factory piece; however, the low-RPM torque will suffer because of its short runner length.

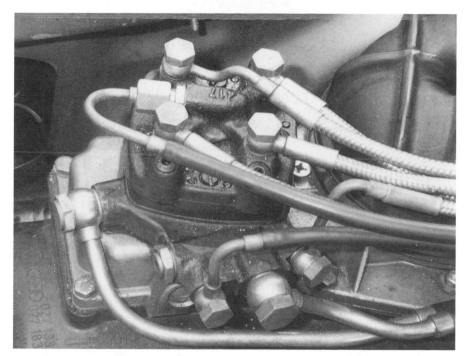

Fig. 5-15. A European fuel distributor has different valving to allow more fuel flow at high RPM. This piece does not have a provision for a frequency valve, an integral part of the oxygen sensor system.

For VWs equipped with Lambda, but not equipped with full-throttle switches (pre-1984), these switches can be retrofitted to the earlier cars. The basic idea of full throttle enrichment is to fool the car into thinking it is cold and thus richen the mixture at full throttle. Install the full-throttle switch on the throttle body (best obtained from a salvage yard) and run two wires from the full throttle switch to the engine coolant temperature sensor that is mounted on the bottom of the coolant outlet pipe on the cylinder head. The full-throttle switch on the throttle body, when closed, will simply connect the two contacts on the engine coolant temperature sensor, making the car think it is cold.

Fig. 5-16. A full-throttle switch enrichens the mixture when throttle is wide open. This can be retrofitted by using the factory mounting system to mount the switch (make sure you get this when you purchase the switch) and then wiring it to the engine coolant temperature sensor located on your head's coolant outflow pipe.

For this to work, you must have a resistor or trim potentiometer (0–5000 Ω). This will allow you to change the duty cycle (measured with a multimeter) to 65%. Without the trim potentiometer, the duty cycle will be 80%, too rich for most applications. The full-throttle switch was marketed in the early eighties as "Lambda Power" by the now defunct company, Drake. Power gains from this modification will be about 4 to 5 hp if extra fuel is needed, assuming there is additional air already flowing.

COMPUTER CHIP INSTALLATION

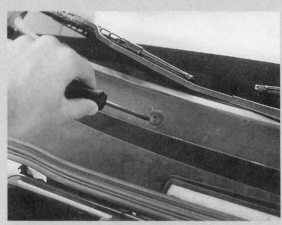

Fig. A. Disconnect the negative battery cable (VW radios will require the anti-theft code to be entered after this procedure; see owner's manual for details). To access the module located underneath the drip tray on the passenger side, carefully unscrew the plastic retainers and remove the rubber weatherstripping that attaches the tray to the car.

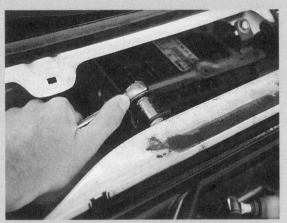

Fig. B. Unbolt the bracket that secures the module to the chassis.

CAUTION —
Installation of an aftermarket computer chip may affect new car warranty coverage. Be sure to check with your authorized Volkswagen dealer regarding warranty limitations before you start this procedure.

Fig. 5-17. A remapped computer chip will take advantage of high octane gas (92+) to increase timing, and fine tune the fuel curve to increase power on Motronic injected cars. In some cases, the chip has replaced hours of dyno tuning for most bolt-on street parts.

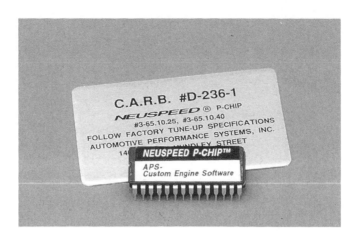

Computer Chips

A2 and A3 cars with Motronic injection systems, including the VR6, can have aftermarket computer chips installed for a 7- to 11-hp advantage (using race gas). The computer chip in the Digifant cars can be replaced, but few aftermarket firms are willing to invest the time to offer upgraded timing and fuel maps. CIS-Motronic and Digifant cars will also benefit from the updating of the entire computer module. Updated units (the latest iteration) are available from Advanced Motorsport Solutions or your local dealership (very costly) and will give you a few more horsepower over the earlier programs.

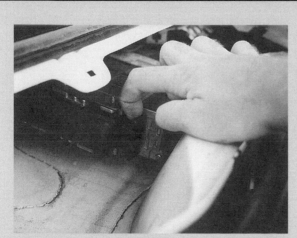

Fig. C. Remove the wiring harness from the module by first pulling the retaining clip toward the front of the car with your finger tips. Be very careful not to damage any of the many pin connectors.

CAUTION —
Not all aftermarket chips are legal for highway use. Always check with your chip manufacturer as well as with the appropriate authorities in your state regarding the legality of the chip you wish to install.

Fig. D. Remove the four six-point star screws (socket available through any major tool supplier) from the end of the module.

cont'd. on next page

STREET FUEL INJECTION

Legality of fuel injection modifications take on a different hue when tuning a street car. Emissions quality is the yardstick on which to base questions about the legality of a certain part. Thankfully, the aftermarket has developed many parts for VWs that are legal for street use, including computer chips, throttle bodies, and air cleaner units.

For street driving, it's best to stick with modifications that only increase air-flow into your engine, since your injection system will automatically compensate, to a certain extent, for the added air with the proper amount of fuel. That means sticking with air cleaner units, throttle bodies, intake mani-folds and the like, as discussed earlier. The exception to this rule is a California Air Resource Board-exempt computer chip for the later cars, which improves the fuel and timing curve as well. After the airflow is improved (including ex-haust), look to the old-fashioned ways to increase hp. Cylinder head porting, mild camshaft grinds, and increased engine displacement will all give great gains in power and will not affect the emission quality of your Volkswagen.

STREET PREPARED FUEL INJECTION

Street Prepared regulations allow any modifications and any fuel injection sys-tem to be installed (except forced induction). This allows aftermarket program-

COMPUTER CHIP INSTALLATION CONT'D.

Fig. E. Slide the cover off of the computer board and metal shield.

CAUTION —

Installation of an aftermarket computer chip may affect new car warranty coverage. Be sure to check with your authorized Volkswagen dealer regarding warranty limitations before you start this procedure.

Fig. F. Before you proceed, make sure your clothes are not static-building (wool, nylon, etc); touch your finger to the metal shield (right) to release any static charge (the module is extremely sensitive to static). Remove the plastic anti-vibration cover (upper left) from the chip.

Fig. 5-18. Street fuel injection modifications should stick to items that only increase airflow into the engine. This will insure legality in terms of vehicle emissions. This air filter unit does away with restrictive portions of the factory's air filter box.

mable systems and modifications of the stock injection. In this "anything goes" area, the point to these changes is not more fuel delivery or air delivery. Instead, it is the delivery of the right amount of fuel and air at the right time. Be wary of tweaks that will increase absolute airflow or horsepower but decrease torque; these modifications will make your car slower.

Fig. G. Gently remove the stock computer chip from the module, prying with a small screwdriver if it is stubborn. Some cars have their chips soldered in from the factory, so your ECU will have to be socketed to install the new chip (most chip makers have exchange programs).

Fig. H. Plug the aftermarket chip in place of the original chip and put the anti-vibration cover back on. Reverse the previous steps to finish.

CAUTION —
Not all aftermarket chips are legal for highway use. Always check with your chip manufacturer as well as with the appropriate authorities in your state regarding the legality of the chip you wish to install.

SHOWROOM STOCK AND SOLO II STOCK FUEL INJECTION

As with all other systems on a Stock class car, there is not much that a competitor in this class can do to improve performance. No porting or enlarging of intake manifolds is allowed, nor is altering the air/fuel mixture in Showroom Stock. In fact, a Showroom Stock car must pass all applicable emissions tests including a gas analyzation of the exhaust.

The first step is to insure that all parts are operating at peak efficiency. This means replacing the air cleaner element every couple of races (or cleaning your K&N), as well as changing the oxygen sensor regularly to keep the fuel injection system in peak condition. The second step is to make sure that any gaskets that seal parts of the intake tract are not obstructing airflow (a good idea for any intake system). If one of the paper gaskets does intrude into the air stream, it will create turbulence and slow down airflow into the combustion chamber. The final step is to check that when the throttle pedal is down to the floor, the throttle body butterfly plates are in the full open position.

IMPROVED TOURING FUEL INJECTION

Improved Touring allows the stock fuel injection system to be modified to increase performance, but no alternative fuel injection systems are allowed. Legal modifications include: changing air filter, modifying air box, and match-porting the intake manifold.

Emission control systems such as the oxygen sensor can also be removed, but unless the sensor was in poor condition, the car will not gain any horsepower at full throttle. On CIS basic (not CIS-E, Motronic, or Digifant) cars, you might want to remove the oxygen sensor (and catalytic converter) if high-octane, leaded racing gas is available at your track, which will prevent knocking and pinging. Sensors and catalytic converters will be destroyed if you use leaded gas in the car. At some tracks there are high-octane, unleaded gasses available that will not harm these parts.

I.T. rules also allow updating and backdating of parts on cars that are listed on the same specification page. This means that a base Golf can be updated to 8-valve GTI specifications. This would be helpful if you had a Digifant Golf; you could replace the entire system with an earlier CIS or CIS-E injection and gain some adjustability and horsepower. The air/fuel mixture should be set as for Solo Stock and most other Volkswagen engine applications, at 2% CO.

Fig. 5-19. In general, the G-60 engine will benefit from exhaust tuning, fuel enrichment, mild cam timing, and increased supercharger speed. There are many hop-up kits on the market to fulfill these needs.

FORCED INDUCTION

Street enthusiasts (few racing organizations allow aftermarket turbocharged cars to compete) can also use forced induction systems on their Volkswagens. By pushing air into the engine instead of letting it be sucked in by a vacuum, you can increase horsepower substantially. This can be done in either of two ways: supercharging or turbocharging. A turbocharger is a combination of two turbines on the same shaft. One pumps air into the intake system, while the other is spun by the exhaust stream. A supercharger is a belt-driven air pump that just pumps air into the intake system.

There are few VW-specific superchargers available on the market today, but in the past, both the aftermarket and the factory have produced supercharger systems. Autotech developed a system in the mid-eighties, but dropped it later due to supply problems. Today, Bellevue Motor Sports offers a Paxton supercharger for the 2.0 A3 cars. This kit will boost horsepower levels to near-VR6 levels at a reasonable price. The factory has developed systems for both the European Polo and the U.S.-imported Corrado. For those who are addicted to power, companies have started developing supercharger systems for the VR6 cars as well.

The Corrado G60 horsepower can be improved substantially with replacement supercharger pulleys, computer chips, and mild camshafts. The replacement pulleys will increase the speed of the blower relative to the engine, thus increasing boost levels. The computer chips operate in the same fashion as in a normally aspirated car, but the chips can take into account the

Fig. 5-20. To install a new supercharger pulley, you must first remove the belt tensioner to loosen the supercharger's drive belt.

Fig. 5-21. After you remove the bolt from the stock pulley, you might have to use a large screwdriver to pry the pulley off of the shaft. Take care that you don't damage the stock pulley in case you want to return the car to stock form.

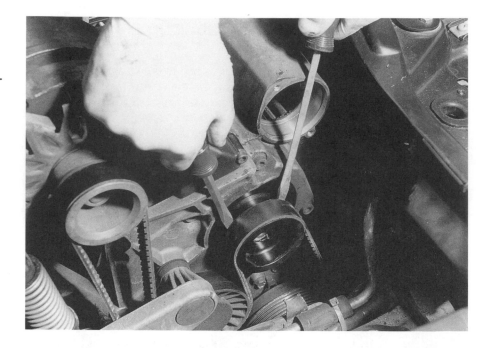

Fig. 5-22. The smaller pulley just bolts in in place of the larger stock piece. The pulley's smaller size increases the RPM that the supercharger spins at, creating more boost.

boost changes due to smaller pulley diameter. Camshafts for forced-induction cars in general will be milder than for normal engines because they can tolerate less valve overlap. Basically, valve overlap is the amount of time that the intake and exhaust valves are open together. If you have a cam with a lot of overlap on a forced-induction car, you run the risk of pushing the intake air and fuel right out the exhaust valve before it is ignited. Neuspeed, Autotech, AutoThority, and Advanced Motorsport Solutions all have developed high-performance parts for this engine.

Fig. 5-23. The larger turbo will yield higher hp, with the downside of added turbo lag.

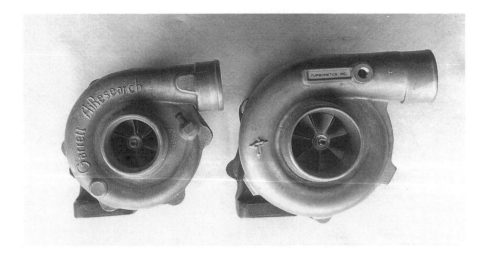

The turbo has been heralded as the best and worst in performance, depending on who you talk to. Historically, turbochargers have given huge horsepower gains, but have been plagued with short lifespans and turbo lag that can be measured with a sundial. Fortunately, most of the bugs have been worked out of aftermarket turbocharger systems, making them a good way to increase your VW's horsepower levels substantially. Earlier design bugs included inadequate oil cooling for the turbo, mis-sized turbos, and improper air/fuel ratios.

New Dimensions, Velocity Tuning, and Advanced Motorsport Solutions all have kits on the market that utilize the most reliable and efficient turbocharger assemblies and support systems. EIP (European Import Performance) is in the process of developing a turbo system for the VR6 cars, with the goal of reaching up to 400 horsepower! Conspicuously absent is the Calloway brand of turbosystems, a mainstay of forced induction VW tuning in the 1980s. The tooling and technology from this manufacturer was bought by New Dimensions and is now marketed under their label, ND Turbosystems.

Fig. 5-24. Sometimes the packaging of a turbo system in a tight engine compartment necessitates long pipes to move air from turbo to intercooler to intake manifold. This will add to turbo lag.

Fig. 5-25. Here is the backside of a New Dimensions turbo system for the A3 2-liter cars. Note the intercooler that gets cooling air from a scoop that is added to the hood.

CYLINDER HEADS

The cylinder head can make or break the entire engine. All of the incoming air has to flow through the intake manifold/gasket/cylinder head interface, through the ports cast into the head, and past the opened intake valve. After the mixture of gas and air is ignited, the exhaust gas has to flow back through the opened exhaust valve, through the exhaust ports, and out the head/gasket/exhaust manifold interface. To deal with the rapidly changing velocity and direction of the air, the cylinder head must have precisely sized ports, properly machined valve seats, and clear, unobstructed manifold interfaces.

The first inclination of any performance enthusiast is to go for the largest valves, ports, and manifolds to get the most air in or out of the engine. This will insure two things: gains in high-RPM horsepower and huge losses in low-RPM torque. The velocity of the gasses must be kept high to gain torque at low

Fig. 5-26. Like a ported intake manifold, the ported head (left) will have larger, rounder ports. This is just the visible portion of a proper porting job. The passages within the head are also enlarged and smoothed to increase flow.

Fig. 5-27. The factory large-valve head (top) has larger intake valves and a different combustion-chamber shape than the earlier small-valve head.

RPM; the total amount of air going in or out is less important. Therefore, even the wildest VW engine will not have the biggest specifications possible; it will, however, be properly engineered and tested. The following shops are popular sources for street or race cylinder heads: Euro Sport, Techtonics, Velocity Tuning, and Autotech.

To do it right, cylinder heads are tested with a flow bench. This device will measure how much air can be pumped into each port and the velocity of that air. Since this tool is both very expensive and hard to use, it is a good reason to leave the actual building of an engine to a professional engine builder. The exception to this rule is port matching (legal in Street Prepared and Improved Touring), which can be accomplished by the owner if carefully done.

Volkswagen engines have come from the factory with a variety of cylinder heads. From model years 1975 through 1982, in the U.S., there was only the single overhead cam, 8-valve head with smallish valves. In model year 1983, GTI models got heads with larger valves (40-mm intake and 33-mm exhaust). In model year 1984, the GTI head gained air-shrouded injectors to improve fuel mileage.

With the introduction of the A2 chassis, the cylinder heads came with hydraulic valve lifters to decrease maintenance. The A2 8-valve heads came with 38/33 valves in the low compression motors and 40/33 valves in the high compression examples. The 16-valve head was introduced in model year 1986 in the Scirocco and model year 1987 in the A2 chassis. The dual overhead cam, 4-valve-per-cylinder design gave increased horsepower. In contrast to the early 8-valve motors, the 16-valve was a cross-flow design (air flows from one side of the head to the other). The elderly 8-valve head's U-turn design reduces air velocity and engine efficiency.

The VR6 motor that was introduced in model year 1993 came with a unique head that mates to both banks of the narrow angle V6 motor. The A3 model with the base 2.0 motor got a newly designed 8-valve head with a cross-flow design. This head, designed to improve crash resistance by moving the intake manifold to the front of the engine, has excellent flow right out of the box.

Fig. 5-28. The last part of a good cylinder head preparation is to replace the valve stem seals and true the valve seats.

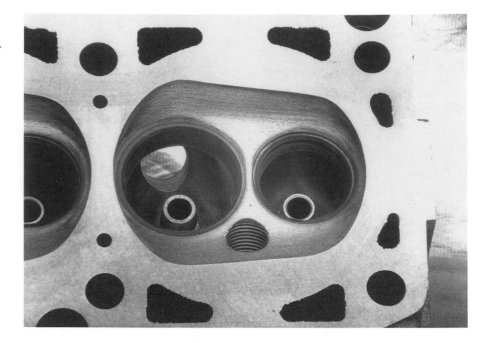

The first step in developing the ultimate head is to find the best factory cylinder-head casting. Production variances will give some cylinder heads bigger ports and better airflow: for example, the 8-valve hydraulic GTI head has two distinct casting types, one made in Mexico, the other in Germany. The German head has better port sizing and the valve seat area is not shrouded as in the Mexican piece. This translates into an increase in air/fuel flow without any additional changes. The German head will also require less port matching if it is used on a Street Prepared or I.T. car.

The remainder of cylinder head preparation entails a high-quality rebuild. If the head is used, all carbon deposits should be removed. The valve guides and seals should all be replaced along with any old or weak hydraulic lifter. The valve seats should be trued and valves should be replaced if worn. As a part of the balancing procedure, the valves should be matched by weight. The valve springs can also be matched for tension, to ensure uniformity across all cylinders. Any casting ridges or excess "flash" can be removed from the cylinder head without cutting into the head itself.

To further balance the engine, the volume of each combustion chamber in the cylinder head should be measured. This is normally accomplished using a burette to feed a precise amount of liquid into a combustion chamber that is covered with a thin sheet of plexiglass. When the combustion chamber is full of this liquid, simply determine how much liquid you injected. If possible you should equalize the chamber size of each cylinder by grinding out portions of the smaller ones to match the largest. This procedure is called "cc-ing" the head. As with other balancing procedures, tech inspectors frown on any grinding of internal engine parts in a Stock class car. If the process is done in conjunction with a head rebuild, it would be possible to adjust how valve seats are installed/trued, how things are cleaned, etc., to equalize the combustion chambers without actually grinding into the head.

The final step is to mill the bottom of the head to the manufacturer's tolerance specification. "Decking" the head will raise the compression ratio and improve power. A more approved way to accomplish this in restricted racing classes is to simply find a head with the smallest deck height. Since most people do not have multiple heads lying around the shop, milling is a logical alternative. Keep in mind that milling the head will retard cam timing; you will need to re-time the cam with an adjustable sprocket.

A good street head should also get mild port reshaping and enlarging. The ports will not grow tremendously and valve sizes will not change. The porting will keep the gasses flowing at high speed (not larger, but smoother passages, with less curves), which will keep your valuable torque for around-the-town driving. Coupled with a mild cam and intake and exhaust mods, the ported cylinder head can help your stock engine immensely.

SHOWROOM AND SOLO II STOCK CYLINDER HEADS

There are no allowable modifications for the stock cylinder head in these classes. For most competitors, this means you do not have to spend any more money on your car. For the top competitors, as in many other systems within the car, "stock" does not mean stock. You can have a high-quality rebuild without any port shaping or enlarging, making it as perfect as possible.

IMPROVED TOURING AND STREET PREPARED CYLINDER HEADS

These classes allow all of the stock modifications, with some changes. The main difference between Stock-type rules, I.T., and Street Prepared rules is the latter two allow port matching. The intake and exhaust openings can be matched to the manifolds one inch into the cylinder head.

Improved Touring rules also allow the head to be milled .025 in. under the manufacturer's minimum specification. Street Prepared only allows the head to be milled to the manufacturer's minimum specs, nothing under. As in Stock classes, the head gasket must be kept stock.

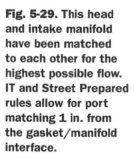

Fig. 5-29. This head and intake manifold have been matched to each other for the highest possible flow. IT and Street Prepared rules allow for port matching 1 in. from the gasket/manifold interface.

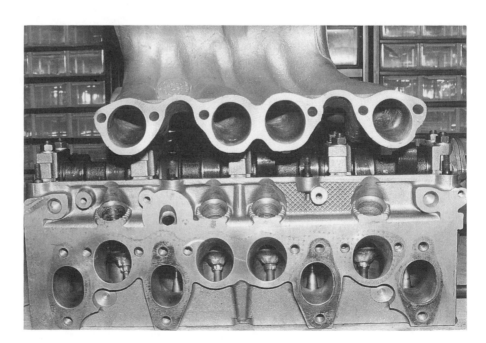

CAMSHAFTS

The camshaft plays a large role in the functioning of a VW motor. By making the intake and exhaust valves open in a particular order with precise timing, the camshaft is the orchestra conductor of the engine. If the conductor is not properly prepared, the music will be off key and tempo. If your camshaft is improperly designed, the engine will be undrivable and any gains in horsepower will be at the cost of low-end torque.

The camshaft determines the powerband of the motor. If the camshaft has exceptionally high lift or long duration, the engine will only run properly at high RPM. The idle will be rough and lumpy, or the engine might even fail to run at low RPM. The stock camshaft, on the other hand, has good idle characteristics and gets good fuel mileage, but runs out of breath at high RPM.

The lift of the camshaft is defined by how far the lobe of the camshaft moves the valves, and can be measured in inches or millimeters. The higher the lift, the more air and fuel that can flow into the combustion chamber for high-RPM horsepower. The penalty attached to this extra air is that its velocity will be lower, costing the low-RPM torque (you can rarely escape that trade-off).

The duration of the camshaft is the amount (in degrees) of rotation during which the valve is off its seat, determining how long the valve is open. Overlap is when the intake and exhaust valves are open at the same time. As the camshaft gains in duration, the overlap will also increase. Too much overlap can cause unburnt fuel and air to be sucked out of the exhaust valve before they are properly ignited, increasing fuel consumption and emissions.

CAMSHAFT INSTALLATION

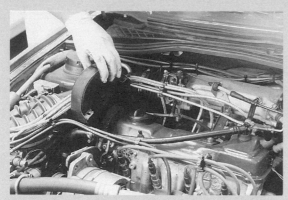

Fig. A. Remove the timing belt cover. It is secured with two nuts on the valve cover and one allen bolt on the bottom.

Fig. B. Rotate the engine (by rolling the car while it is in gear) so that the mark on the timing belt sprocket lines up with the edge of the valve cover.

CAUTION —
If you lack the tools or experience necessary to remove and install the camshaft, this work should be left to an authorized Volkswagen dealer or qualified repair shop. Attempts to remove and install the camshaft without the proper tools are likely to cause serious injury.

Fig. 5-30. This curve shows a stock 1.8 head (high compression) vs. a ported head/cam combination. Notice how there is no difference in hp gains until 4000 RPM is surpassed.

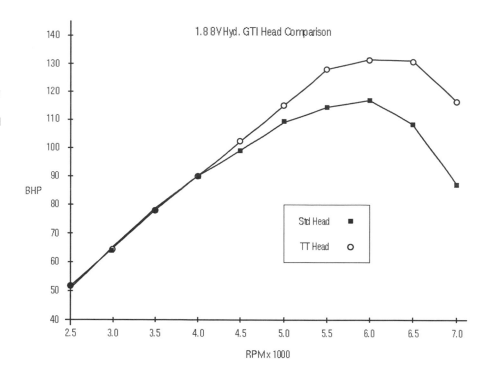

1.8 8V Hyd. GTI Head Comparison

BHP

Std Head ■
TT Head ○

RPM x 1000

Fig. C. The Top Dead Center mark on the flywheel should be in the center of the view hole. Remove the threaded plug from the view hole if installed.

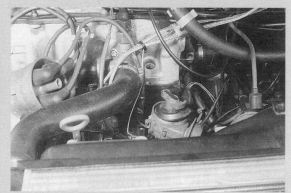

Fig. D. Also make sure the distributor rotor is pointing towards the no. 1 cylinder.

cont'd. on next page

Fig. 5-31. An asymmetric camshaft will have differently shaped intake and exhaust lobes. This will allow a smoother idle with good power.

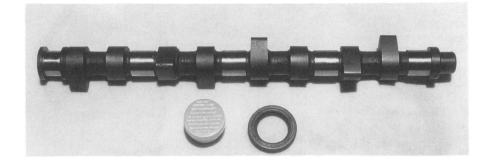

Other camshaft characteristics are just as important. Lobe shape and ramp profile will determine how things happen and at what speed, changing emission characteristics and how the engine pulls the next cylinder's air and fuel into the combustion chamber.

The timing of the cam, which is the point in the engine's revolution that the cam will open or close a valve, determines where the camshaft/engine will produce power. One way to move the powerband around on a camshaft, stock or high-performance, is to change its position relative to the crankshaft. By advancing the cam timing, you get greater low-end power; by retarding the cam timing, you get greater high-end power. This horsepower movement will gain you several hp at one end, with a corresponding loss at the other end.

CAMSHAFT INSTALLATION CONT'D.

Fig. E. Remove the crankcase ventilation hose from the valve cover, and loosen all of the nuts on the valve cover.

CAUTION —
If you lack the tools or experience necessary to remove and install the camshaft, this work should be left to an authorized Volkswagen dealer or qualified repair shop. Attempts to remove and install the camshaft without the proper tools are likely to cause serious injury.

Fig. F. Remove the valve cover and its gasket. Make sure you remove all of the gasket material.

CAUTION —
Be careful when removing the gasket, especially if it is stuck. Damage to either surface will cause leaks. Use only a gasket-removing tool designed for this purpose.

The way to get the best ratio of these different characteristics is to compromise and get a cam that is both livable and will net some horsepower gain. Luckily, VW camshafts are an easy bolt-on, rarely taking more than a couple of hours. Simply bolting in a good sport camshaft can liven up a stock motor. Camshaft power gains can be substantial on any car. These gains will be best seen on cars that have had their airflow improved both into and out of the engine. It is recommended to at least modify both the intake and exhaust system to get the full benefit of a sport camshaft for your Volkswagen.

Street and sport camshafts come in several distinct groups. Early cars (A1) came equipped with solid lifter heads. The later cars (A2 & A3) came with hydraulic, self adjusting lifters that require different camshafts. Supercharged Corrado engines require a milder sport camshaft than normal hydraulic cams; this mild cam will also work in the normally aspirated engine. Incidentally, the 260-degree camshafts for the supercharged G60 cars are the only California Air Resource Board-exempt sport camshaft for the 8-valve cars. Sixteen-valve cars with their dual overhead cams can change either the intake (Neuspeed's is California Air Resource Board-exempt) or the intake and exhaust cams to boost power. VR6 owners who are unhappy with the engine's power output can swap both camshafts in their cars for extra power (the 260-degree cams seem to help this motor the best).

People who race their Volkswagens in the grassroots classes are not as lucky as the street crowd; camshaft mods are not allowed in Showroom Stock, Solo Stock, I.T., or Street Prepared. This is quite a shame for most I.T or Street

Fig. G. Remove the oil spray shield if your car is so equipped.

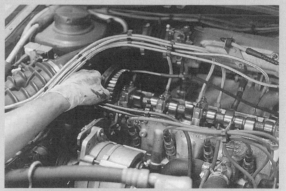

Fig. H. Remove the timing belt from the timing sprocket; you can use a bungee cord to keep tension on the belt so that you don't misalign the crankshaft pulley with the idler pulley.

cont'd. on next page

CAUTION ———
Rotating the crankshaft or the camshaft with the timing belt removed can cause interference which can damage pistons and valves.

Prepared competitors, as the tweaked fuel injection systems, aftermarket fuel injections, or dual sidedraft carburetors beg for a more radical camshaft. In the racing classes, there often comes a point when further modifications will not help, as the camshaft is the limiting factor.

The solution for this problem is obvious to those who are used to racing with a rule book. Find out the factory camshaft specification, add the tolerance levels to the stock values for lift and duration, and have a camshaft reground. Neuspeed and Havoc Motorsports have both done their homework and can sell you a "Spec" cam for your engine. It will have the most lift and duration that is theoretically possible with a stock-manufactured camshaft. Horsepower gains will not be nearly as great as a straightforward sport camshaft, but the gains will be measurable. This is a step in the whole engine blueprinting and balancing procedure that shouldn't be left out.

Adjustable Camshaft Sprockets

An adjustable camshaft sprocket allows you to change the cam timing without changing the camshaft. These are only legal in Solo II Street Prepared but would also be really helpful for a street car. For tight, low-speed autocrosses or most around-the-town street driving, it would be beneficial to advance the cam timing for extra low-end power. Such gains in low-end horsepower are normally only found with increased engine displacement. If the autocross course is wide open, you can retard the cam timing to give higher peak power. Several companies market these manually adjustable sprockets: Autotech, Techtonics, Euro Sport, and Eurospec.

CAMSHAFT INSTALLATION CONT'D.

Fig. I. Using a rag-wrapped, large adjustable wrench, hold the camshaft in place while you loosen the bolt that secures the sprocket to the cam.

CAUTION —
If you lack the tools or experience necessary to remove and install the camshaft, this work should be left to an authorized Volkswagen dealer or qualified repair shop. Attempts to remove and install the camshaft without the proper tools are likely to cause serious injury.

Fig. J. Loosen the camshaft bearing caps. Make sure that you remember which one went where, because you'll have to reinstall them in their original positions. This is easily accomplished by storing them in order.

Fig. 5-32. An adjustable camshaft sprocket allows you to move the power band around. Advancing cam timing will give good low RPM torque, retard cam timing and increase high RPM power.

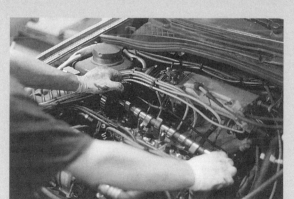

Fig. K. Lift the camshaft out of the head.

Fig. L. Use an impact wrench to secure the sprocket to the new cam (or you can simply secure it with hand tools now), and then tighten it while it is on the car with the adjustable wrench-and-rag method. Installation is the reverse of removal. Be sure to torque all fasteners to the factory specifications found in your service manual.

Fig. 5-33. The automatic camshaft sprocket shows marginal, but real, gains, both at high and low RPM ranges.

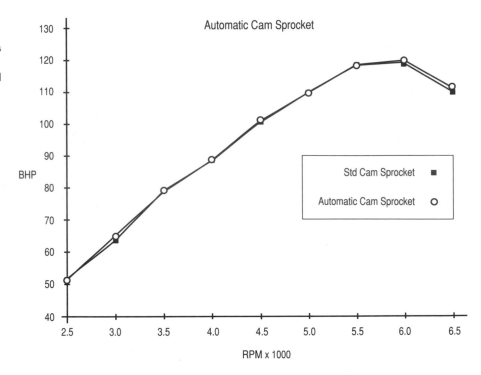

There has been a lot of bad press surrounding the alternative to a manual adjustable camshaft sprocket. The automatic sprocket, which starts out at full advance at low RPM and retards at high RPM, has been called a waste of money. The argument basically states that it only gives several horsepower for three hundred or so dollars. Techtonics has tested this with a 2-hp gain, which is substantial since it was on the low end. The automatic sprocket does give you a good boost in low-end torque with no loss at high RPM. It is constructed of a complex arrangement of weights and springs that centrifugally retard the camshaft timing as RPM increases. This is a great idea for a Street Prepared competitor who needs both low-RPM torque and high-RPM power (who doesn't ?). Furthermore, the average Street Prepared competitor has already tried other ways to boost horsepower, many that are much more expensive than this. This sprocket is manufactured by Franco Industries.

Camshaft sprockets are easy to change when installing a camshaft or changing the timing belt. Just install the adjustable sprocket in the place of the stock one during reassembly. Ignition timing, timing belt tightness, and other maintenance specifications are unchanged.

One note on the timing belt: you should replace it more frequently than the factory recommends, if the car is driven hard. Timing belts on 8-valve cars should be changed at 60,000 miles for street cars or every 2 seasons for racing cars. Sixteen-valve cars (and cross-flow 8-valves) should have their belts changed more often. If the belt on a 16-valve breaks, most of the valves will be bent—a very expensive proposition. Recommended change intervals are 40–50,000 street miles or once a racing season.

Chapter Six
IGNITION SYSTEMS

Fig. 6-1. An aftermarket coil is usually unnecessary. They are usually used as replacements for failing early-model points-type systems.

To properly ignite the air and fuel mixture that is rushing into the combustion chamber, a spark that is strong enough needs to be produced at exactly the right moment. The stock electronic ignition systems easily accomplish this feat. The points style used prior to 1981 (1980 in California) should be upgraded to a later factory electronic system for greater reliability and lower maintenance. The factory electronic ignition systems will give the same power as a custom ignition system, will most likely be more reliable, and the parts are readily available worldwide. The exception to this rule is the Electromotive crank-fired system for highly modified Street Prepared cars. This system is available with the fuel injection system or without. If you do not use the entire Electromotive fuel injection and ignition system, only use the seperate ignition system as a replacement for an early points-type ignition system.

The factory electronic ignition systems come in two flavors, knock-sensing or not. Both types of ignitions are available through salvage yards and can easily be swapped for one another. The standard electronic ignition was used from 1981 through 1987. The knock-sensing system was introduced on the high-compression GTI and GLI in 1985. The timing map was changed in 1986 for a 2-hp improvement.

1985 cars can be converted to the later timing curve by cutting the wire that runs between pin No. 11 and pin No. 3 in the large connector plug that connects to the knock-sensing control unit (the wire is brown; check your service manual for the pin locations in the connector). Knock-sensing ignition systems are also in place on all Digifant- and Motronic-equipped cars.

Since an easy path to high performance is to replace an aging engine with a late-model high-compression one, it is often recommended to also switch to an ignition system with a knock sensor. There are two reasons for this. The first is

Fig. 6-2. The knock-sensing control unit on the 1985 GTI (with boot rolled back to show connecting wires).

available fuel quality. In the Midwest and Western United States, the best fuel available is sometimes only 90- or 91-octane, making the 10:1 compression ratio engine knock badly when hot. The second reason is that carbon deposit build-up in the combustion chamber on cars will raise the compression even higher, further exacerbating the knocking problem.

If you have these problems with fuel quality and carbon build-up, the only solution is to install the knock-sensor system. For people who live in areas which have 94-octane gas or for people who only run racing fuel, there should be no problem running a 10:1 compression ratio engine without knock sensing. Some people can even get away with using 92-octane gas without a problem, if the engine is getting enough fuel (true for racing, but you might still want a knock sensor for street use). Newer engines or engines that are frequently run at high RPM will not have substantial carbon build-up and can also do without the knock-sensing system.

Fig. 6-3. You should use only OEM Bosch replacement parts.

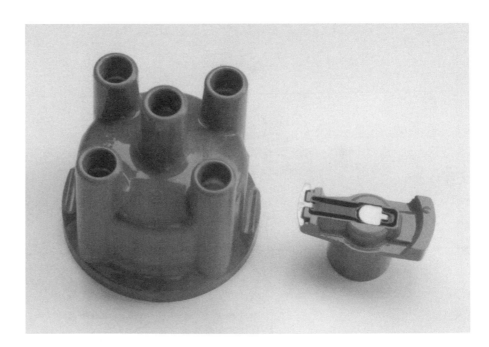

Fig. 6-4. The owner of this 16-valve car was complaining about a lack of power—with a distributor rotor that has melted in two, no wonder!

For optimal performance make sure that maintenance of the ignition is done routinely. This means replacing spark plugs, distributor caps, and distributor rotors often. The factory system and all systems in general will work best when all parts are in good condition. Luckily, maintenance costs for all ignition systems are cheap and should not break your budget.

The type of gas that you use is also important, since not all gasolines are created equal. If you are racing a car, you should invest in the highest octane gas that is available as it will help your car put out the most horsepower with no pre-ignition. This is especially helpful in any VW with a high-compression motor and knock-sensing ignition. For most people this means 92- to 94-octane gas that is sold at the corner gas station. This is the only type of gas that is legal for Showroom Stock and Solo Stock competitors. For Improved Touring and Solo Street Prepared, there are specially formulated racing gasses with octane ratings of over 100 available at most race tracks. These very-high-octane fuels should be used only if your car has high enough compression to require such octane ratings; otherwise, they will hurt your performance.

STREET, STREET PREPARED, AND IMPROVED TOURING IGNITIONS

The rules and regulations for Street, Street Prepared, and Improved Touring ignition systems are very liberal. The fact remains that very little can be done to improve a factory ignition system. Indeed, the best racing set-up is also the best for the street.

Spark plugs can be replaced with any other type, the best for a Volkswagen being the Bosch Platinum type. The platinum-tip electrode will warm up quicker, have less misfires, and will last longer than a conventional spark plug. For cars with knocking problems, you can use a spark plug that is one heat range colder.

Fig. 6-5. High-quality after-market spark plug wires will last longer than the original wires. They will also usually be cheaper than those available at your VW dealer.

Fig. 6-6. Advancing the timing on high-compression 8-valve engines will yield 4 to 5 hp at the top end with no loss at the low end.

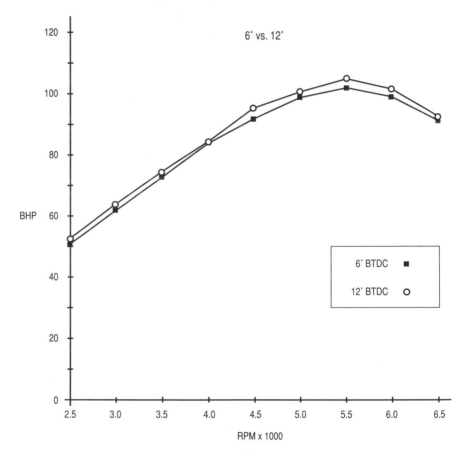

Spark plug wires can also be replaced. For best performance, the plug wires should be constructed with silicone insulation and factory-style terminals. Stay away from all bargain brands available at local "one size fits all" auto parts stores. The most popular brands on the market are Bosch, Neuspeed, Autotech, Advanced Motorsport, and Blue Ignitors (from Rapid Parts). These kinds all have silicone-insulated wire and factory-style terminals for long life.

Another modification that can improve performance is to advance the timing from stock on the high-compression (with knock sensor) 8-valve cars. The stock setting is 6 degrees before top dead center (BTDC). If your car does not show any signs of knocking, you can advance it to a setting of 12 degrees BT-

Fig. 6-7. The Electromotive twin-coil system eliminates the distributor. This system is not used to improve on the factory ignition system; it is used to add the ability to match the timing and fuel curve to each other.

DC. This will give most cars up to a 5-hp boost. Some cars equipped with a high-compression motor and no knock sensor can even handle this timing advance, giving additional power for no cost. The power gains that are given for a knock-sensing ignition over a standard electronic are often made with the assumption that you shouldn't advance the timing on the latter. In fact, most people can, giving the same horsepower increase as a knock-sensing car.

On cars with computers that control fuel and ignition, an aftermarket chip will handle advancing the timing for you. For the most part, the majority of the hp gain seen with a computer chip is due to changes in the timing curve.

Since Street Prepared and I.T. (and street, for that matter) allow updating and backdating of parts, the only swapping that is necesary is the updating of the points-type ignitions to factory electronic (or Electromotive for the well-funded). If you are replacing a Digifant system, you must also change ignitions. You can use either a standard or a knock-sensing ignition system to replace the integrated Digifant electrical system. This will require the entire ignition system from a donor car. This would include the distributor, the coil, the ignition module, the harness, and the knock sensor if you are using one.

SHOWROOM STOCK IGNITIONS

Like most other automotive systems, ignition systems are highly controlled in SCCA Showroom Stock racing. In fact, no parts can be changed from factory standard, including spark plugs. Additionally, the factory ignition settings must be adhered to. Frequent replacement of caps, rotors, and plugs is the only chance for performance advantage in this class.

SOLO II STOCK IGNITIONS

SCCA Solo II Stock rules allow just the spark plugs and wires to be changed. Use the recommendations for Street use in this class. All other adjustments must be stock.

Chapter Seven
POWERPLANTS

Fig. 7-1. It takes a lot of skill to make these parts work for the best power and reliability. When in doubt, pay for quality.

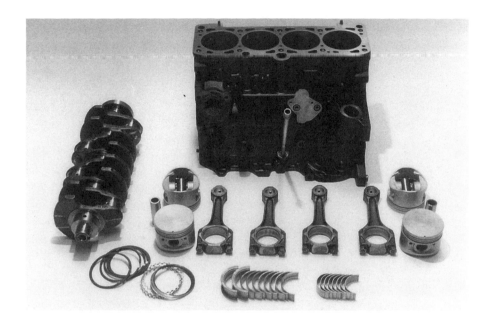

Volkswagen owners are especially lucky with regard to engines—the VW water-cooled engine has the great combination of reliability and power. Racing and high-performance street use will not overtly shorten the life of the engine; stories of high-mileage racing cars abound. Proper maintenance is all that is required to enjoy your VW's powerplant for a long time.

Engines found in VWs come in four broad types. The most common engine is the basic 8-valve, single-overhead cam unit with stock displacements between 1.5 and 1.8 liters. The second type is the 16-valve, dual-overhead cam, 1.8- and 2.0-liter displacements. The third engine is the 2.8-liter narrow-angle V6 engine (or VR6) found in Corrados, Passats, and in the A3 chassis. The last engine type is the 8-valve, cross-flow head, 2.0-liter engine found in the base model A3 chassis.

Engine rebuilding and modification is not a job for the novice or just any generic engine builder. It takes a huge amount of experience and shop time to learn the proper techniques in engine building for street or racing, so your money and time will be best spent with an experienced engine builder. The results will be better in terms of power, reliability, and cost. You can spend all the time you would have wasted where it can do more good, such as suspension development or driver training.

You will find that the average, local foreign-car repair shop will charge an arm and two legs for a decent engine overhaul. Discussing a performance rebuild will make most mechanics stare at you with a vacant expression denoting the daydream of the new house you're helping them finance. Your best bet is to contact a major VW performance shop on engine rebuilding, such as Techtonics, Velocity, or Euro Sport. Shops such as these will be cheaper and less frustrating than a local shop, and since engine building is nearly all they do, it will

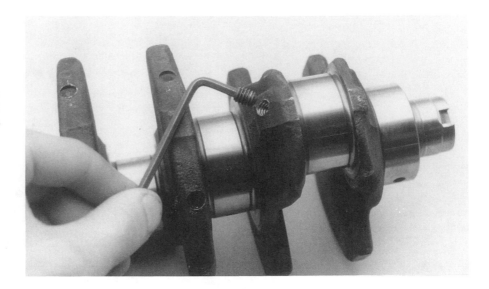

Fig. 7-2. Engine preparation includes tricks like tapping the oil galley plugs in the crankshaft. This will make it easier to clean out the oil galleys in subsequent rebuilds and is easier to deal with than the pressed-in plugs that need to be drilled out.

be better than if it is done by someone with little or no experience with high-performance rebuilds. You can specify whether you want merely a stock re-build, a rebuild for a specific racing class, or a big-bore 2.0-liter, and they will deliver. In the immortal words of television, "don't try this at home, kids."

In racing, especially in classes with strict engine rules, the engine should be the last place you spend money after all other performance modifications have been undertaken. In contrast to the engine mods you might undertake for street performance, legal power gains from performance engine rebuilding will be small in the racing classes discussed in this book; but after all else has been done, it will be necessary in order to compete at the national level.

For street drivers, the engine should also be the last place to look for performance, but since there are no rules, the horsepower gains can be much higher. In the end, it is the age-old cliche that rules: "Speed costs money—how fast do you want to go?"

Engine preparation for Showroom Stock, Solo II Stock, Street Prepared, and Improved Touring is approximately the same for each class. Engine displacements must be at stock (Showroom Stock), bored to the first factory overbore (Solo II Stock) or second factory overbore (Street Prepared and Improved Touring). The stock classes do not allow any machining to balance engine internals. The I.T. or Street Prepared competitors are only allowed to remove enough material from each piece to balance the assembly. This whole process of boring and balancing is called *blueprinting* (as discussed in the suspension chapter).

BORING

The bore of the engine will determine the size of the piston that can be installed. Larger pistons will produce more vacuum to suck more fuel and air into the chamber. This will produce more power. The factory blocks will allow some overbore to increase the displacement of the motor. There will be an upper limit to how much larger the pistons can actually be. If you bore too much, the wall between the cylinders will be too small or the outer wall of the block will get too thin. The block needs to be sufficiently thick to prevent flexing and cracking, a destructive possibility.

Limiting bore sizes for each class does not prevent builders from taking advantage of factory tolerance specifications. Some builders will bore the engine block to the largest legal size (normal bore + overbore [if allowed] + factory percent tolerance) and then fit a more average piston in the bore, leaving a lot of room between the piston and cylinder wall. As the piston expands when heated, this extra room will prevent scuffing and friction under high-heat racing conditions. An engine bored in this manner will rattle when cold, like a diesel, before the pistons warm up. This will also cause increased oil consumption as the oil will seep past the piston rings more readily.

For Solo II Stock the first factory overbore is allowed (pistons .020 in. larger than stock). In normal non-racing applications this overbore is commonly used for engine rebuilding, making the slightly larger pistons readily available. I.T. and Street Prepared are allowed to bore to the second overbore (.040 in. over stock). This would bring a stock 1.8 engine from 1781 cubic centimeters to 1825 cc. This is a small change in displacement (44 cc) but will give a few more horsepower over stock. The second overbore size is slightly harder to find, but many high-performance and racing VW shops stock them.

In Improved Touring and Street Prepared classes, you can exchange your cast pistons with forged ones, which are lighter. The problem with this change is that the SCCA mandates that the pistons must be of the same weight as the stock cast type, which would eliminate most of the performance advantages of using forged pistons. Moreover, it is difficult to find a forged piston that weighs as much as a cast unit. For all-out racing applications, however, such as Prepared classes or Modified classes, where piston weight is not regulated, you can take advantage of the benefits forged pistons offer. The disadvantage of forged pistons is that they will expand more when they are hot; this will require more cold tolerance between the piston and the cylinder wall. This increased

Fig. 7-3. Forged pistons, on the right, offer lighter weight for better high-RPM power than cast pistons, but at the cost of higher oil consumption.

Fig. 7-4. This is the top view of an assembled, balanced, and blueprinted 1.8-liter Street Prepared motor. The top of the block has been milled to the minimum factory specs, the pistons have been balanced, the block has been bored .040 in. over, and the crankshaft has been balanced. It all looks stock, right?

tolerance will cause the same problems as using larger overbores with stock-size pistons for more power.

STROKING

The crankshaft will determine how far the piston will move with each revolution. The longer it moves, the more air/fuel can be used. Also, in terms of torque and hp, a longer stroke will give more fill time and thus more torque; but the trade-off is less hp. The upper limit for crankshaft stroke is determined by its clearances with the block. Too large a stroke will cause the crankshaft to hit the block. Aftermarket crank shafts are available from many tuners to increase your engines displacement.

BALANCING

The other part of building an engine is balancing the internal moving parts. This can be accomplished in one of two ways. First, you can simply machine off small amounts of material from each part to balance it with the rest. This mod is strictly against the Stock-class rules but is legal in I.T. and Street Prepared. For the latter classes, only enough material can be removed to balance the part. This is a very imprecise rule; competitors do take advantage of the gray zone and lighten each part slightly. Some Stock-class engine builders will duplicate the factory machining/balancing process on each part (i.e., making the actual grinding marks look similar), making detection of overt balancing difficult for technical inspectors.

The second type of balancing is legal for all types of racing. Batch-balancing is the process of starting with large amounts of pistons, connecting rods, and other parts and simply picking out the ones that are both physically most similar to each other and closest to the performance optimum. By performance optimum, I mean that the pistons would be the lightest (to rev faster), the connecting rods would be the longest (to increase compression ratio), and the crankshaft would have the most stroke (to increase displacement). By taking every advantage of normal factory build tolerances, it is possible to come up with a "stock" engine with increased displacement, higher compression, and lower reciprocating weight than any motor normally assembled.

Fig. 7-5. This piston is being matched to within 1 gram of the other pistons for the engine. When you match pistons, don't forget to also match the wrist pins as well; they contribute a good portion of the assembly's weight.

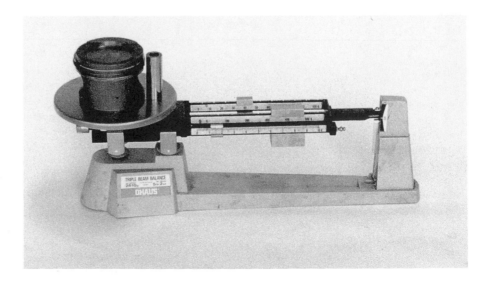

Fig. 7-6. The crankshaft can be balanced by removing weight from the counterweights. Some people even "knife edge" the counterweights. This makes the crank lighter and allows it to spin through the crankcase oil with less parasitic drag.

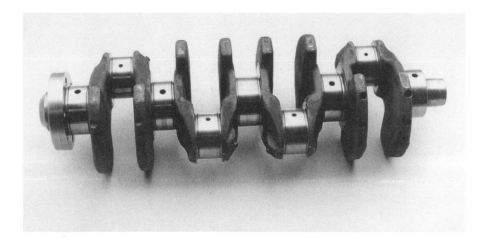

Fig. 7-7. Weight is removed from the crankshaft counterweights by drilling holes. These holes were drilled at the factory as a part of the engine's original build process.

The vast capital outlay involved in batch-balancing is another reason to leave engine building to a professional. Some low-buck competitors can accomplish this with a trip to the local salvage yard. This would require both a healthy relationship with the proprietor and a huge investment of time to dig through parts.

PUTTING IT ALL TOGETHER

There are a large number of non-reusable parts in a VW engine. These pieces are usually unrestricted in all racing classes. This is because they will not usually increase horsepower, but they will increase longevity. For example, the piston rings should be replaced with new ones, such as the Total Seal type. The connecting rod bolts and head studs should be replaced with non-factory high-performance parts. Raceware and ARP make such heavier duty hardware that can prevent headgasket failures in racing and turbocharging usage. All other miscellaneous fasteners should be checked and replaced if they aren't perfect. It doesn't make sense to trust a suspect 10-cent fastener in an engine rebuild.

UPDATING/BACKDATING

In the classes that allow updating and backdating of parts (I.T. and Street Prepared), upgrading to a larger displacement factory long block is a quick and dirty performance gain (you must update both the head and the block). In ITB, engines can be changed within the Golf 8-valve cars from the small-valve, low-compression 1.8-liter to the GTI (or Digifant) 1.8-liter 8-valve. The Digifant motor will normally be cheaper than a GTI motor because of the high demand for the latter. The only real difference between the two is that the Digifant motor does not have air-shrouded fuel injectors. Street Prepared cars can also interchange the 16-valve engines in C-Street Prepared (CSP) and the 8-valve engines in D-Street Prepared (DSP). For A2 cars in DSP, this means going to a GTI or Digifant engine, possibly even the cross-flow 2.0-liter, from an A3. All A1 cars in DSP can update to model year 1983-84 GTI specifications, coupling the light weight of older Rabbits and Sciroccos with the horsepower of a GTI. The factory-updated long block can then be rebuilt, balanced, and overbored for even more performance.

Street enthusiasts who are looking for more power will also find that updating engines is a cheap and quick way to increase performance drastically. The logical choice would be to update to a late model GTI/Digifant 8-valve engine or, if you can afford it, a 2.0 16-valve engine. This would give immense power gains over most stock VW engines with factory reliability.

The best bet when hunting for one of these powerplants is to search local salvage yards for a low-mileage example. Instead of asking for a GTI 16-valve engine, you can ask for a base Passat engine which is the same 2.0-liter 16-valve engine. Since the Passat is assumed to be lower performance (and therefore, will have less demand), you might find that salvage yard owners will let it go cheaper. A salvage yard engine will also be cheaper than any rebuild you can find, making it a logical choice for many engine swaps.

The optimal starting point for any no-holds-barred street motor is a late model GTI/Digifant or a 2.0-liter 16-valve engine. It does not make sense to

Fig. 7-8. The 2.0-liter 16-valve engine is a good engine to swap into an older car. They can be found in GTIs, GLs, and Passats. They offer good hp and torque, and many parts are available for even more performance.

Fig. 7-9. A typical "big-bore" engine kit. Your block will need to be machined to be able to fit these parts.

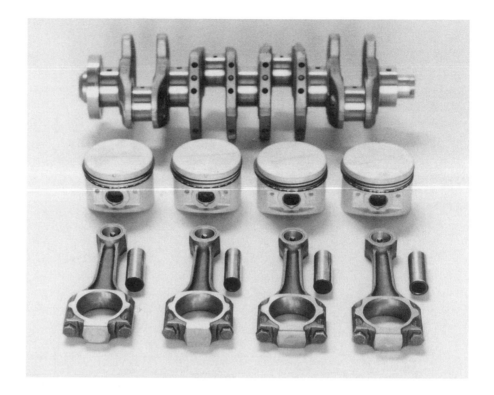

Fig. 7-10. 84.5-mm pistons are the largest that can be installed in the VW block; coupled with a 99-mm crankshaft stroke, this yields over a 2.2-liter motor.

start with one of the smaller engines if you have to spend a lot of money just to make it equal a late-model piece. The late-model 16-valve engine will have a big valve head with 40-mm intake and 33-mm exhaust valves, high-compression ratio, and a larger cylinder block. If you have an earlier A2 motor with smaller valves and lower compression, you can simply get a GTI head and mill the cylinder head deck height to raise the compression to make up for stock pistons. Alternatively, you can buy a custom head gasket that compresses further than stock, yielding higher compression. Autotech and Techtonics both sell custom head gaskets that will raise the 8.5:1-compression engine to 9.4:1.

People who desire even more power can proceed from there. The maximum displacement possible for a 1.8-liter 8-valve motor or a 1.8 16-valve is 2.0 liters, due to the size of the bores and the crankshaft clearance. This is easily accomplished with readily available "big-bore" kits or short blocks from

Fig. 7-11. This head gasket for a 2.1-liter motor shows the cylinder bore limitations that all 4-cylinder VW motors face. The bore just cannot be made any larger. Displacements over 2.1 liters are accomplished using longer strokes.

most high-performance shops (kits are available to 2.2 liters, but not for these non-tall or "bubble-block" motors). The late model 2.0-liter 16-valve engine can be bored to 2.1 liters due to its "bubble-block" design, which allows clearance for longer stroke crankshafts. This increase in displacement is possible using kits from many tuners. For the displacement crazy, late model 2.0 8-valve owners can bore their engines out to 2.2 liters. This is possible because of the block's taller design, allowing for room for a longer rod.

The ultimate transplant is the VR6 engine. While highly time-consuming, the swap into an A2 chassis is possible. Many items will simply bolt on to the earlier chassis. However, the wiring of the VR6 engine-management system is another matter. The VR6 engine also requires the replacement of the transmission and driveline. This could also include the uprated "plus" suspension system featured on the VR6 cars with five-lug wheels. The massive amount of parts that would be required makes it advisable to simply buy a wrecked VR6 car so that you know where everything goes to begin with.

Fig. 7-12. A VR6 engine awaiting transplant.

Fig. 7-13. You can find G60 engines for fast transplants from wrecked Corrados such as this one. Most VW-only salvage yards would be able to find one for you.

The big VR6 engine can be easily modified from stock with all sorts of parts. Computer chips, air cleaner assemblies, and high-performance throttle bodies are all available. With very little massaging, the VR6 engine can put out over 200 hp, making a great addition to a lightweight A2 chassis.

Fig. 7-14. You can see that the VR-6 is a tight fit in this A2 engine compartment, but the added power is worth the hassle.

Chapter Eight
EXHAUST SYSTEMS

Fig. 8-1. A mandrel-bent exhaust system will not be pinched, as the tubing goes over the rear axle.

Now that the air/fuel mixture has been mixed and ignited, the next step is to let the upward-traveling piston push the spent mixture out the exhaust port. To get more air in and out of the engine to produce power, the exhaust system has to have as little restriction as possible. The tubing diameter plays a large part in restriction: if you double a tube's diameter, you will improve exhaust flow by a factor of 16! This sensitivity to change means that the size is crucial to high flow and low restriction. At some point, however, any additional tubing size increase will cease to make a difference. It doesn't really help much if it improves theoretical hp at 10,000 RPM, since your engine won't turn that. As in the intake system, the need for high velocity is as important as total volume moved through the system. If you increase the diameter too much, it will hurt low RPM torque. This means that the exhaust manifold and whatever exhaust system you install must be free-flowing but properly sized.

In addition to size, the way the pipe is bent is important. A properly-designed system will have pipes shaped with a mandrel bender. Most tube benders will crimp the tubing at each curve, reducing flow. A 2-1/4 in. pipe that is bent on a conventional tube-bending machine will be necked down to about 2 in. A mandrel-bent tube will remain the same inner size diameter throughout its length. Mandrel-bending machines are very expensive, making it unlikely that the local muffler shop would have one. This is not a practical concern. The ready-made high-performance exhausts on the market are much less expensive than any locally obtained system. The icing on the cake is the fact that they can raise horsepower substantially.

Another consideration in your exhaust system is muffler design. The stock VW mufflers have large amounts of baffles and restrictors to reduce sound. A good high-performance muffler will have less restriction, albeit with higher noise levels. For some people, the added noise is annoying. However, most enthusiasts revel in the added music.

Street drivers should be aware of the federally mandated smog laws that are in effect. While some states do not do any emission testing, the majority of the country is cracking down on polluters. Luckily, powerful engines and clean air are not mutually exclusive. Exhaust manifolds can be updated or backdated as long as the oxygen sensor and catalytic converter placement are the same as stock. This would also mean that tubular racing-type headers are allowed if they have the necessary smog provisions (except in California, unless the part has exempt status). Of course, everything behind the converter can be changed legally as long as it meets any sound ordinances. This means the restrictive factory exhaust systems can be replaced with free-flowing types for great, cheap power gains. Indeed, the exhaust system is the first place where you should look for more power on any VW.

Fig. 8-2. This factory exhaust section shows a crimp-bent pipe that has reduced diameter where it goes over the rear axle; this will lead to reduced flow.

With emissions laws getting ever stricter, the catalytic converter is now a permanent piece of automotive engineering. The catalytic converter, as evident in its name, catalyzes a chemical reaction to change harmful emissions to benign ones. Volkswagen catalytic converters have improved since VW started using them in the seventies. The horsepower losses attributed to the cats have gradually decreased as the factory has learned how to make clean power. The best catalytic converter design will only reduce power around 4–5 hp. It is not recommended (and illegal) to remove or disable any smog-control device on a street-driven vehicle. For racing and track use only, it is highly recommended to remove or disable most smog-control devices as they will cost some horsepower. This will relegate your car to being a "trailer queen," but if you must have the last iota of horsepower. . . .

Since modification to the exhaust system can produce serious horsepower gains, SCCA and other rule makers strictly govern what can and cannot be modified. Nothing in the exhaust system can be modified in the Showroom Stock class. The only preparation to be done is to check all fittings and pieces for misalignment and possible obstructions. The catalytic converter should also be checked frequently for any signs of plugging. As soon as the catalytic converter becomes plugged from overheating or poor air/fuel mixture, it is useless and can cost a lot of horsepower. Solo II Stock allows any exhaust system to be fitted beyond the catalytic converter. Street Prepared and Improved Touring allow any exhaust system that terminates behind the driver.

EXHAUST MANIFOLDS

Designing the ultimate exhaust manifold for a VW is no easy task. There are many engineering problems that must be solved before a workable manifold is created. The manifold must have large enough ports and tubing to allow sufficient exhaust volume and, consequently, sufficient horsepower. The tube from each cylinder must be of the proper length to keep the powerband in a useful range. Each of the four tubes must be joined together in such a way that the combustion pulse from one cylinder does not adversely affect another. The exhaust manifold assembly has to allow for the unavoidable engine movement that is characteristic of a transverse-engined car. If it doesn't allow for the flexing, it will crack very quickly. Finally, the actual material has to survive heat cycles and damp or wet weather without rusting through.

Fig. 8-3. Flex joints can prevent cracking of headers and downpipes caused by engine movement.

There are some factory exhaust manifolds that fulfill these criteria. It is rare to find a tubular header that can do the same. The good factory manifolds will only give up a little high-end power to the tubular header, while lasting much longer. If a cast-iron manifold is completely ported out (read: Extrude Hone), it could even match the tubular header in power. This would be the best choice for street cars and people who want to install a part and forget it. In general, I recommend stock manifolds, but racers might want a header.

The best factory exhaust manifolds can all be described as 4-2-1 design. This means that each of the four tubes is paired with another, creating a dual downpipe which then joins together at the bottom of the car. This design will allow good high-end power and great mid-range torque. There are three different types of this design. European A1 cars had this design with a widely spaced bolt flange on the manifold-to-downpipe interface. Pre-1981 cars had a similar manifold with a closer-spaced bolt flange. The final type is the A2 and A3 dual downpipe manifold with a distinctive flex joint on the downpipe for increased longevity (i.e., forever). This excellent manifold can be found on model year 1986–87 Jetta GLIs, all 16-valve engines, all non-VR6 Corrados and Passats, 1988–89 Digifant equipped cars, 1990–92 non-California Digifant cars, and the 2.0 A3s. The VR6 cars also have properly designed manifolds which should be retained.

For the salvage yard hunter, keep in mind that the 16-valve manifolds have different exhaust port shapes than the 8-valve, so the manifolds will not interchange. The 2.0 A3 manifold also has a different port design, making it an unfeasible swap to an earlier 8-valve. The only manifolds that would work on an A2 to replace a restrictive one are from the model year 1986–87 8-valve GLIs, 1988–89 Digifant cars, or the 1990–92 non-California Digifant cars. If you only find the manifold and not the downpipe, don't worry. The downpipe and cat from the 16-valve and 2.0 A3 will bolt on. The model year 1982 and newer A1 owners should look for a 1981 or earlier car for its dual downpipe manifold. Fox owners should find the dual-downpipe manifold from the mid-seventies Dasher. This particular manifold, when mated to an aftermarket downpipe, will liven up the bargain-basement Fox.

Volkswagen has a funny habit of making things either excellent or horrible, with no middle ground. Such is the case with exhaust manifolds. If your car doesn't have the dual-downpipe manifold, it needs one. Swapping to one of the good manifolds can net you up to 10 hp before any other modifications. To add insult to injury, some of the more awful factory manifolds will crack as often as a poorly-designed tubular header. An example of this is the 1990-1992 California Digifant cars. The single downpipe manifold that these cars come with has a very low life span if any high-performance driving is attempted. A good indicator of the lack of performance this manifold offers is the fact that the manifold-downpipe flange and downpipe itself is exactly one half of the better

Fig. 8-4. Six-bolt manifolds flow very well.

Fig. 8-5. This is about the worst VW manifold available: note the 4-1 design with a small manifold-to-downpipe flange.

Fig. 8-6. A long tri-Y header design will give good torque and horsepower. This header has a flex joint at the end to prevent cracking.

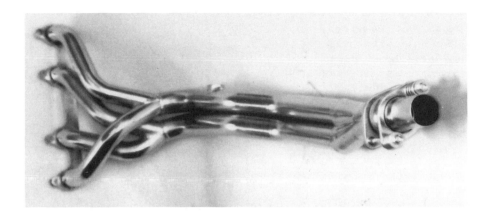

dual-downpipe design. This, of course, will technically give you half the exhaust volume. Yuck.

A good tubular header design will have the following characteristics. The basic layout will be a 4-2-1 or Tri-Y design. The alternate 4-1 design will give slightly more high-end hp with little low-end torque (a common problem of aftermarket parts, it seems). The material that the header is constructed of should be at least 14-gauge steel; anything thinner (16-gauge or less) will be too weak for extended use. Additionally, the thinner tubing will rust through quicker. The flange that bolts to the cylinder head should be all one piece instead of four little flanges for each cylinder port. This will give better sealing and higher strength because it is easier to align all of the tubes if you are welding to one common flange, allowing for a more precise flange surface. Finally, the header should incorporate some sort of flexible joint to allow for engine movement.

Of the dozens of VW header manufacturers, there are only a few in the U.S who meet these criteria: Autotech, Velocity Tuning, Wolf Sport, and Euro Sport. For the racing-only crowd, the Euro Sport, Techtonics, or Velocity headers are the only way to go. They do have an oxygen-sensor flange (basically, an 18 x 1.5 nut), but instead of the cat flange, they have extra-long down tubes before merging into one collector. This will yield greater torque and, since there is no cat, horsepower is also increased.

Before a tubular exhaust manifold (or even a cast-iron manifold) is mounted, it should be given a protective coating. Most paints will quickly burn off in a matter of minutes on a hot exhaust system; stove and exhaust paints may last somewhat longer. For the ultimate coating, try ceramic. This coating is available either as a service in which you send the part in to be coated (HPC or Swain Technologies) or as a raw product that you can apply yourself (Jeg's). In addition to preventing rust-through, the ceramic coating will improve power. By preventing heat from escaping the exhaust manifold itself, it helps in two ways. First, hot gas will flow faster than cool gas, and high velocity equals high torque. Second, the radiant heat won't be allowed to heat up the intake manifold that is usually situated directly above the exhaust manifold. The cooler intake manifold allows for cooler intake air, improving horsepower and reducing the chance of knocking and pinging.

Halfway in between a header and a stock manifold is the European-style long-tube downpipe. This will connect to a stock cast-iron manifold and completely do away with the catalytic converter. The downpipes end up being about a foot longer than the short stock ones, enhancing torque. The euro-style downpipes have to be constructed with the same care and materials as a tubular header. If the downpipes are constructed of 16-gauge steel or thinner, they will crack very easily.

Fig. 8-7. Fox owners can either replace their manifold with a Dasher unit or they can use a header like this one. The short piece of pipe can be used to replace the catalytic converter on a racing car.

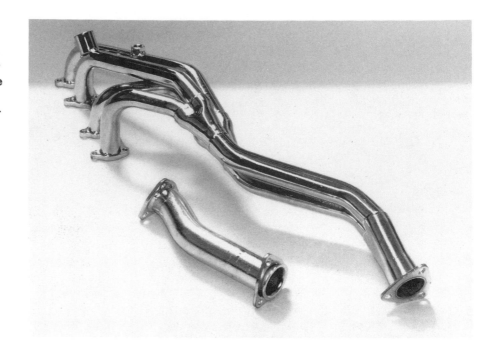

Fig. 8-8. Short vs. long downpipes. The latter offer close-to-header performance, while lasting longer.

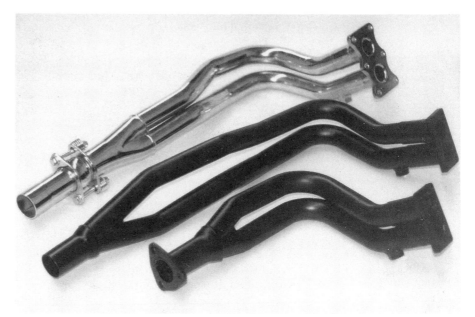

GENERAL MANIFOLD RECOMMENDATIONS

The Stock racing classes will all have to make do with their stock, unmodified manifolds. If a street-driven (smog-legal) car does not have one of the good manifolds, visit a neighborhood salvage yard for the proper dual downpipe replacements and Extrude Hone it, if necessary. If that is impossible to accomplish, try the Autotech header. Street Prepared and I.T. competitors should run the Euro Sport header if smog legality is not a concern. Alternatively, you could use a good, ported, factory exhaust manifold and replace the cat with a straight piece of pipe that is the same diameter as your exhaust system. Yet another possibility is the long-tube Euro-style downpipe which will also be smog-illegal.

CATALYTIC CONVERTERS

The internal design of the catalytic converters usually differs depending on who manufactures it. Fortunately, VW has always used the most free-flowing design. The three-dimensional matrix forms hundreds of tiny chambers in which chemical reactions reduce harmful emissions.

The performance difference in the VW cats is based on both the size of the matrix and the inlet and outlet sizes. Rabbits and other A1s were equipped with small converters with 42-mm inlets and outlets. The original A2 converters came with 47-mm openings; these were later increased to 55 mm. All of the A3 cars have at least this 55-mm size, while the VR6 cars get an even larger catalytic converter. The later, larger devices will yield more horsepower. The only downside to the larger catalytics is the extra weight. Since the larger converters are constructed out of heavy-duty stainless steel, they can weigh as much as 15 lbs. more than some of the small examples.

Great power gains that are smog-legal can be had by swapping a later factory cat in the place of your smaller one. Since a new catalytic converter costs about $600, a used one seems like a good option. This might be easier said than done, as the EPA has prohibited the sale of any used catalytic converter for quite some time. This means if a salvage yard or any other shop sells a used cat, they are liable for fines and prosecution!

Another option is to purchase a generic high performance catalytic converter from a high-performance automotive shop. Available from such manufacturers as Summit, the high-flow cat was designed for large American V8 engines. The high-exhaust demands of these engines insure more than adequate performance on a VW. A popular design in the market place is manufactured by Walker under the Dynomax label. As in the factory design, this cat is constructed out of heavy-duty stainless steel with a brick-type matrix. It would be perfectly legal to simply weld on the proper flange to mate with your downpipe, or simply slip it on the end of your header's collector. Techtonics makes a sport cat specifically designed to fit on the VW.

Racing classes either specify absolutely no modifications or state that you can remove all pollution control devices, including the catalytic converter. For the classes that must remain unmodified (the Stocks), simply make certain that

Fig. 8-9. A late-model catalytic converter such as this one is a good design because of its large size and tubing diameter.

Fig. 8-10. The larger catalytic converter from a 2.0 16-valve car (bottom) offers a larger inlet flange, a large outlet pipe, and a larger case; these all help increase exhaust flow.

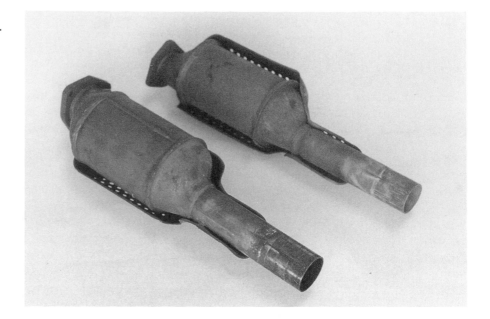

your stock cat is in peak condition. This is quite easy to do. Just unbolt the cat from the downpipe and shine a flashlight into the housing itself. If there is any plugging of the matrix or if there is any looseness of the matrix in the outer canister (usually accompanied by rattling or the sound of "rocks in a tin can"), it should be replaced. Improved Touring and Street Prepared competitors can simply remove the cat with a header that has no provision for it or with a straight piece of pipe that is mated to a good manifold. Street Driven cars should update to the best factory cat or a Dynomax version.

EXHAUST SYSTEM DESIGN

The exhaust stream that exits your header or catalytic converter is packed with energy in the form of sound—ear-splitting sound, to be exact. The old formula for a racing exhaust system is to simply have the exhaust pipe go straight back from the header for about 2 ft., take a 60-degree bend, and exit right behind the driver's door. The resulting shriek did allow the most horsepower by far, in a time when there were very few low-restriction mufflers.

Fig. 8-11. The Dynomax Super Turbo offers good performance and a low price. It is used in many budget performance exhaust systems. This cut-away shows the exhaust pathway through the muffler. Notice the semi-circular pieces that guide the exhaust when it makes its U-turn in the muffler.

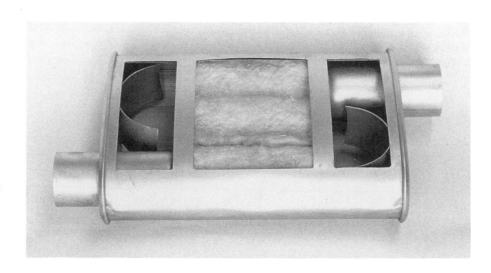

The number of racing venues that still allow unrestricted exhaust systems is slowly decreasing. The rapid encroachment of residential areas on race tracks has required racers to be good neighbors. Faced with noise regulations, competitors have demanded low-restriction exhausts that are quiet too; and VW street enthusiasts have come to expect that their modifications be livable in a day-to-day fashion. The aftermarket responded to this need well.

A properly engineered high-performance exhaust system differs from a poorly-designed one in several ways. First, a good system's tubing should be constructed out of 14-gauge aluminized steel or 304 stainless steel alloy. The lighter 16-gauge exhaust systems will only last about a year in a state that uses salt to de-ice roads in the wintertime. For racing teams that need to reduce weight wherever possible, the 16-gauge tubing will take off several more pounds over the weight loss normally associated with a 14-gauge high-performance exhaust. A racing car will also most likely never see a snowy road, making rust-through improbable.

The actual tubing size for the best high-performance exhaust depends on the engine size of the car and the chassis. The A1 chassis should use a 2-in. tubing size on engines of 1.8 liters or less displacement, or on street driven vehi-

Fig. 8-12. The Dynomax UltraFlo has a straight-through design for unrestricted exhaust flow. The exhaust gas doesn't have to make any turns in its trip through the muffler.

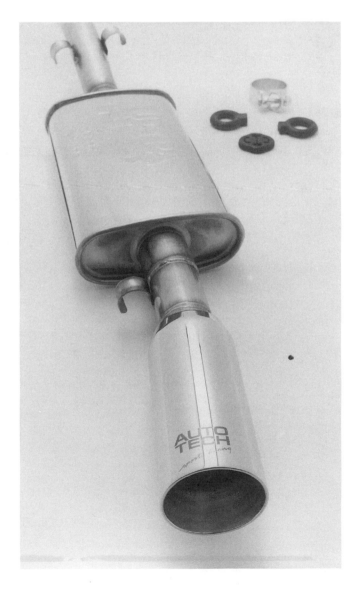

cles. The 2.25-in. size should be used on racing A1s with 1.8-liter and larger engines. The reason this size is only recommended for racing is that it will likely rub on the chassis, creating rattles that most street drivers will not be able to tolerate. The A2 and A3 chassis cars should use a 2.25-in. diameter exhaust tubing size. The newer chassis have more room for larger exhaust tubing, making this larger size an easy fitment. The VR6 cars may need 2.5-in. tubing, but their factory systems are very good out of the box and only minimal gains can be found here.

Muffler design should be as straight through as possible with little restriction to the exhaust stream. There are several types of these muffler designs in use today. The one most commonly found in high-performance exhaust systems is the "super turbo design." This type is similar to a stock muffler, where the exhaust stream travels back and forth through the main chambers, finally exiting the other end. The passages in the super turbo's casing will be larger and more free flowing. A good example of this type of design is the Walker Dynomax Super Turbo. The exhaust tone that is produced is louder than stock, but the deep mellow tone is not offensive.

The second type of high-performance muffler is the straight-through design. Here, the exhaust stream simply enters one end, travels straight through, and exits at the other end. The advantage is obvious, as the exhaust stream is not slowed down a bit. Horsepower will be greater than with a super turbo. The exhaust system will be louder with this configuration. The exhaust is actually in the muffler a short amount of time, making substantial sound-deadening im-

EXHAUST SYSTEM INSTALLATION

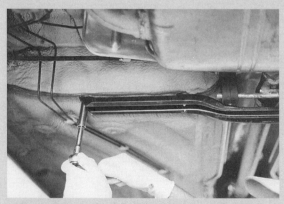

Fig. A. Remove both brackets that span the exhaust system tunnel. Both the rear bracket (shown here) and the bracket immediately behind the catalytic converter are secured with 13-mm nuts. Some earlier cars don't have these brackets.

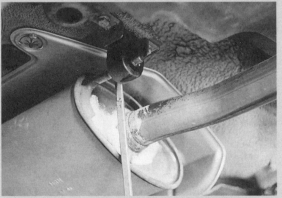

Fig. B. Remove the exhaust hangers from the original exhaust system. A large screw driver works well in prying these rubber hangers off.

CAUTION —

If you lack the tools or experience necessary to disassemble the exhaust system, this work should be left to an authorized Volkswagen dealer or qualified repair shop. Attempts to disassemble the exhaust system without the proper tools are likely to cause serious injury.

possible. The most common mufflers of this type are the Borla and the Walker Dynomax UltraFlo. These mufflers are constructed out of stainless steel (Walker is partially stainless steel) , are available at local automotive stores, and are usually offered as upgrades when purchasing an entire system.

The third type of muffler seen on high-performance exhaust systems, the Supertrapp, started as a spark arrester for off-road motorcycles used in desert racing (to prevent brush fires). The Supertrapp reduces sound levels by forcing the exhaust stream through discs on the end of the unit. The more discs you have, the more holes the exhaust can escape through (less restriction), leading to higher noise levels. The less discs you have mean less holes and less noise but correspondingly more restriction. The Supertrapp is loved by some and hated by others, the former group are racers who like to run with the Supertrapp because they can take all the discs off and run straight. The latter group argue that the Supertrapp does not flow well, especially when all the discs are installed. It's a matter of personal preference. The Supertrapp is available either as simply the discs and an adapter to be welded on the end of the exhaust pipe, or with a glass-pack muffler preceding the discs. The glass-pack design is the one that is recommended for most people because the discs alone are very loud. This muffler comes in either stainless steel or carbon steel. Since the muffler is rebuildable, go with the stainless to make it last for a long time.

There are no complete exhaust systems available for VWs that incorporate the Supertrapp, but it can be done. The easiest way to get a working system with this muffler would be to first buy the center section and the over-the-axle

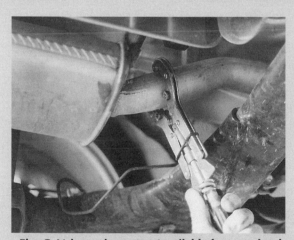

Fig. C. Using a pipe cutter (available from any hardware store) or a cutting torch, cut the stock system in front of the rear muffler. This step is only necessary on the later models which have a one-piece middle resonator/rear muffler section.

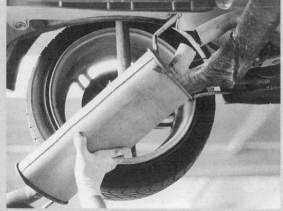

Fig. D. Remove the rear muffler once the pipe is cut through.

cont'd. on next page

CAUTION —
Consult your factory service manual for torque values for all fasteners.

Fig. 8-13. On the tuneable Supertrapp, the removeable discs at the end can be used to increase or decrease noise levels: more discs mean more power and noise, less discs mean less power and noise.

piece of a Euro Sport, Techtonics, or Autotech exhaust system and the Supertrapp itself. Then, install the tubing sections and figure out what sort of pipe you need to connect the Supertrapp to the rest of the system. There shouldn't be any bends required to fit this, making any local muffler shop the easiest source for the needed section.

EXHAUST SYSTEM INSTALLATION CONT'D.

Fig. E. Unbolt and remove the middle muffler section.

CAUTION ——

If you lack the tools or experience necessary to disassemble the exhaust system, this work should be left to an authorized Volkswagen dealer or qualified repair shop. Attempts to disassemble the exhaust system without the proper tools are likely to cause serious injury.

Fig. F. Unbolt and remove the exhaust pipe from the catalytic converter. It sometimes helps to use a large pair of channel locks to pull the pipe off.

Fig. 8-14. A typical budget exhaust system that uses a glass-pack muffler in the center section as a resonator. The system can be considered "budget" because of its use of uncoated aluminized tubing, inexpensive clamps, and a "turbo-style" muffler. Performance will be quite good with this system.

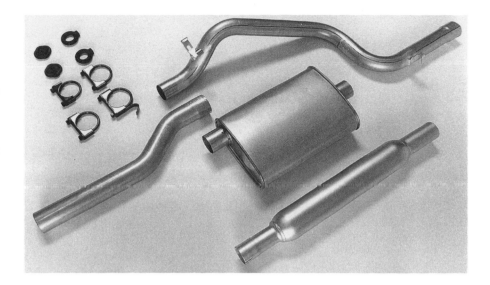

Exhaust systems designed for street use have a second muffler. A straight-through glass-pack muffler (like a Cherry Bomb) is welded into either the center section or the section that goes over the rear axle. The purpose of this muffler is to act as a resonator, removing high frequency, raspy noise from the exhaust. This secondary muffler will cost a few horse-power over 6000 RPM,

Fig. G. Thread the aftermarket over-the-axle section between the rear axle and the unibody.

Fig. H. Hang the section with the factory hangers.
cont'd. on next page

CAUTION —
Consult your factory service manual for torque values for all fasteners.

but it is necessary for most street drivers. If your car has a catalytic converter, try not using the resonator; the cat will act in the same manner.

The final characteristic of a high-performance exhaust is weight. The stock exhaust system is quite heavy; many aftermarket kits also weigh a considerable amount. A good exhaust system should be substantially lighter than stock while still being resistant to cracking and rust-through. Changing from the stock exhaust system to a lightweight system with no resonator, no catalytic converter, and a header instead of the cast-iron manifold will save you about 40 lbs. Just changing the exhaust from the cat back will shave off an average of 10 lbs (w/resonator) to 15 lbs (w/o resonator). The disadvantage of extra weight in the exhaust system is twofold: it's not good for performance and the heavier the exhaust system is, the sooner the rubber exhaust hangers will fail. The solution to this second problem is available from most companies who sell high-performance VW parts. There are rubber hangers that have a metal chain molded inside the rubber to prevent stretching and breakage; they cost more than stock hangers but they will last a long time.

There are many complete exhaust systems for VWs on the market today. Each brand has its own claim to fame, making the choice seem difficult. Fortunately, the best exhaust system design for most enthusiasts is the budget type. These systems, marketed by Euro Sport, Techtonics, New Dimensions, and Autotech, will give the largest horsepower gains, lightest weight, and the lowest price. Enthusiasts worried about rust should consider stainless-steel systems such as those made by New Dimensions, Techtonics, or Autotech.

EXHAUST SYSTEM INSTALLATION CONT'D.

Fig. I. Slide the center resonator section over the catalytic converter, and attach it to the over-the-axle section. Don't tighten up any clamps yet.

Fig. J. Install the rear muffler section. Rotate the muffler so that the exhaust pipe is centered in the cutout in the rear bumper.

CAUTION —
If you lack the tools or experience necessary to disassemble the exhaust system, this work should be left to an authorized Volkswagen dealer or qualified repair shop. Attempts to disassemble the exhaust system without the proper tools are likely to cause serious injury.

Fig. 8-15. The donut exhaust hanger on the right is used on the rear muffler of A2 cars, the hanger on the left is the normal type for A1 and A2 cars, and the middle hanger is the chain-type hanger for heavy-duty usage.A3 cars have a redesigned hanger system that is both strong and isolates the exhaust system vibrations from the chassis.

The "designer" exhaust systems from Europe will be as heavy or heavier than stock, with only moderate horsepower gains. An example of this type is the Leistritz system; some dyno tests have been run that found no horsepower gain over the stock system. Basically, those polished exhaust tips and wrinkle-coated finishes will do nothing for power. If you must go with a European tuner for an exhaust system, try the Gillet or Supersprint systems. The Gillet system is used by European factory-backed rally teams and offers good longevity. The

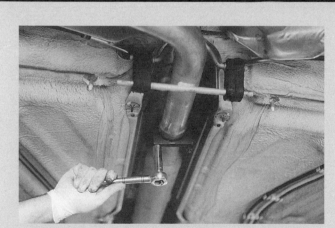

Fig. K. After aligning the exhaust system and making sure that there is no contact between the system and any chassis part, tighten the exhaust clamps.

CAUTION —
Consult your factory service manual for torque values for all fasteners.

Fig. 8-16. A2 GTI exhaust systems are better than some of the earlier systems, but a 5-hp gain in peak power can be achieved with a well-designed exhaust upgrade.

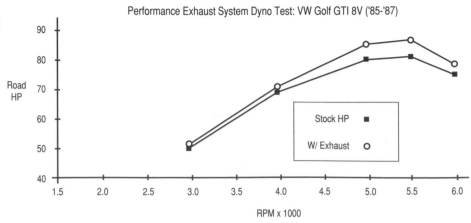

Fig. 8-17. The stock Fox exhaust system strangles the engine above 5000 RPM. An aftermarket sport exhaust will yield a 7-hp peak gain, and a 14-hp gain at 5500 RPM.

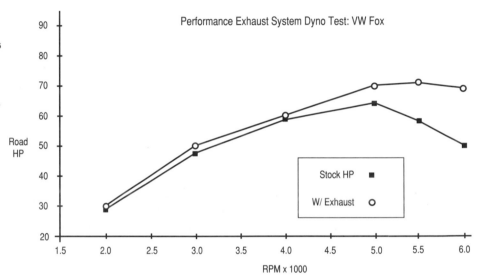

Supersprint exhaust system can give good power, but it weighs even more than a factory exhaust system, not to mention that it costs an arm and a leg.

THE BOTTOM LINE

Exhaust system horsepower gains are often exaggerated and misapplied and depend largely on how bad the original system was. For most A2s and A3s, the normal gain in power found by switching from a stock system to the best system (from the cat back) is 6 to 8 hp. Rabbits and Foxes, with their unusually restrictive system, will gain 9 and 14 hp, respectively, over stock. If you are running without a center resonator, you can add a couple more hp above 5000 RPM. Switching from the worst exhaust manifold (model year 1983–84 GTI or 1990–92 California Digifant) to the best manifold will give you 8 more hp with the catalytic converter intact. Removal of the catalytic will give you between 3 and 5 more hp of power. These values are for a normally aspirated motor; turbos will benefit more from exhaust work. If you couple these power gains with modifications to the intake system, you can see up to 30 percent more horsepower without opening up the engine.

Chapter Nine
LUBRICATION

Fig. 9-1. The oil change should be performed on a regular basis. Use a new drain plug washer each time, and use a high-quality filter.

Engine oil plays a crucial role in the internal combustion engine. It will reduce friction by forming a protective coating between tightly fitted parts, allowing the engine to run cooler. Less friction means less heat and more horsepower. By protecting engine internals, the oil will contribute to an engine's longevity. A properly-designed lubrication system will lubricate, cool, and have a filtration system to properly clean the oil.

There are three levels of maintenance and modification for a lubrication system: your level will depend on your high-performance driving needs.

LEVEL ONE

The first level of lubrication system maintenance and modification should be completed by anyone who wants to take excellent care of their car. This level should also be completed by everyone who is competing in a motorsports event, or even high-performance street driving. The recommendations in this level are legal for all racing classes, even the most restrictive.

The first step is to change your oil often. Old oil will not properly lubricate an engine for two reasons. First, it becomes dirty as the filter fills up with dirt and contaminants from your engine. Second, oil will break down after a while, with each molecule shearing apart when subjected to high heat and pressure.

The oil change is probably the most basic maintenance procedure that you can do on any car. If you are unaccustomed to mechanical work, it is a good starting point from which to learn. It is also a learning experience that needs to be repeated on a regular basis.

For conventional oils, this means you should change your oil every 7,500 miles. People who run synthetic oils should change fluid every 10,000 miles (or every six months), with a filter change at 5k. Synthoil, which is neither a conventional or synthetic oil but somewhere in between, is claimed to last 50,000 miles with filter changes at 5k. Racers stick with a premium grade synthetic instead of the Synthoil. On a race car, the added longevity (in terms of thousands of miles) is not at all important. A typical VW race car, even one used in endurance races, will rarely see more than one or two thousand miles a year.

The second step is to change to the best oil that you can afford. A conventional petroleum oil at $1 a quart will not lubricate as well as a synthetic type. The extra money will not be wasted; you will see lower oil temperatures and lower friction with the synthetically produced oil. This translates to the best protection for your engine, better fuel economy, and even a slight improvement in horsepower (1-2 percent). There are two distinct levels of synthetic oil. They are not the same formula, and not the same price. The "bargain" synthetics are those available at any automotive parts store, including Mobil 1, Castrol Syntec, etc. They are normally $4 a quart. The next level includes the premium-grade synthetics. These are typified by Redline, Spectro, or Amsoil, and are the choice of many racers. They cost more than "bargain" synthetics at about $7 a quart, but the differences are worth it. The higher grade oils will be less likely to break down under high-heat conditions, allowing the oil pressure to remain constant. They will also have even lower friction levels, equating to more horsepower and lower heat.

The third step in Level One is to use only high-quality oil filters. This means you should not use anything except filters from the following manufacturers: Mann, Bosch, or Fram (only the Extra Guard). Many street and racing enthusiasts have had lesser quality filters fail under stress. VWs, especially early ones, run very high oil pressures: 150 psi or more at cold startup. In fact, the factory specifies either Bosch or Mann filters on new cars. These filters are slightly more expensive than cheapo ones. Bosch and Mann filters can be purchased by the case, which will save you money in the long run.

Fig. 9-2. You can stop valve cover leaks by using unshouldered studs and a late-model 2.0 8-valve gasket.

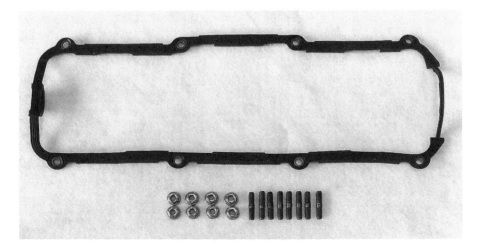

Fig. 9-3. This is the low-budget way to equip your car with an oil cooler. The lines are a high-pressure rubber and a sandwich adapter plate is used. This method may be problematic, however, with earlier cars, which can exceed 150 psi on a cold start. The solution: use oil lines with a burst strength of 250–300 psi and make sure the fittings on the sandwich plate are barbed. Otherwise, use stainless lines.

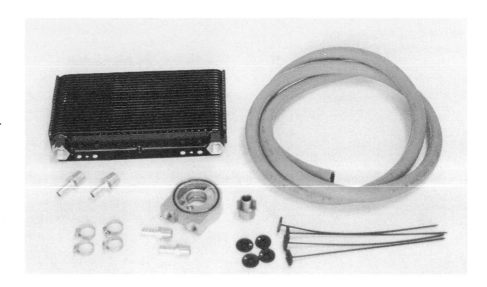

LEVEL TWO

If your street, I.T., or Street Prepared VW is still experiencing high oil temperatures (over 225 degrees) you should install an oil cooler. The oil cooler is simply a radiator for the oil, normally dropping temperatures a minimum of 25 degrees. In addition to the air-cooling effects of the oil cooler, it also will increase oil capacity. This means that it will take longer to overheat the oil, because there is more of it. The factory had an interesting oil cooler on the GTI and GLI models. It used the coolant (anti-freeze) to cool off the oil. It is a unique piece and should usually be removed only if you are fitting a conventional oil cooler, unless there is enough room for both in your particular car. Techtonics sells a water-to-oil cooler as a complete kit if you want to retrofit it on your car.

There are two ways to get oil out of the block, into a cooler, and back again. The hard way is to remove the oil filter mount and replace it with one that has fittings for external oil lines. That is expensive as the only such examples are from European GTIs. The easy way is to install a "sandwich" plate between the oil filter and its mount. Some of these adapters will have a thermostat to prevent oil flow through the cooler until the engine has reached operating temperatures. This would only be necessary on a daily driver in a cold climate (frequent winter temperatures below 20–30 degrees). The actual lines that run between the adapter and the cooler can be either high-pressure, fabric-covered rubber lines or braided-stainless-covered lines. If you can afford it, go with stainless. Otherwise, rubber is just fine for most anyone, as long as it is a true "high-pressure" line.

The oil sitting at the bottom of your engine block does not stay in one place. Turning, accelerating, and braking will make the oil slosh around inside the oil pan. There are several problems with this. The oil, if it is splashing around, will not be near the oil pump suction tube. This will starve the engine of oil during hard cornering. The oil will also be splashed onto the crankshaft as it is spinning around. This will cause high RPM drag and thus, lost hp. The crankshaft, by splashing in the oil and causing bubbles, will introduce air into the oil pump and oil passages. Air is not a lubricant! Often you will hear a VW come off a race course with its hydraulic lifters "ticking." The oil pump was sucking air during hard cornering, allowing the hydraulic lifters to lose pressure.

A baffled oil pan will solve the oil-splash problem. It is essentially a stock appearing oil pan with baffles inside to control the oil's motion. The pan should

Fig. 9-4. Baffles keep the oil near the oil pump pick-up tube.

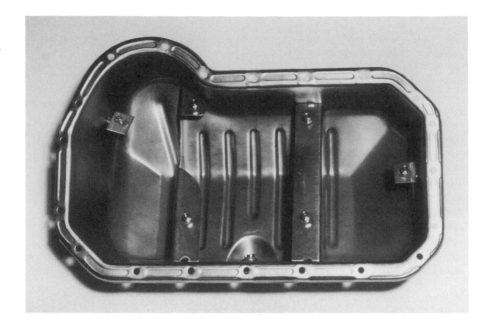

also have one-way trap doors mounted in the baffles. This will allow oil to go towards the oil pump pick-up tube, but not away from it. Most baffled oil pans will also have the advantage of larger oil capacity to increase the thermal reserve of the engine.

The baffled oil pans on the market today are either constructed out of cast aluminum or steel. Aluminum pans are available from Neuspeed and Autotech; modified steel pans are available from Autotech, Techtonics, and Havoc Motorsports. The aluminum has its advantages and disadvantages over steel. The aluminum pans will cool the oil with cooling fins on the bottom and the material itself has better heat dissipation properties. The aluminum is more expensive than steel, and it is much more fragile. If you hit something with a steel oil pan, it will bend. If you hit something with a cast-aluminum pan, it will crack and spill the engine's oil. Steel pans would be a better choice for most racers. They are cheaper, stronger, and work just as well as the expensive aluminum ones.

To prevent oil from splashing onto the spinning crankshaft, install a windage tray. This part will install on top of the baffling to create a roof for the baffled chambers. Oil will not be able to hit the crankshaft, saving one or two horse-

Fig. 9-5. This typical aluminum pan has the advantage of being able to cool the oil with its fins, but it will be more fragile than a steel pan.

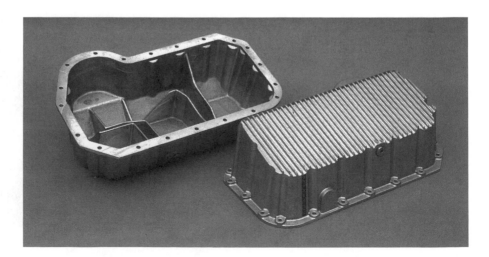

power at high RPM. The windage tray will also remove the air from the oil that drips from the crankshaft by forcing it through a metal screen. Windage trays normally come with the steel, baffled oil pans.

Some VWs actually have a small windage tray that attaches to the oil pump. There are two sizes of this tray, one found on the 8-valve engines and one found on the 16-valve engines. The 16-valve windage tray is larger than the other, and would be a good retrofit in any car where a baffled oil pan is illegal for its racing class. It also looks so similar (except in size) that it could be used in stock-type categories without fear of disqualification. It will have some of the benefits of a full windage tray, but will not be nearly as effective.

The final upgrade for Level Two is to replace your oil pump to increase lubrication. On solid lifter engines, replace your 26-mm gear pump with a 30-mm pump. On hydraulic lifter engines, upgrade to a 36-mm pump.

Fig. 9-6. Steel oil pans work as well as expensive aluminum ones. Note the windage tray that keeps oil from splashing onto the spinning crankshaft. Oil hitting the crankshaft at high RPM can slow the motor down!

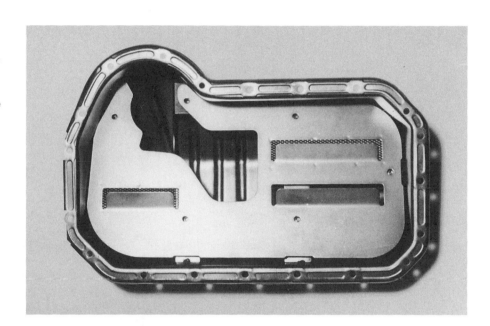

Fig. 9-7. The factory oil baffle works in conjunction with the stock oil pan. It offers the same benefit as a windage tray while being quite inexpensive (less than $20).

LEVEL THREE

This level is entirely unnecessary for almost all racers. If you are running in a racing class such as Prepared, Production, or G.T. and you are still having oil-related problems, you will want to install a dry-sump lubrication system. Instead of the oil being at the bottom of the engine, it will be stored in a reservoir and pumped from there. The advantage of this system is the total lack of the oil-control problem, superior oil flow, and minimal parasitic loss due to oil hitting the crankshaft.

Fig. 9-8. An Accusump will store extra oil that can be released when the system senses low oil pressure.

Chapter Ten
THE WATER-COOLING SYSTEM

Fig. 10-1. The factory recommends phosphate-free antifreeze.

When VW switched from air-cooled cars to water-cooled in the seventies, they must have been paranoid about overheating. The water-cooled VWs have amazingly effective and reliable cooling systems if they are functioning properly. There are few modifications to be made that will actually improve cooling; the Volkswagen engineers did their homework. The basic design has been nearly unchanged since the first A1 cars. The old saying, "if it ain't broke, don't fix it" obviously applies to the Volkswagen water-cooling system.

All of the racing classes that are being discussed are allowed to change antifreeze type; all classes except Showroom Stock can also change thermostats. The classes that allow updating/backdating can upgrade their coolant system by fitting later-model parts. If the car is street-driven and you are having overheating problems you should simply change things until the problem goes away. The modifications that are recommended are listed below in the order of their importance.

RECOMMENDED MODIFICATIONS

The Volkswagen factory recommends that only phosphate-free antifreeze be used in the cooling system. The phosphate is said to attack the various metals inside the engine. The only conventional brands on the market that meet this phosphate-free criteria are Volkswagen's OEM ethylene glycol coolant that is available at the dealership, or Sierra, a non-toxic propylene glycol coolant. The Sierra is available from any auto parts store. It is quite inexpensive and is better for the environment than conventional coolant.

Both of these should be mixed in a 50:50 ratio with water. Many people simply pour in the whole gallon of antifreeze and fill the rest with water, but this will not achieve the proper water-to-coolant ratio in many of the smaller-capacity cooling systems, often leading to overheating problems. You should find out the cooling system capacity (owner's manual or Bentley manual) and add half that amount of antifreeze, then fill the rest with distilled water; or you can pre-mix equal parts water and coolant before filling the tank. This will often cure hot running problems that are caused by the wrong mixture in the system.

An unconventional coolant that is available is also formulated out of propylene glycol, Canton-Mecca's Evan's Cooling. This fluid, with different properties than Sierra, is reported to be highly effective at engine cooling. It is not mixed with water as is the case with other antifreeze fluids; it is poured in full strength. The cooling system's greater efficiency with this fluid will ward off knocking and pinging of the engine. With a knock-sensor-equipped car, this will allow the system to advance the timing more, and advanced timing (to 12° BTDC) will give more horsepower.

There is an antifreeze additive on the market today that can improve the cooling capabilities of your regular coolant. Redline's Waterwetter reduces the surface tension of the water in the system. By reducing surface tension, you will also reduce the amount of bubbles that are formed in the hotter areas of the engine. These bubbles will reduce the efficiency of the coolant because air is not a good heat-transfer agent. One bottle of this product will treat the entire coolant mixture. It should be replenished when you change your antifreeze (once a year is sufficient).

With conventional coolants, you can lower the thermostat heat range, allowing the coolant to flow into the radiator sooner. This will lower engine temperatures quite effectively. The most common temperature-range thermostat is

Fig. 10-2. A 180-degree thermostat will allow coolant to flow through the radiator sooner. It will look identical to your stock unit, so make sure it comes in its original packing.

Fig. 10-3. Like the 180-degree thermostat, a lower-temperature fan switch will look exactly like your original.

the 180-degree type. It will open when the coolant is 15 degrees cooler than with the stock thermostat. The thermostat is in the inlet pipe of the water pump.

To match the lower opening temperature of the thermostat, you can install a fan switch that turns on the cooling fan at the same 180 degrees. This will help greatly in stop-and-go traffic, when natural airflow is minimal. There are two types of switches available. One switch has two terminals for one-speed fans, the other has three terminals for two-speed fans. To find out which one your car has, simply unconnect the connector from the switch itself and count the wires. The fan switch is located on the bottom right side (if you are looking into the engine compartment from the front of the car).

Another trick is to wire in a switch that will manually turn on the fan. This would be extremely helpful when waiting in stage lines for a race. You should put it close to the driver in the cockpit, for ease of use. The fan has a ground running to it (brown wire), and one or two switched positive wires. To run an additional switched power source, you need to have a wire going from the positive side of the battery to the switch. From the other switch connection, you

Fig. 10-4. Updating to a larger factory radiator will increase your cooling capacity. The small unit on the top is from a Cabriolet, while the larger unit is from a A2 GTI.

need to have a wire going to the positive wire that is connected to the fan. There will be a choice of two positive wires on fans with two speeds. Pick the higher-speed wire (usually the wire is red with a black stripe).

Street drivers and Improved Touring and Street Prepared competitors should update to later factory radiators to cool the engine better. The cheapest source of parts is the local foreign-car salvage yard. You should beware that some fragile parts such as the radiator are easily damaged in accidents. Most salvage yards will give very short-term warranties; install and check the part shortly after you buy it. The easiest swap is to install the radiator from an air-conditioned car in a non-air-conditioned car. It will be slightly larger and will cool any engine quite well. Another helpful swap would be the addition of the factory coolant expansion tank on a car that did not have one. This will increase coolant capacity by about a half a gallon, and it makes checking coolant levels easier. For this swap you will need the radiator from a car with the tank; companies such as Techtonics sell adapters to provide the outlet from the radiator to the expansion tank.

Fig. 10-5. The factory late-model coolant tank is an easy upgrade for cars without them. It will allow for more coolant, which means more thermal reserve. You will need an adapter for your radiator's outlet for this update.

Chapter Eleven

THE DRIVELINE

Fig. 11-1. The factory uses Sachs clutches; make sure when you replace yours that you use the same. Properly cared for, the clutch should last well in excess of 100,000 miles.

Getting the horsepower and torque—on which you have spent a lot of time and money—to the ground is the job of the driveline. The clutch, transmission, differential, final drive, and axles all play a part in power transfer. Weak clutches will waste horsepower and not allow fast acceleration. The gear ratio will determine acceleration and top speed, while the differential will allow power to be put to the ground when the car is cornering.

THE CLUTCH

The clutch on a water-cooled Volkswagen is absolutely amazing. It is routine to hear about a VW clutch lasting upwards of 150,000 miles, some even 200,000! Personally, I have had a clutch outlast the engine on a daily driver/weekend racer. After 130,000 miles and 80 races, the hydraulic lifters and piston rings were shot, but the clutch still had plenty of life left. One of the only times that you will hear of clutches lasting less than 100,000 miles will be when the engine's rear main oil seal goes bad. This will allow oil from the crankcase to soak the friction material of the clutch, rendering it useless.

When the clutch does go bad, clutch replacement can cost in excess of $400, a high percentage of which is labor time. Since only a small portion of the clutch-replacement costs are parts (clutch disc, pressure plate, rear main oil seal, and clutch pushrod seal), you should replace them whenever you have the engine or transmission out of the car, insuring that the clutch will have a long life without premature failure. For best results, Sachs is one manufacturer that produces excellent factory clutches.

The stock clutch also has the capability to handle vast amounts of horse-power over factory levels. If you are running a stock clutch, you can have your engine put out up to 170 hp before you see slippage problems, regardless of the racing that you do. It is often thought that you should replace the earlier, smaller clutch (190 mm) with the later 210 mm unit. This should only be done if your clutch's friction material is wearing out unreasonably quickly.

The larger clutch was used by the factory to increase longevity of the system. It does not have higher holding pressure to resist slip because the tension on the clutch disc's springs is the same as the smaller clutch. It will last longer because there is more actual friction material bonded to it.

If you are running in excess of 170 hp, you should install a Sachs sport clutch package, which costs about four times more than a stock Sachs clutch, so it's an option only for people who actually need the extra holding power. You might be tempted to just purchase the sport clutch disc to be used with a stock pressure plate. This will work worse than stock and cost more—not the smart thing to do. Using the stock disk and sport pressure plate can, however, help and give good results for less money than an entire sport clutch system.

For the ultimate in holding power, you can install a four-puck racing clutch. which has four metallic holding pads instead of the circular friction material of the standard type. It will be extremely harsh for street use and should only be considered for racing use (still a little overkill). For autocrossing, where you have to start smoothly every time for the quickest finish, the four-puck clutch would actually make your start slower. The massive "stick" of the clutch would stall the engine instaneously if the engine revs were not high enough. Then, when the clutch grabbed at that high RPM, the tires would spin excessively.

Eight-valve cars with 210-mm clutches can gain some extra holding power cheaply by using the pressure plate from a 2.0 16-valve car. This pressure plate should only cost about $20 more than the 8-valve piece. It will have higher-rate springs in it, to increase the pressure that it will exert on the clutch disc. The 16-valve car's clutch disc will not work on an 8-valve engine because of its differently-sized output shaft splines.

In Solo Stock and Showroom Stock, clutches must be stock. Street Prepared and Improved Touring racers can install any clutch. The recommendations for these latter classes and street are the same. Stick with the stock (or 16-valve pressure-plate upgrade) on all cars with less than 170 hp. If your engine is putting out more than that, go with a sport clutch unit. When these clutches fail you, you can try the four-puck racing clutch, though I suspect the problem at that point may not be with the clutch.

Fig. 11-2. Pressure plates from the 2.0 16-valve cars are a good upgrade for 8-valve cars. The 16-valve pressure plate has higher rate springs, increasing holding power.

Fig. 11-3. The manually adjusted cable (left) is a low-cost replacement for the more expensive automatic adjusting unit (right). The downside of the manual is that you do need to make clutch adjustment a part of your maintenance procedures. The downside of the automatic is that it can fail, causing abnormal wear on your clutch; but when working correctly, the automatic keeps the clutch cable adjusted perfectly.

Some clutch failures have been attributed to a bad adjusting mechanism in the automatically adjusting clutch cable. This type cable was fitted on some A2 and all 4-cylinder A3 cars. When the adjusting mechanism is not working properly, it will overadjust. This will quickly wear out the clutch. The solution is either to replace it with another expensive automatic cable or try the less-expensive manually adjusting type. The cables are interchangeable, making the swap an easy 15-minute job.

TRANSMISSIONS

There have been several basic types of manual transmissions fitted to water-cooled VWs. These range from four-speed, wide-ratio to five-speed, close-ratio configurations. The wide-ratio transmissions are designed to give better fuel mileage with long-legged gearing to make the engine run at a low RPM on the highway. The close-ratio transmissions are meant to give the best acceleration by reducing the RPM drop from one gear to the next. Reducing the RPM drop in a gear change is good; it will better keep the engine within its powerband.

The A1, A2, and A3 020 transmissions can all fit into a different chassis with little or no custom modifications. This does not make each swap as easy as another. The transmissions are easiest to change when you are switching within chassis types. The A1 transmissions will fit into an A2 but you need to change a few other parts to make the swap. The 8-valve and 16-valve transmissions are also different, requiring different axles flanges to fit on some early A2 cars. You will save some headaches, therefore, by staying within the same chassis type. The 00A transmission that is fitted to the Corrado, Passat, and all VR6 cars utilizes a cable shift linkage, requiring that you swap all of the mechanisms (and a hydraulically actuated clutch on some models).

Like many other expensive parts on your Volkswagen, replacement transmissions are best found in a salvage yard. The close-ratio transmissions are found in the sport models such as the GTI and the GLI. They are also found in many of the Wolfsburg-edition cars. One problem with this close-ratio transmission is that during the design process, VW elected to use a rivet head to retain internal differential components instead of circlips. This has resulted in failures where the final drive will actually machine a hole in the side of the transmission. Unfortunately, this will require an expensive repair by an expert. The solution is to upgrade to a bolt kit and circlips for the differential.

All of the other VW models have wide-ratio transmissions, the one exception being some late-model A2 8-valve cars (later Digifants). The transmissions on the late-model A2 8-valve cars have all of the close-ratio gears except for second. This second gear is the same as the wide-ratio's. This oddball transmission will therefore have a large RPM drop between first and second without a big drop in the other gears and will probably work best on the faster tracks.

Swapping your four-speed transmission for a five-speed is a great modification to make to your Volkswagen. The added gearing will make your car much more flexible, and it will give faster acceleration with better highway cruising. The swap itself is quite straightforward. The required parts besides the different transmission are the clutch pushrod, the five-speed clutch and pressure plate, the transmission mounts, and the shift linkages. All of the five-speed pieces will bolt right on in place of the four-speed parts.

The five-speeds come in two basic flavors: close- and wide-ratio. They can be interchanged easily if so desired, but for the racing classes that allow changing the transmission, there is no clear-cut advantage for doing so. I.T. and Street Prepared rules, with their normal updating/backdating procedures, allow changes within the same classification (stock racing classes allow no transmission changes or modifications). Improved Touring racers will have to decide which of the transmissions will work better at their speeds. The shorter tracks will benefit from the close-ratio transmission, while the faster tracks will not. This is because the close-ratio boxes will have a lower fifth gear (higher numerically), while the wide ratio will have a higher fifth gear (lower numerically).

The advantage of the close-ratio transmission on an autocross course depends on the speed and layout of the track. If the course allows speeds up to 60 mph, then a wide-ratio transmission might be better. This is because you will not have to make the change from second to third gear, saving precious time. If the course is very tight with speeds less than 45 mph, the close ratio transmission will have the advantage. Most courses will have a combination of slow and fast sections; time lost in some areas might be made up in others. If the region where you race likes short, tight courses, you should run a close ratio. If it doesn't, don't automatically switch to one without thinking it through.

Another option is to swap individual gear ratios inside the transmission. This is not generally feasible for most people except in some isolated conditions. Individual gear sets are very expensive for the VW transmissions. It is always cheaper just to find the complete transmission with the desired ratio. Changing gear sets is also illegal in all of the racing classes discussed in this book. In addition, the labor involved to swap all of the gears and synchronizers is quite extensive. Basically, changing the ratios would only be desirable if your racing

Fig. 11-4. A custom or racing gear set is overkill for most racers. The advantage is that you can tailor-match your car to different tracks so that the engine is always in its powerband.

class allowed it, and you could afford it. Changing ratios, besides swaps of entire transmissions, is totally unnecessary on a street vehicle.

The factory five-speed ratios are more than adequate for street driving, except for the one that is installed on the close-ratio transmissions. This fifth gear is designed to give great fifth-gear acceleration; unfortunately it also makes the engine run at a high RPM on the highway. For most cars, this fifth gear turns the engine at 3500 RPM at 70 mph. This is too high for most people. An easy remedy is available to remedy this problem: fifth-gear conversions are available from Neuspeed, Autotech, and others. This kit will change the factory close-ratio fifth gear (.91) to an overdrive fifth (.76 or .80). This fairly straightforward swap will save you money in gas if you do a lot of highway traveling.

Fig. 11-5. An Autotech 5th-gear conversion will lower 5th-gear RPM for good economy on the freeway; they are available for both 8- and 16-valve cars.

FINAL DRIVES

You can also change your car's gear ratio by swapping the ring and pinion. This will either lower (higher top speed) or raise (better acceleration) the overall ratio, while leaving the gear spacing intact. This modification is only allowed in I.T. racing, but a street driver looking for quicker acceleration could use it too.

The aftermarket ring and pinion gears are extremely expensive, and are hard to find. The factory does sell different ratios through its VW Motorsport branch in Germany; these are imported by some companies to the U.S. Autotech has the best selection of both final drives and transmission gear sets here in the states. Most alternative ring and pinion gears are a numerically higher ratio than stock, giving better acceleration at the expense of top speed. At some road-racing tracks, this would be beneficial; at others it wouldn't. Generally speaking, if you are running out of RPM on the straights at your local track, don't even think about an alternative final drive.

There is one alternative to expensive aftermarket final drives. The Rabbit, Golf, and Jetta Diesels have a higher numerical ratio to help their lackluster performance off the line. This gear set (best found in a salvage yard) can be bolted into any of the 8-valve transmissions, giving good off-the-line performance. For the Street Prepared competitor, since updating and backdating of

Fig. 11-6. A lower (numerically higher) ring and pinion set will lower the overall ratio, while keeping gear spacing the same. A lower ratio will have a smaller pinion gear and a larger ring gear.

complete assemblies is allowed, this mod would give the diesel transmission the gear spacing and final drive ratio that some people need.

Changing your car's final drive will require a complete teardown of the transmission. It would be smart to do this at the same time as other repairs or modifications, such as when installing a different differential. You should also keep in mind that if you raise your car's final drive, you will alter the calibration of the speedometer. If this is a concern, you can consult the supplier of the alternate ring and pinion about possible solutions. If you have purchased a diesel ring and pinion, you could just swap the speedometer drive gears.

SPECIAL DIFFERENTIALS

When a car is going around a curve, the wheels on the inside of the curve have to travel a shorter distance than the wheels on the outside, so there has to be some method of allowing this action in the transaxle. A differential allows the outside wheel to travel further and faster than the inside to allow for this.

Fig. 11-7. The factory open differential does not provide any limited-slip action; power will take the path of least resistance. Unfortunately, that means the wheel with the least traction will get the most power.

Most early VWs are equipped with what is called an open differential. This is a basic non-limited slip design that is inexpensive to produce and is very easy for the average driver to drive with. The driven wheels will break loose gradually and early on in the corner. Unfortunately, when the inside wheel starts to spin as weight is transferred off of it in a turn, the differential thinks that it is the outside wheel. It will then give that already overloaded wheel more power. In a high-performance Volkswagen, this is disastrous for cornering speed.

Modifications to the differential are excellent for street and racing use. On the street, the added traction will make the VW both faster and safer. Racing cars in Street Prepared and Improved Touring will benefit with substantially improved lap times. Stock class Volkswagens that are equipped with the factory's differential should make sure that it is operating at peak efficiency.

The handling balance will change when using a limited-slip differential. The front wheels will have much greater traction, causing some corner entry oversteer. However, as the car exits a turn under power, the two front wheels will lose traction at the same time, leading to understeer. This difference in handling behavior can be used to your advantage once you get used to it.

There are several different types of limited-slips available for front-wheel-drive Volkswagens. The first is the friction or clutched differential. In this design, springs exert force onto the differential gears, effectively locking the entire differential solid. The amount of locking is dependent on adjusting the preload of the springs with shims. The more shims, or spring pressure, the more locked the differential is. This is measured by a value of what percentage of inside wheel spin is allowed, and how much is transferred to the non-spinning wheel. Most aftermarket friction/clutch limited slips will allow about 40 percent of the power to be applied to the wheel that has traction (40% locked).

Volkswagen actually has its own differential of this type of design on its later-model front-wheel-drive cars. Often called the "Minislip," this factory differential system uses springs and a brass, tapered washer that apply pressure between the drive flanges and the differential gear/housing assembly. The O20 series transmissions all have this feature, installed on nearly every car since the 1983 GTI. The springs, although originally used to lessen noise and vibration in the differential system, do provide the system with some limited slip.

Fig. 11-8. For effective operation, the brass washers on the factory differential (for model year 1983 on) must not be worn or broken.

Fig. 11-9. The Velocity Tuning shim will increase spring pressure.

Fig. 11-10. This tool, included in the Velocity kit, is used to compress the factory springs so that you can remove and install the drive flanges.

While this factory differential does not have a fantastic amount of locking ability, it does help. Showroom Stock and Solo Stock competitors should rebuild this assembly at least once a season. The brass, tapered washers should be replaced when they wear or break, which happens fairly often. The springs that actually apply the preload should also be replaced before they lose temper. As a part of the blueprinting process, you should find the best examples of these springs, judging by the length and rate of the spring. To get the best factory differential, the springs should be as long and as stiff as possible.

Velocity Tuning has developed a shim kit to modify this factory differential system. The kit consists of heat-treated shims that are installed between the spring and the brass, tapered washer. The shim increases preload on the gear

Fig. 11-11. Velocity tuning kits include everything you need for added traction.

assembly, increasing the amount that the differential effectively locks (possibly up to 40%). This kit also includes a tool to remove the drive flanges, the drive flange seals, and new upgraded brass, tapered washers. The Velocity Tuning modified differential is a substantial improvement over the factory differential. Traction is greatly improved, and often lap times will drop as a result.

Perhaps the most convincing argument for installing this differential kit is its cost effectiveness, offering nearly the traction gains of the more expensive gear driven limited slips for 1/8 the price. Also, it can be installed in a few hours, without removing the transmission. A complete differential would require complete disassembly of the transmission, a $400-plus job at most VW shops.

The gear-driven torque slip differential is the ultimate for your front-wheel drive Volkswagen. It uses a complex series of gears to proportion power to the wheel that has the most traction. The Quaife-type differential is an entire differ-

Fig. 11-12. The Quaife limited-slip differential provides excellent traction, but it is expensive and requires a complete teardown of your transmission.

ential unit which replaces the stock piece. This design gives the most traction gains of any torque slip differential ever made—up to 75% of power can be applied to the wheel with the most traction—but the cost is high. Quaifes retail for around $1000 and installation can add another $400 to that.

The VR6 cars also come with a limited-slip system with a different design. The traction control device on the VR6 relies on the wheel-speed sensors that are a part of the anti-lock braking system. When the computer senses that one wheel is spinning faster than the other during acceleration, it applies braking force to that wheel, reducing wheel spin and allowing quicker starts on loose surfaces. This system is effective on loose terrain, and will help many inexperienced drivers accelerate quickly, but may not be the hot ticket for an experienced driver on a race track. If you are already planning a VR6 swap into an earlier car, you might want to swap the entire braking/traction control system as well.

The final type of locking differential seen on VWs is one with no differential function at all. The completely locked differential solves all of the problems associated with the wheel with the least traction getting the most power. Since both axles are locked together, they cannot spin faster than each other. The inside wheel will, however, have to spin slightly to keep up with the outside wheel, increasing steering effort and wheel scrub drastically at low speeds. A cost-effective mod for I.T. racers, for whom low-speed turning is not an issue is to remove the stock differential, weld all of the gears together and reinstall it—sounds cheesy, but it is effective at increasing high-speed traction. This mod is only for track use, *not* for autocross or street.

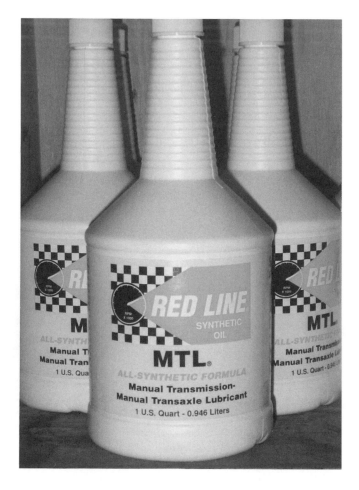

Fig. 11-13. A synthetic transmission fluid will speed up synchronizer action and lower friction levels.

TRANSMISSION FLUID

Like the engine, the manual transmission requires proper lubrication to function well. The molecules in poor-quality transmission fluid will quickly shear apart, reducing their capacity to reduce friction. While the factory does not list transmission fluid changes as a part of routine maintenance, it is an excellent idea for people who want to take extra care of their VW.

The engine is not the only place where synthetic oil performs well. Synthetic transmission fluids (Redline's MTL, for example) have been developed to reduce heat and power-robbing friction and help the transmission synchronizers. This fluid is used by many top racers and thousands of street enthusiasts.

Fig. 11-14. Some short-shift kits are adjustable. This one has two settings, 30% and 50% reduction in shift throw.

SHIFT LINKAGES

To reduce the throw of the shift lever as you change gears, you can install a short-shift kit. This will significantly reduce the distance you have to move the shift lever. With reduced shifting time, the driver can concentrate on the road or track better. These linkages are manufactured by many different companies for all of the water-cooled VWs. Some of the better manufacturers will even include new bushings for all of the linkage connections; this will get rid of loose

Fig. 11-15. Weighting one of the linkages can improve shifting feel. Aftermarket examples mimic the factory's A3 design.

and sloppy movement in the shifter. You should also expect high-quality powder-coated finishes, or a zinc plating on the aftermarket pieces.

Short-shift kits are legal in Street Prepared, Improved Touring, and they are an excellent idea for the street. Unfortunately, there are only a few short-shift kits available for the cable-shifting cars, such as the Corrados, Passats, and all of the VR6s, and they are expensive.

The factory added a weight to one of the shift linkages in the A3 cars, making the shifting smoother and less notchy. The weight adds momentum to the linkage arm's movement, causing the shifter to drop positively into each gear. Weighted linkages are sold by many of the manufacturers of short-shift kits.

MOTOR MOUNTS

Securing the engine to the chassis is not an easy task. The mounts have to be solid enough to actually keep the engine in place, while they also have to absorb the inevitable engine vibrations. These problems have spawned several different factory-produced motor-mount types: some work, others do not.

Fig. 11-16. The cylinder mount will not fail catastrophically like the hydraulic versions will.

The standard enthusiast's response to engine movement is to fit stiffer motor mounts to their car. This will limit engine movement and transfer all available power to the ground. Unfortunately, it will also increase chassis vibration immensely, making the car unpleasant to drive. An added benefit of stiffer motor mounts, particularly the front, is that exhaust manifolds and downpipes will last longer when the engine is more securely held.

The only engine mount changes that are recommendable for street use are different front mounts. The side and rear mounts are adequate for high-performance street use, while the front is not. The easy solution for the A1 cars is to simply install the aforementioned polyurethane or stiffer rubber front mount. This will solve almost all engine rocking and clunking. Unfortunately, this change is illegal for the stock classes, Street Prepared, and Improved Touring. On an A1 chassis that is raced you must either hope no one protests you or change the stock front mount once a season.

A2 cars came equipped with two different types of front engine mounts. The early version is similar to the passenger side mount, a cylindrical rubber piece fitted within a circular band of steel that is attached to the engine. The other, later type is a hydraulic mount that is constructed like a jelly-filled donut; it is a steel-and-rubber shell filled with a silicone gel material to absorb vibration.

The problem with the hydraulic mount is that it can pop apart under extreme conditions. The rubber outer shell will tear, and the gel will leak out. This will cause extreme engine rocking and clunking. Simply replacing the mount is one option that most people take. However, it will soon rip again if the car is driven hard. The only real solution is to retrofit the early cylindrical mount in its place, as it is nearly indestructible. This change requires the cylindrical rubber mount, the bracket that bolts to the block, and the U-shaped bracket that bolts to the front subframe. This is an excellent and legal update/backdate for street, Street Prepared, and Improved Touring use. Again, stock-class competitors can either switch, and be illegal, or change the hydraulic mount each time it breaks.

Fig. 11-17. The hydraulic "doughnut" front mount. The engine, as it rocks, will pull upwards on the threaded bolt. If the mount fails, this bolt fitting can tear away from the rest of the mount, leaving the engine unrestrained.

The no-compromise racer (Prepared, Production, GT, or Modified) or street enthusiast will want to change all of the motor mounts to either polyurethane or harder durometer rubber. The polyurethane types are stiffer than rubber, but they transfer more vibration to the chassis. Hard-rubber mounts are said to be a compromise, offering good engine stability, while not being as rough as the poly mounts.

Fig. 11-18. These VW Motorsport mounts look identical to their stock counterparts, the difference being that they are made of stiffer rubber.

Polyurethane motor mounts are available from most high-performance shops, while hard-rubber mounts are only produced by VW Motorsport. The latter are imported to this country and are available through Neuspeed. Unfortunately, they are much more expensive than the polyurethane types. For you rule-benders out there, the VW Motorsport mounts look exactly like the factory pieces, they just have different part numbers on them.

Chapter Twelve

BALANCING WEIGHT FOR PERFORMANCE

Fig. 12-1. Corner weights are obtained by weighing each wheel separately. This Longacre scale system includes a computer to make the job simpler.

Of all the modifications and tweaks that you can perform on your car, there is nothing you can add to simultaneously make it quicker, brake better, and handle better. There is something you can take off, though, that will accomplish all of these things: weight. If you have two cars with the same engine, chassis, and brakes, with one car weighing even one pound more, the lighter car will be faster. While the best drivers have a difficult time telling differences in car performance due to weight losses or gains within 20 lbs., it is still true that every bit counts. How much weight you decide to take off your street car depends on the usage it sees. If you live in a hot climate, the performance advantage of no air conditioning might be outweighed by the discomfort that it causes. A typical street car is a compromise; how much comfort you are willing to forego for the last bit of performance is up to you. For a racing car, compromise assures that you will run mid-pack, since racing by definition is a competitive sport.

HORSEPOWER/WEIGHT AND CORNER BALANCING

When talking about the weight or the horsepower of a car, the hp/weight ratio can be used to compare one car to another. To compute this ratio, you simply divide the weight of the car by the horsepower. There are two main ways to determine how much your car weighs. The weight of the car can be measured by scales used for large tractor trailers which are accurate to within 10 lbs. These are usually located in industrial areas at scrap metal or building supply facilities. The fee for getting your car weighed is usually between $1 and $5, if you ask for a non-certified weight. You will usually encounter strange looks as you pull your diminutive VW on a weight platform that is five times your car's length, but a weight is a weight.

Fig. 12-2. The balance of the car can be determined by the weight on each wheel. This Jetta has a weight distribution of 58% front and 42% rear bias. While this isn't fantastic compared to a rear-wheel-drive car, it is quite good for a front driver.

A more useful way to get the weight of your car is to use racing scales. These are four purpose-built scales that you put under each of your wheels. This will give you total weight along with the weight on each wheel (or corner weight). These scales cost around $1500. However, if you attend any Solo II divisional or national event, you can usually drive up on them when they aren't being used, for free. These scales are usually present at many road-racing events. You might also ask around within your SCCA region for fellow competitors who have a set of these scales. That way you could get your corner weights and have time to change things to get the desired settings. Some racing shops will rent the use of their scales; if you have no other option, this is a good idea.

The desired settings for corner weights, with driver, are such that you get equal diagonal values: in other words, left rear plus right front equals right rear and left front. You should also get the front-to-rear balanced a little better; whereas most VWs start out at approximately 65% front / 35% rear, you can get them to 57/43, creating a well-balanced racer. One thing to consider is that

Fig. 12-3. The Tunnells had excellent luck campaigning this 1987 Jetta in E Stock; it only weighed 2130 lbs.!

having more weight on the front to some extent is not bad, since that is where the driving force is on a front-wheel-drive car. If you reduce the front weight to an extreme amount such as 50/50, the car will be unmanageable in wet track and road conditions. To change corner weights, you either need to change weight distribution or ride height at each corner (as discussed in Chapter 2).

The other part of the horsepower-to-weight ratio is horsepower (hp) which can be obtained using a chassis or engine dynamometer. For a stock Golf III, the ratio would be 23 lbs. per horsepower, while a Street Prepared Rabbit could have a ratio of 15 lbs. per horsepower. The car with the lower number will be quicker on the track or the street.

CREATURE COMFORTS

The first things that should be removed, or never put on in the first place, are the comfort options and accessories. That means no sunroof (30 lbs.), air conditioning (50 lbs.), or for the serious racer, even radio (8 lbs.).

It is often hard to find cars with no options on them, even at dealerships. In 1987, there were only seven Wolfsburg Jetta 2-doors made with no options. Bob and Patty Tunnell, both national champions in E-stock, found one such beastie. Prepared to full E Stock Solo II specifications, this car weighs 2130 lbs. and puts out 115 horsepower, a great combination for a "stock" car. This particular car has won four national championships, one with Alan McCrispin driving and the other three with the Tunnells. With a horsepower-to-weight ratio comparable to most 2-liter GTIs, in Bob's and Patty's very competent hands it is a force to reckon with. Most of the no-option cars that were imported into this country were snapped up by Showroom Stock racers, making them hard to come by in a pristine state. Furthermore, since the only places that wouldn't need air conditioning or sunroof also have lots of snow, these examples might be rusty and not fit for racing.

Luckily, it is not difficult to find a rust-free example in a warmer climate and remove all of the unwanted pieces. The air conditioning pump and plumbing can be removed, and alternate brackets and belts can be fitted. The bracket that holds the A/C pump, P/S pump, and the alternator is constructed out of cast iron and weighs about 10 lbs. A cheap way to change over from A/C to non-A/C on a power-steering-equipped car is simply to cut off the portions of the

Fig. 12-4. The heavy cast-iron power-steering pump bracket is used on A/C-equipped cars.

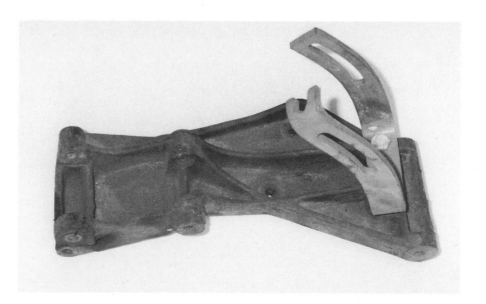

bracket that are not needed, bringing weight down a pound or two. A lighter way to do it involves ordering the correct aluminum piece (VW part #053 145 515) from a dealer as it only weighs one pound. There are also portions of the A/C system inside the cockpit. To allow usage of the ventilation system once you remove the evaporator, you can block off the resulting holes with sheet aluminum. One side benefit of removing the condensor in front of the cooling system's radiator is greater engine-cooling efficiency, as air does not have to pass through the condenser before it reaches the radiator.

The radio is easy to remove, and resultant holes can be filled with a trip to your local VW dealership which stocks lightweight, plastic block-off plates. Speakers, antennas, and all wiring can also legally be removed. Some interior trim pieces that house speakers such as the lower door pockets on 1988 and newer cars are also available without speakers. The antenna hole can be plugged with a rubber piece from VW that simply snaps in. For street drivers who want to race occasionally, try using an anti-theft removable stereo and removable speaker enclosures. This will allow you to have your tunes when you want them, and to have the lightest weight when you need it. It will also prevent the practically unavoidable break-ins.

Fig. 12-5. This aluminum power-steering pump bracket for non-A/C cars can help you lose a few lbs. when removing the A/C.

The sunroof is slightly more difficult to remove. One option is to replace the entire roof sheet metal, which necessitates removal of all the glass. This is the only way to remove the sunroof and stay legal in most racing classes. As an alternative you can remove just the sunroof, cut out all of the tracks and sunroof supports, and then weld the sunroof panel in. This could be sanded and filled until it would indistinguishable from a normal roof. While being difficult, removing the sunroof is worth the trouble. The extra weight placed high in the vehicle increases body roll and makes the car less nimble.

In classes that allow updating/backdating, one trick is to replace the knee bolster on newer cars with the plastic trim piece from earlier ones, for a weight loss of 20 lbs. This will also make your car more pleasant on the street for those drivers and passengers equipped with long legs. For I.T. racers who want to install a kneebar on their rollcage, you must also remove this piece; the plastic trim that replaces it will fit, albeit with some trimming. Removal of the knee

Fig. 12-6. Although the extra panels and bracketry do not weigh a lot, it is their placement that hurts. This I.T. Rabbit is only allowed to remove the headliner and bolt the sunroof closed; no other modifications are allowed.

bolster should only be done if you have replaced the stock passive-restraint system with a racing-type harness.

In Improved Touring, you can remove carpet, sound deadening, headliner, and the rear seat, reducing weight by another 75–90 lbs. Some people will replace the carpets after stripping the sound deadening from underneath. This makes a lot of sense as the carpet only weighs around 5 to 7 lbs. and can prevent a good portion of the car's noise from reverberating around the cockpit. This would be a blessing during Improved Touring endurance races, reducing driver fatigue. In the Solo II Prepared and Modified classes and the road-racing Production class, you can strip the interior entirely, including the dashboard, and substitute lighter-weight body panels such as fiberglass hoods and trunk lids. Prepared, Production, and Modified classes can also substitute window glass with race-approved Lexan (RTM).

Power steering is one option that some racers prefer. For autocrossing and street driving, the 20 lbs. weight penalty is overshadowed by the quicker ratio of steering-wheel lock to lock movement, and the ease of effort. Volkswagen power-steering systems are excellently weighted and come in handy on tight lock-to-lock autocross courses. For road racing the benefits are not as great,

Fig. 12-7. Glass sunroofs weigh more than their steel counterparts. The best solution would be to order a new car without one. Otherwise, the entire roof panel and headliner will need to be replaced.

Fig. 12-8. Just the bare essentials for this Production class Rabbit.

and the added power drain of the pulley system is not wanted. Neither the removal nor the installation of this system is extremely difficult, and the manual or power rack and pinion systems are available at most salvage yards. You will need to swap the racks and the tie rods, and you will either need to install or remove the pump and plumbing.

Some performance parts also save weight. With the replacement of both front seats with racing buckets, you can save 50 lbs. (I.T. competitors can only replace one). If you replace your stock wheels with lighter examples you can save another 15–50 lbs. depending on whether your car came with aluminum or steel rims. If you design your suspension without anti-roll bars, you can cut another 50 lbs. off your car's curb weight. Changing the exhaust system on a Street Prepared or I.T. car will let you lose as much as 40 lbs. if you replace the catalytic converter with a tubular header. Even street drivers can cut 20 lbs. by changing to a lightweight system that retains the catalytic.

While all of this might seem like a lot of effort for not much gain, if you add up all of the deletions, the car can become quite light. If you then look at the horsepower-to-weight ratio of most Volkswagens, the loss of 100 lbs. is worth about 5 hp. It also increases handling and braking ability, making the car quicker at the track or to the grocery store. An additional point to ponder is that as you lighten the car, the required spring rates for your suspension are reduced. If you lighten your car substantially, you might want to rethink the spring and anti-roll bars that you have planned to install.

Some weight loss can be accomplished on the day of the event for people who autocross and time trial. You should remove the car's spare tire, jack, and tool kit. This adds up to about 30 or 40 lbs. for most cars. Furthermore, any loose items in the cockpit should be removed. This includes floormats, stereo speaker boxes, and any other junk that litters the average car interior. Another reason for removing these loose items is that they could be tossed around the cockpit during sharp cornering, distracting the driver. For an additional weight loss, you should even drain your car's windshield washer reservoir.

One weight-loss tip seems obvious, but is often overlooked. The amount of fuel that you have in your gas tank can contribute substantially to your vehicle's weight. One gallon of gas weighs around 7 lbs.; multiply that by 14 for the capacity of an A2 gas tank and you get 98 lbs. of ballast. The A2 and later cars

Fig. 12-9. Racing cars do not need a spare tire and jack, about 30 lbs. of cargo.

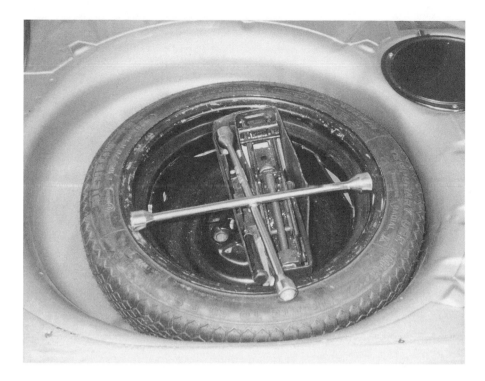

can make do with around a gallon and a half in the tank without fuel starvation in turns. This means that you can save 87.5 lbs. by racing with only 1.5 gallons instead of 14. In practice, an autocrosser can simply plan on having a sixth of a tank of gas on the morning of a race, which will provide a safe margin of fuel for the entire day's runs. Some A1 cars (Sciroccos in particular) have fuel starvation problems with anything less than a quarter of a tank of gas. You should experiment with how little gas you need, to save as much weight as possible. This is a great "modification" for beginning autocrossers; it costs no money and makes the car quicker. Road racers and time-trial participants will need more fuel, depending on the time spent on the track. An extra margin of safety can be supplied with a portable 5-gallon gas tank filled with your favorite fuel. Of course, if the driver could also stand to lose some weight. . . .

THE ULTIMATE LIGHTWEIGHT

Another way to reduce weight in any car is to start with the body itself. An entire "body in white" is available through the Volkswagen of America dealer network. This bare shell is the optimal starting point for a serious race car. The first notable difference is the lack of all undercoating (up to 50 lbs. worth). The second difference is that it allows the competitor to "acid dip" the entire shell more easily. This questionable practice (from a rules and regulations perspective) entails dipping the shell in a gigantic vat of acid. This removes all paint and wax rust-proofing, and makes the metal slightly thinner. While most companies who do acid dipping are located in Southern California, there are other facilities throughout the United States.

After the shell is dipped, the builder can reinforce all spot welds where the car is seamed together with continuous welds. This seam welding creates a stiffer chassis that resists fatigue better (illegal in some classes, but hard to see if covered with the seam and joint sealer that is used at the factory and many body shops). The most effective place to do this is around the front suspension towers and control-arm mounting points. From there, a proper rollcage is in-

Fig. 12-10. Before constructing a weld-in cage, you should learn where you need more strength and where you need weight.

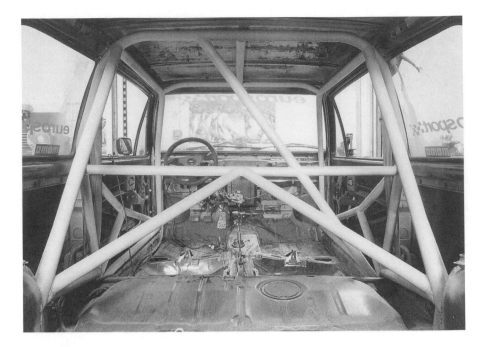

stalled and the entire assembly is coated with a thin layer of paint. Thus, the ultimate lightweight VW is formed.

How to Gain Weight Effectively

For classes with no minimum weights, or street-driven cars, this diet regimen for your car is a straightforward success. If, however, you are in a class where there are minimum weights, such as Showroom Stock and I.T., and you took off too much weight, you can add the weight back on where you want it. The rollcage structure is an excellent place for adding weight.

If the rules for your class limit extra braces in the rollcage structure, then you can construct the cage out of tubing of larger wall thickness. The thicker the wall of the tubing, the heavier it is. On the other hand, as the wall thickness of tubing increases so does the compressive and torsional strength.

Placement of extra weight using additional bracing is determined by the corner weights of the car. If the passenger rear of the car is light, then this area is a likely candidate for more bracing or thicker tubing. Most Volkswagens will perform better with weight in the rear and on the passenger side to offset the driver's weight. Some competitors have gone as far as inserting cement into certain tubes in the cage structure. This is illegal, but undetectable, as SCCA forbids the use of ballast in both Showroom Stock and I.T. The optimal set-up would also have weight positioned low in the car for a lower center of gravity.

Another way to put weight where you want it is to move the battery to the back of the car. This is only allowed in Street Prepared, Prepared, and Modified Solo II cars. If you don't use the entire capacity of your trunk in your daily driver, you might want to try this also. Moving the battery to the trunk gets weight off of the nose of the car to limit understeer. This modification is easily accomplished with a battery relocation kit supplied by Summit Racing, which includes cables, terminals, and a plastic marine battery box.

Fig. 12-11. The full washer reservoir and battery can add up tp 50 lbs. to an already heavy corner.

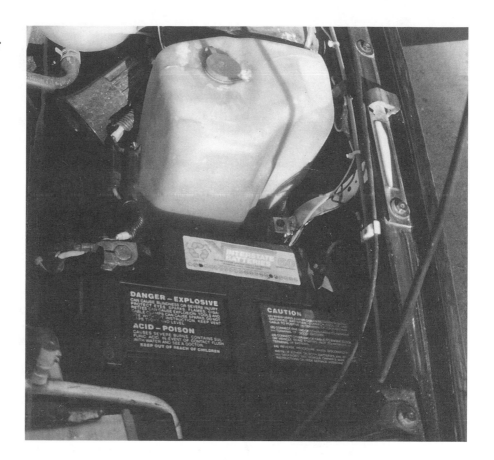

Fig. 12-12. Voila! A more balanced chassis.

Fig. 12-13. Tucked in this Rabbit's trunk is the battery in a protective marine-type box.

By losing weight where you do not want it and gaining it where you do, you can change the balance of the car for the better. Additionally, the corner weights of the car will be more in line with a high-performance set-up. Fine tuning of corner weights can be accomplished by threaded body shock absorbers (or coilovers).

Chapter Thirteen
SAFETY EQUIPMENT

Fig. 13-1. It doesn't matter if you drive your high-performance Volkswagen on the street or on a racetrack: you should always include additional safety equipment in your modification plan.

It is a rough-and-tumble world out there. The physics involved with 1-ton, 2-ton, or even 3-ton cars traveling on public roads at high velocities are staggering. If you throw in the added threat of poor drivers, crumbling roads, and ever-changing weather, the trip to the grocery store seems extremely dangerous. The government has mandated certain levels of safety equipment for every car sold in the U.S., going a long way toward improving your safety odds, but there is more that could be done to make your VW safer. If you like to drive your street car fast, or if you want to race, additional safety equipment is essential. The trade-off for increased driver and passenger safety is the added discomfort from the very things that protect them.

The safety requirements for racing classes vary; as the speeds encountered on the track increase, so does the required safety level. Here is a brief synopsis of what is required. Solo II requires just a standard seatbelt, a helmet, and a safe and well-maintained car. Time Trials require a roll bar (some higher classes require full cages), automotive racing helmets (SA rating), five-point harnesses, full fire-retardant clothing and footwear, a window net, and a fire extinguisher. Showroom Stock requires a bolt-in full roll cage, SA helmet, five-point harness, window net, fire extinguisher, and fire-retardant clothing. Improved Touring safety requirements are essentially the same as Showroom Stock, with the exception of the ability to use a welded-in cage.

HARNESS BELTS

Another safety requirement that also makes for faster driving is the competition five- or six-point harness. These consist of two shoulder straps, two lap belts, and one or two "crotch" straps. The crotch straps prevent the driver from slid-

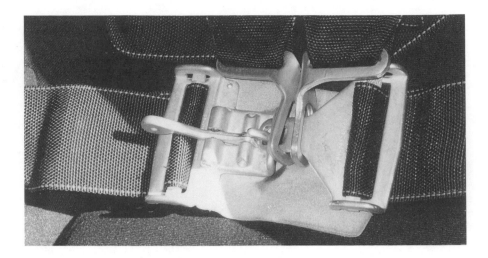

Fig. 13-2. This is a latch-link harness buckle. Harnesses with this design are legal for all types of racing and they are inexpensive.

ing under the lap belts and thereby sustaining internal injuries during a frontal collision ("submarining"). The racing harness, while improving safety tremendously, allows you to drive faster by keeping you firmly in the seat. Instead of hanging on for dear life, you can concentrate on the course.

There are many different brands of harnesses on the market, and they can be narrowed down into three distinct types. The first is not actually an SCCA-legal road-racing harness, but rather a DOT-legal, high-performance street belt. The Schroth harness-belt system is very popular with the street and Solo II crowd. It is a good belt because it holds you into the seat, is safer than the stock belt, and isn't overly uncomfortable in day-to-day driving. However, if you are planning to move up to time trials or road racing, it doesn't make sense to buy this belt because you will have to replace it later.

The second type of harness is the latch-link type. This is the simplest and least expensive racing harness on the market, and it is no less safe or effective than the more expensive types. Pyrotect, Simpson, and M&R all make high-quality latch-link systems that are legal in all types of racing.

The third type of harness is the cam-lock system. This more expensive type of harness attaches all belts to one central hub that releases with a touch of a lever. Schroth, Simpson, and others make good examples of these. While some find this type easier to use, it is no safer or better for driver placement than the latch-link type. You should use the money saved here on something that would either make you go faster or keep you safer.

Safety harnesses are an excellent idea on any vehicle, increasing driver stability within the seat and providing safety in the event of a collision. While the stock seatbelts are effective in reducing injuries, they are designed as a compromise. Performance enthusiasts should be willing to sacrifice the comfort of a stock seat belt for the safety and placement of a racing harness. Of the harnesses on the market, Schroth units are the most convenient on the street and can be used for Solo II events. You will adapt quickly to the initial inconvenience of a racing harness; soon a normal seat belt seems inadequate and downright scary compared with the additional restraint of an aftermarket unit.

A quick word is in order about the stock passive-restraint system used on some Rabbits and on model year 1988 and newer cars, to comply with the federally-mandated passive-restraint laws. This system uses a door-mounted shoulder harness, a separate lap belt (easily forgettable,) and includes a knee bolster in the event you forget the lap belt.

Since the shoulder harness is mounted to the door, it is highly dependent on door integrity to keep you strapped into your seat. In the event of a serious side

Fig. 13-3. The cam-lock system allows for easy fastening and unlatching. All of the belts are plugged into the central hub and a flip of the lever will release them.

impact, it is possible that the door could fly open, rendering the shoulder belt ineffective. If you also forgot to buckle the lap belt, the consequences could be even more severe. For any racing activities, it is recommended that you replace this system.

ROLL BARS AND ROLL CAGES

The important thing to remember about the added steel structure of a roll cage is that for the most part, it will make you a faster driver. This sounds strange, given the weight that a roll cage adds to your car, but it's true. A bolt-in roll cage or roll bar makes a car handle better than its normal counterpart and a welded roll cage helps even more. As mentioned in the chapter on weight, a roll cage makes a car stiffer and a stiffer car will handle better. The minimum tubing size and thickness for all classes with Volkswagens present is 1.5-in. in diameter with a 0.12-in. wall thickness.

Roll cages that are bolted into the chassis are legal in Showroom Stock, Solo Stock, and Street Prepared. They are also an excellent idea for a street-driven

Fig. 13-4. Roll cage structures vary from class to class.

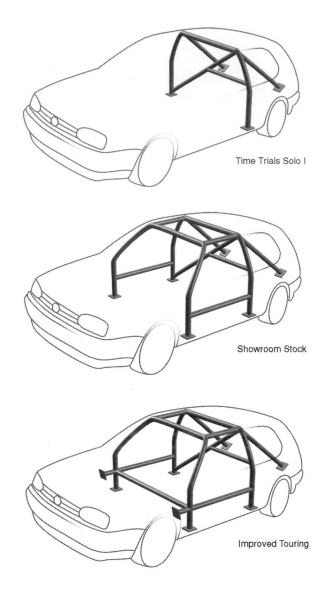

Time Trials Solo I

Showroom Stock

Improved Touring

high-performance Volkswagen. Some people will find that a cage is rather claustrophobic and ingress and egress from the car do require some practice. If the added safety of the forward portion of the cage is a bit of overkill, you should consider the more traditional roll bar. Front-seat access is unaffected with this design, and the safety margins of the car are still much improved. For street use, you can also opt for a removable diagonal crossbrace, which allows you the freedom to use your back seat on the street.

Bolt-in cages, by definition, are installed with normal hand tools. The only modification that you will need to make on your car is to drill 3/8-in. holes in the floor pan and rear wheel wells. Installation is quite simple if you take your time and follow a few guidelines. The first step is to remove all four seats. Try to do this with clean, degreased hands to avoid ruining the fabric. With the help of a friend, install the rear roll bar portion into the rear-seat area. Make sure that the bar is evenly installed side to side and that it lays against the floor and wheel wells without rocking. Then, before any drilling, fit the forward portions of the cage together. Again, make sure that everything fits well before drilling.

Fig. 13-5. This roll-cage backing plate is quite close to the brake lines. Be very careful not to drill through these lines when you are installing the cage.

The actual drilling of the chassis and roll cage tubes should be done while the car is sitting level on the ground. If the car is on jacks, or if it is installed on jackstands that are crooked, the entire structure will be twisted. If the cage is fitted when the chassis is twisted, it will stay twisted forever. For this reason, some racing teams will fit the cage while the car is on a body shop's frame-alignment machine. In this way, the trueness of the structure is insured.

When installing a roll bar or cage, remember to watch where you are drilling. This may sound pretty basic, but there are fuel and brake lines running where most cages attach behind the front seats. If the lines are in the way, you can unsnap their fasteners and gently pull them aside.

When the cage is completely drilled and you are ready to reinstall the seats, go for a test drive, and see the amazing improvements . . . STOP! Go wash your hands before you reinstall the seats. All of the grease and grime on your paws will quickly trash nice seats. Extra time taken during the installation process will insure a quality job.

After the cage is installed, you must cover all parts of the cage that are in near proximity to the driver's (and passenger's) head with energy-absorbing padding. The best kind of padding is called "offset" padding (available at I/O Port Racing or Pegasus); the hole through the pad is offset to one side, creating a thick and thin side. The thick side of this padding would go nearest to the person, while the thin side would conveniently go between the cage and car roof where fitting is typically tight. (This padding is *not* flammable pipe insulation.) The padding on the cage is best installed with nylon tie-wraps approximately 12 to 14 in. in length. Padding is extra important in a street-driven vehicle. Since people do not wear helmets on the street, any head contact with the cage during even a minor collision will cause injury.

Each joint in a bolt-in cage can flex, reducing the structural integrity of the car. The solution to this distortion is to weld the entire cage together while it is inside the car. This modification is legal in Improved Touring and all of the Prepared, Modified, and Production racing classes.

Welding in a cage is too difficult for the average person to handle, but the structural enhancement is substantial, so it's worth having done. The entire interior will have to be removed from the car during the cage fitment because of

Fig. 13-6. Padding is an essential part of a roll bar or roll cage installation. Note also how the driver's-side shoulder harnesses are attached to the cage while the passenger's is not. Attaching to the cage is much safer.

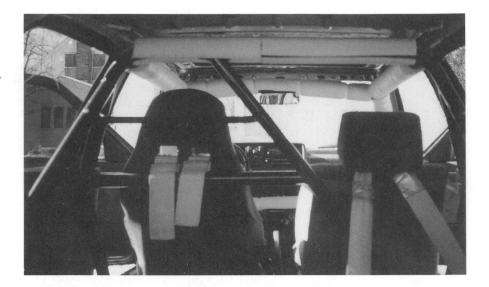

Fig. 13-7. This design, with a large, flat plate welded to the wheel well, spreads the load over a wide area.

the inevitable sparks and heat generated during welding. If the carpet is left inside, it will most certainly catch fire.

The bases of welded cages are constructed with pads that are first welded into the floor pan. These pads will serve to spread forces over a larger surface to make the entire structure stronger. The actual tubes of the cage are then welded onto these pads. Some cage manufacturers have found that they can weld these pads to the sills of the car instead of to the floor pan. This will help immensely as the sills are actually intended as structural members, in contrast to the floor pan which is just thin gauge sheet metal. If you wish to construct your cage this way, you should consult OPM Motorsports, VW Specialties, or other

Fig. 13-8. This under-dash reinforcement is allowed in I.T. racing.

racing prep shops. They have had good luck with this cage design, and could direct you to an appropriate custom tube bender.

For I.T. racing, where weld-in cages are allowed, you can also add a bar passing under the dashboard to either side of the cage. This both stiffens the cage structure and helps prevent the intrusion of the engine and driveline into the cockpit in the case of a dire mishap. The safest method of installation is to run the bar in front of the steering column, getting it out of the way of your knees. This is difficult, however, requiring some rearrangement of the dashboard internals.

I.T. also allows a welded brace between the two main roll-hoop supports which are between the two rear shock towers. This will prevent roll cage deformation in side impacts. From a performance standpoint, this is beneficial because it takes the place of a bolt-on rear-shock tower brace that is illegal in this class. By stiffening the rear-suspension mounting points, the car will flex less and have less understeer.

Fig. 13-9. This Production-class Rabbit has reinforcements extending forward to the bulkhead. I.T. racers can also utilize this design.

Fig. 13-10. This car has an excellent shoulder harness bar welded to the cage, but the owner is not using it!

New regulations in Improved Touring allow an eight-point roll cage instead of the normal six. These two extra points are allowed to go forward from the front roll hoop to the bulkhead. The cage cannot, however, go all the way forward to the top of the front strut towers as is allowed in advanced racing classes. Safety will be improved by keeping the forward portion of the cockpit area from crumpling in the event of a serious collision. In addition to the added safety, these extra points will further stiffen the body structure. The maximum structural integrity will be found by attaching the cage to the exact point on the firewall where the strut towers meet it on the engine compartment side.

Another option that is allowed by all racing categories is the shoulder-harness bar. This is simply a bar that runs behind the driver's seat (and behind the passenger seat if it too has a harness) and prevents the seat from moving backwards in a collision; it also offers a place to mount the shoulder harnesses.

Mounting the shoulder harnesses on this bar is safer than mounting them on the floor behind the driver. Whereas a bar-mounted harness pulls the shoulders horizontally back into the seat, a floor-mounted harness will pull the driver's shoulders down, possibly causing compression injuries of the spine.

There are three main manufacturers of bolt-in and weld-in cages in the U.S.: Autopower, Safety Devices, and Kirk Racing Products. These companies all offer cages in both bolt-in or weld-in configurations. Some racing teams will produce their own roll cages with the help of a tube bender, depending on their own design criteria.

FIRE EXTINGUISHERS

Fire extinguishers are a required piece of equipment in some racing classes, but they are an excellent idea for all racing competitors and even for street use. While a standard 2.0 lb dry-chemical, kitchen fire extinguisher meets the letter of the rule, a Halon 1211 type is a more effective fire-fighting tool, with the added benefit of having no sticky yellow powder to clean up. Halon, being a chlorofluorocarbon, is becoming harder and harder to obtain. In the U.S. it is

Fig. 13-11. A shoulder-harness bar makes for a safer restraint system.

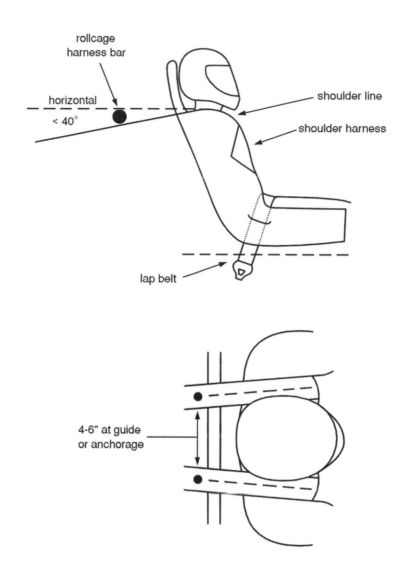

rollcage
harness bar

horizontal
< 40°

shoulder line

shoulder harness

lap belt

4-6" at guide
or anchorage

being banned for its effect on the ozone layer. As it does get harder to find, new types of fire extinguishers, such as CEA-614, are being developed.

The minimum poundage for a fire extinguisher in road-racing categories is 2.0 lbs. While this is usually enough for small fires on board a car, a 5-lb. bottle would be better as would an on-board fire-extinguishing system. An onboard fire extinguishing system is a permanently mounted system with nozzles mounted in the engine compartment; it is activated by the push of a button. For garage, tow vehicle, and home use, I would recommend at least a five-pounder, if not a ten. Whatever type you use, keep it nearby, and if possible, take a class on the use of a fire extinguisher. Your local fire department should have a class on fire-extinguisher use or be able to tell you where there is one. This is a skill few people know or realize that they need to know.

Other safety equipment such as helmets, window nets, and fire-retardant clothing are available through most racing supply houses. With products such as these, as long as the item meets all applicable rules and regulations, choices can be based on personal preference.

Fig. 13-12. This 2.5-lb fire extinguisher is barely larger than the SCCA minimum of 2.0 lbs for road racing.

Fig. 13-13. This is a typical on-board fire extinguisher system. The bottle is permanently mounted and metal tubing transfers the chemicals to nozzles in the engine compartment.

Chapter Fourteen
INTERIOR AND EXTERIOR MODIFICATIONS

Fig. 14-1. While this Jetta can hold all four of its passengers in place during hard cornering with deep side bolsters, ingress and egress are compromised.

The Volkswagen enthusiast who wants to hop up his or her car for high-performance driving has fairly utilitarian needs when it comes to interior and exterior modifications. Some street drivers will want to make changes that primarily affect looks; but for the true high-performance driver, on the street or on the track, the modifications worth making are the ones that improve driving efficiency and speed.

INTERIOR DESIGN

The interior of a car is designed with several main criteria in mind: namely, the number of people and amount of luggage it can hold, the comfort of the driver and passengers, and the ease with which the driver can control the vehicle. The last is not as easy as it sounds. Seat design, steering-wheel size, instrumentation, and shift-lever placement all have to allow drivers of vastly different sizes and body shapes to operate them safely.

Your Volkswagen has been designed to offer high quality and good performance for a low price. As such, there are many aftermarket interior products that simply dress up an otherwise plain package. Performance-wise, however, there are only three things, besides safety equipment, that you should change: seats, steering wheels and gauges. Other custom products will merely make the drive to work more pleasant.

Seats

Like many other things in life, automotive interior design is a study in compromise. The easiest seats for ingress and egress are wide and flat, while deep buckets with large side bolsters provide the best driver placement. The base-model seats that Volkswagen designed allow easy entry for the average car buyer, but provide little additional support for performance driving.

Like aftermarket and racing seat belts, a properly designed, performance oriented seat can improve your lap times. They can also make spirited driving more pleasurable, allowing you to concentrate on the road instead of trying to keep from flying into the passenger while cornering. While flat bench seats are a great idea at a drive-in movie, they leave a lot to be desired for both racing and street use.

Street enthusiasts will have the best luck with a reclining sport bucket seat. This would be exemplified by any of the reclining Recaro seats, most Koenigs, Flofits, and the Corbeau GTB. These seats will all have good lateral support and still allow back-seat access with their reclining design. If you don't need to get to your back-seat area easily, a non-reclining seat is also an option. The Corbeau Clubman and the GT8 are both steel-framed seats with deep buckets, good for street use and weekend racing. The shell-type seats, typically seen in purpose-built race cars, are uncomfortable for day-to-day driving.

The GTI and GLI models, being Volkswagen's performance products, come equipped with well-designed sport seats. These seats are excellent for street performance use and are even adequate for some racing. There have been two different types of sport seats available from VW: the original factory-produced

Fig. 14-2. Aftermarket sport recliners are only marginally better than factory sport seats.

Fig. 14-3. The "Clubman" design seat is popular with grassroots racers because of its light weight, low cost and good support.

sport seat and the Recaros that are found in the 16-valve cars. The Recaros have larger side bolsters to keep the driver firmly in place. Unlike other after-market sport seats and even other Recaro models, these Recaros do not require adapters to fit in the stock seat-track locations.

If your car came with either of these sport seats from the factory, and you are not worried about losing some of your car's curb weight, you really do not need to change them. In conjunction with a proper harness, they do a superb job at keeping the driver in place. VW owners whose cars came with the factory base seats may want to update to the factory sport units. They are available from many salvage yards. Because they are so popular, however, you may have trouble locating them. The sad truth is that many GTIs and GLIs were stolen merely for these seats. You might have luck locating some through Wolfsport,

Fig. 14-4. The VW factory sport seat is an excellent retrofit for cars that do not have them. They were used in all GTI, GLI, and GLX models, among others.

Bug World, or BMVW—salvage yards that deal only with VWs and are used to shipping parts nationwide.

Racing drivers should consult their rule books before deciding on an after-market seat. Solo Stock competitors will have to make do with their stock seats, although with a good competition harness this is not a major problem. All of the other racing categories discussed, including Showroom Stock, can replace the driver's seat with any high-performance unit. Street Prepared competitors can even change the passenger seat as well. The advantage of changing to a racing bucket is twofold. First, the racing seat will keep you in place. Second, most racing seats weigh substantially less than their stock counterparts—as much as 30 lbs. less per seat.

Racing competitors should replace their stock seats with either a steel framed or shell-type bucket, as these offer both the lightest weight and greatest support. The Corbeau Clubman and GT8 are very popular steel framed seats because they offer low cost and low weight. For the ultimate racing bucket, you should consider the shell type. These are generally made out of Kevlar™ or aluminum, with a thin layer of padding. Sparco, Corbeau, Recaro, and Cobra all make Kevlar™ seats that can be used in your Volkswagen. Kirkey and RCI make aluminum seats that are becoming popular with the budget racer. These can be as light as the Kevlar™ brands, while costing substantially less.

Fig. 14-5. Kevlar™ shell seats are ultra-lightweight and strong; they are also expensive.

Fig. 14-6. This affordable aluminum seat is comfortable for most racers, but I would recommend trying one before you buy a set.

Fig. 14-7. Most aftermarket seats require seat tracks and brackets. These are usually available from you seat supplier. Make sure that they are the bolt-in kind, so that your stock seats can be used later, if need be.

Steering Wheels

The stock steering wheel is designed to give the lowest steering effort without being so large that it interferes with other driving tasks. While the average bus driver might appreciate this, a quick jaunt on a twisty road will convince most enthusiasts otherwise. A smaller diameter steering wheel will result in a quicker steering ratio and more road feel. Excellent aftermarket steering wheels are produced by Momo, Personal, and others.

If your car doesn't have power steering and you run very wide rims and tires, you might want to stick with a larger diameter steering wheel to keep steering effort at a manageable level. One suggestion is to use the factory leather wrapped steering wheel from later 16-valve A2 cars. It offers a slightly smaller diameter with a nice, thick, leather wrapped rim.

Cars with power steering can use fairly small diameter (down to 12.8 inches) wheels without any difficulty. The only other consideration with smaller wheels is to make sure that all of the dashboard gauges are still visible with your new steering wheel installed.

Gauges

You cannot very well drive around with your head stuffed into the engine compartment. Because of this, you need adequate gauges and sensors to tell you how things are running; and you will benefit by installing aftermarket gauges to keep an eye on your car. Many enthusiasts will take this to the extreme with gauges that will tell everything from outside temperature to the water pressure

STEERING WHEEL INSTALLATION*

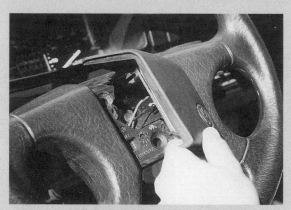

Fig. A. Pry off the horn cover/ button from the steering wheels, and disconnect the wire from this cover.

Fig. B. Mark the steering column (using the steering wheel as a reference) at the place where the road wheels are pointed straight ahead.

CAUTION —
If you lack the tools or experience necessary to disassemble the steering wheel, this work should be left to an authorized Volkswagen dealer or qualified repair shop.

WARNING —
Do not perform this modification on your car's steering wheel if your car has airbags. Tampering with your car's airbags is illegal and may lead to injury.

Fig. 14-8. Gauges can be placed out of the way in unused storage bins. This is a good place to put a gauge only if you don't need to see it during driving. for functions such as oil pressure, It's better to use a more visible location.

in the windshield squirter bottle. Too much information is as bad as too little—unnecessary gauges will break your concentration by catching your eye.

The essential gauges listed in order of their priority are: speedometer, tachometer, oil temperature, oil pressure, water temperature, and voltage. If you have a turbocharged or supercharged car, you should also install a boost

*Illegal for Cars with Airbags

Fig. C. Loosen the nut that secures the steering wheel, and remove the old wheel.

Fig. D. These splines determine where the steering wheel is on the shaft: do not damage them.

cont'd on next page

Fig. 14-9. The Autometer shift light is a good supplement to your tachometer. It lights up when you reach your desired shift point.

gauge. To help tune aftermarket fuel injection or carburetors, a exhaust gas pyrometer or air/fuel monitor with oxygen sensor can be installed.

One neat alternative to the standard dial gauge is the high intensity warning light. Pioneered by Autometer, the Prolites will tell you basic information in

STEERING WHEEL INSTALLATION* CONT'D.

Fig. E. Install the new hub: it will usually be marked where the top is, so align this with your mark on the steering column.

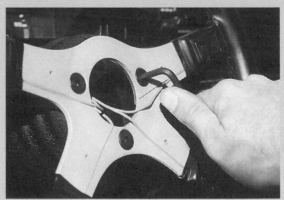

Fig. F. Bolt the new wheel to the hub.

CAUTION —
If you lack the tools or experience necessary to disassemble the steering wheel, this work should be left to an authorized Volkswagen dealer or qualified repair shop.

WARNING —
Do not perform this modification on your car's steering wheel if your car has airbags. Tampering with your car's airbags is illegal and may lead to injury.

Fig. 14-10. Racing cars, such as this DSP Rabbit, rarely have Aero doo-dads, as they can add weight and most often are useless.

such a way that you can't help but get the point. This lights are a very high intensity LED that should be installed in your peripheral vision. When oil pressure drops or when the proper shift point has been reached, the light goes on. It makes catching shift points very easy, instead of concentrating on a moving dial for a long time, you can fully concentrate on the road before the light says "Hey, stupid, SHIFT!"

*Illegal for Cars with Airbags

Fig. G. Tighten the nut that secures the hub to the steering column.

Fig. H. Attach the horn wires to the horn button, and install the center cover.

Fig. 14-11. As a VW enthusiast, I feel that the factory design is beautiful with only minimal enhancement.

EXTERIOR STYLE

Modifications to the exterior of a Volkswagen are primarily the realm of the street driver. Over the years, extensive exterior modifications have become less and less popular. The "aero-kit" boom of the eighties has declined somewhat and people are concentrating on other ways to improve the looks of their VWs. A tasteful combination of larger wheels and tires, lighting upgrades or tame air-dams can make your car stand out without looking tacky. Cars that see racing use will not have many of these apearance items, they are either illegal or can add weight or don't do anything useful.

Fig. 14-12. The European four-headlamp grille with Kamei grille spoiler.

Lighting

The U.S. Department of Transportation has literally kept the American motorist in the dark. The Federal regulations limiting lighting output and design for use on new automobiles has left us far behind what the rest of the world has to offer. Anyone who drives their car at night can attest to this fact. U.S. spec lights give off a yellowish, murky pattern that is very easy to out drive. Upgrading to European specification lights is an effective cure, but they are illegal for use on public roads. Some states will check what lights you have during yearly safety inspections; you should consult your local inspection station to see if they actually care what lights you have. Many states are simply glad that you have lights at all. Competitors in endurance-type races will find that additional lighting is a must for both fast lap times and lessening driver fatigue.

There are three ways to upgrade your lights. The first is to add supplemental driving and/or fog lights. This will, in general, be both easier and cheaper than changing your stock headlamps. Hella, Bosch, PIAA, and Cibie all make excellent high intensity add-on lights. The problem many people have with this solution is that the new lights will look tacked on. Later model cars, if not already equipped, can install the factory fog lights that are mounted in the bumper. Being factory parts, these fog lamps will look great and are an easy swap. Salvage yards are an excellent source for these lamps, if you can find them.

The clean and neat way to upgrade your car's lighting is to change your headlights to the Hella H4 variety. On the A1 and A3 cars this is a straightforward swap, with no real problems. On A2 cars you can either switch just the large rectangular "aero" headlights, or you can install the four-headlamp grille seen on later-model GTIs and all of the European GTIs. Many U.S. VW performance shops sell this kit for roughly the same amount of money.

Recently a company called High Performance Bulbs started importing high-watt replacement bulbs for the 9004-series bulb used in U.S. halogen headlamps. These bulbs simply plug in in place of the anemic stock units, and at around $20 a piece they are a very cost-effective way to achieve better lighting. Some cars, such as U.S.-built Golfs, will require additional relays for this type of bulb, installed to prevent overloading of that circuit. Consult with the manufacturer before swapping these lights, and be aware that high-wattage bulbs can also cause connectors to melt and burn out. You're still stuck with the mediocre U.S. lens pattern.

One extra add-on for the European GTI grille and most other VW grilles is the Kamei grille spoiler. This flexible plastic trim piece blends in the space between the grille and the hood for a clean, custom look. While other aero doodads are unpopular, these trim pieces find their way onto many custom VWs.

Other European lighting upgrades, in addition to headlamps, are very popular. Euro side-marker lights are seen on almost all cars featured in the national magazines. Not only do they look cool, they also increase safety in traffic by allowing drivers in other lanes to see your turning intentions more clearly. One tip for an inexpensive side-marker light is to find Audi 4000 front parking lights in a salvage yard. They are nearly identical to the more expensive VW type, and they can be easily glued on and wired to your front turn-signal lights.

Fig. 14-13. These Audi 4000 side-marker lights are available at most salvage yards. While lacking the clips of a factory VW light, they can be glued on and wired to the front signal lights.

Fig. 14-14. These tail-lamps look like expensive Hella tinted units, but using VHT tint spray, they only cost about $7 to modify.

Tinted taillights and turn-signal lights have been popular for quite some time now. The expensive way to accomplish this modification is to purchase complete light units from Hella that are molded in a darker tint. The cheap way that can, with practice, yield excellent results is to use a spray-type tint. Marketed by VHT, Nightshades is a tinting spray that can be applied directly to the outside of the lens. The more you spray, the darker the tint becomes. If you try this product, you should try to find higher wattage bulbs so that your lights are still readily visible. Halogen taillight bulbs are also available from Neuspeed.

Fig. 14-15. The Hella A-2 body kit offers high quality, but is not a simple bolt-on. European bumper supports are required and the kit needs to be sanded, primed, and painted to match your car's paint.

Fig. 14-16. The Zender kit adds a brawniness to this GTI.

Aerodynamics

Front airdams are the centerpiece of most aerodynamic enhancements made for Volkswagens. By limiting the amount of air that is allowed to travel underneath the car, the airdam reduces lift at high speeds. There are several downsides to these pieces. To be most effective at their job, airdams need to be close to the ground, which makes them highly susceptible to damage from curbs and speed bumps. They are also easily damaged on autocross courses if they are not flexible enough, and are less effective on low-speed autocross courses.

Since airdams prevent air from going under the car, they also prevent cooling air from reaching the brakes. I.T. regulations allow for this and specify that you can run brake cooling ducts to solve overheating problems. Since Street Prepared rules specifically prevent brake cooling ducts on cars that were not otherwise equipped, and even soft pylons can really beat up a front spoiler, I would recommend sticking with one of the small factory lip spoilers.

If money is no object, you can get full aerodynamic kits with front spoiler, side skirts, and fender flares. But while we're talking about money and your car's exterior, you should consider installing armored door plates to protect your investment—a small price to pay for peace of mind.

Fig. 14-17. Armored door plates will protect your investment from pry-in theft.

Fig. 14-18. European bumpers look clean and save weight, but they are not designed to give the same level of protection as the U.S. units. They are also illegal in all but the Prepared classes of racing.

Full aero kits, at first glance, seem to be a bolt-on mod, but this is not the case. The average body kit will require extensive fitting and shaping to match the contours of your individual car. It will also require proper paint prep with a flexible primer to insure adhesion even when the piece gets bumped. With the introduction of the factory "aero" kit in late 1990, many people have stopped buying aftermarket kits. Available at almost any salvage yard, the factory pieces can be sanded down, prepped, and painted to match the rest of the car, creating the look of an expensive aero kit, with easier fitment, and lower cost.

Bumpers

Street drivers who wish to change their car's appearance and remove some weight can change to European specification bumpers. Early A2 owners can also update to the later full-bumper covers that came equipped on the 1990 and later models. These plastic covers are more integrated into the overall styling design of the A2 chassis. You will also not experience any weight gain with this swap as it allows you to remove the front metal valance panel. The only required parts to complete this swap are: front and rear bumper covers, four new bumper-fender clips, and new turn signals. Being flexible plastic, the new bumper covers will need to be properly prepped for paint by a professional before they are color-matched to the car.

Appendix

PERFORMANCE BUDGETS AND SUPPLIERS

With an unlimited budget, your only limit for modifying your Volkswagen is how much imagination you have. For racers, the rule books pose additional constraints; but in general, the more money that you throw at a VW, the better it will be. This approach is not feasible for all but a few enthusiasts—it comes right down to how much disposable income you have and what you would like to do with your VW. Even the choice of project car is affected by your cash flow. You could have enough money to purchase a five hundred dollar Rabbit as a daily driver, or you could have just purchased a $25,000 Corrado SLC as a weekend toy. This fifty-fold range makes setting a general budget a difficult task.

Below, I have outlined a budget for street enthusiasts who are not planning on racing. To make things easy, I have broken down the budget into $500 increments, with each level building upon the previous one. High performance tuning is a matter of balance. Each of these levels addresses handling, power, and braking. The prices listed are in 1997 dollars, the fact is that these prices have been stable for the last 8 years, leading me to believe they will continue to remain the same. These budgets assume that the base project car is mechanically sound and will not blow up. Those of you who race should consult your trusty rule book before spending any money.

If you had $500:

- Budget performance exhaust such as Eurosport or Techtonics ($200)

- Quality front end alignment ($50)

- Replace brake pads with high performance alternative such as Repco, Ferodo, or Performance Friction ($50)

- K&N air filter ($30), cut holes in air box on side furthest away from hot engine.

- Bosch Platinum plugs ($10)

- Install all of the available stressbars for your car ($120 for A2 & A3, and $150 for A1 cars)

- If you shopped wisely, install 180 degree thermostat and fan switch.

$1000 is burning a hole in your pocket:

- Boge Turbo Gas shocks ($200)

- Fuel injection modifications (throttle body changes on A1s, alternate computer chips on later cars, $250)

- Braided stainless brake lines ($50-$75)

Wow! what a good tax refund! $1500:

- Sport suspension springs ($180)

- Mild camshaft ($100-$200)

- Install vented rotors if not otherwise equipped ($60)

- Front and rear anti-roll bars ($220-$350)
  Skip a step and go buy a nice set of rims and tires
  with at least a 7 inch rim size. ($1000)

So who's counting? $3000:

- Emissions legal manifold/downpipe upgrade,
  or emissions legal header ($200)

- Install four-point safety harness ($100-$160)

- Upgrade upper strut bearings ($100)

- Install Velocity Tuning's limited slip differential
  upgrade ($150) and have fun!

SUPPLIERS

Advanced Motorsport Solutions
3040 S. Robertson Blvd.
Los Angeles, CA 90034
(310)-559-7764

Autobahn Designs
2900 Adams St. Suite B-27
Riverside,CA 92504
(909) 351-9566

Autobahn Performance Inc.
484 Mitchell Road
Norcross, GA 30071
(770) 409-8288

Auto Meter
413 West Elm St.
Sycamore IL 60178
(815) 895-8141

**Automotive Performance Systems
(Neuspeed)**
3300 Corte Malpaso
Camarillo, CA 93012-8762
(805) 388-7171

Autotech Sport Tuning
32240-E Paseo Adelanto
San Juan Capistrano, CA 92675
(714) 240-4000

AutoThority
3769-B Pickett Road
Fairfax, VA 22031
(703) 323-0919

AVO Shocks Corporation, USA
3940 Prospect Ave., Suite K
Yorba Linda, CA 92886
(714) 577-9574

BBS of America, Inc.
5320 BBS Drive
Braselton, GA 30517
(800) 422-7972
(770) 967-9848

Bell Auto Racing
P.O. Box 927
Rantoul, IL 61866
(800) 237-2700

Bellevue Motor Sports
13500 Bel-Red Road
Bellevue, WA 98005
(206) 747-3278

BF Goodrich
6061 BF Goodrich
Jacksonville, FL 32226
(800) 366-8945

Bilstein Corporation of America
Sales West
8845 Rehco Road
San Diego, CA 92121
-or-
Sales East
320 Barnes Road
Wallingford, CT 06492
(800) 537-1085

BIS (P21S Products)
550 E. Main St.
Branford, CT 06405
(800) 215-9442

Borbet GmbH Metallgiesserei
Hauptstr. 5
59969 Hallenberg, GERMANY
49 (02984) 3010

Borla Performance Inc.
5901 Edison Drive
Oxnard, CA 93033
(805) 986-8600

Brookside Import Specialties
550 East Main St.
Branford, CT 06405
(203) 488-6569

Bug World
3600 Recycle Road
Rancho Cordova, CA 95742
(916) 635-6469

BW Auto Dismantlers
(Volkswagen Used Parts Specialists)
Roseville, CA
(916) 969-1600

Canton Racing Products
2 Commerce Dr.
N. Branford, CT 06471
(203) 484-4900

Carrera Racing Shocks
5412 New Peachtree Road
Atlanta, GA 30341
(770) 451-8811

Corbeau USA
9503 South 560 West
Sandy, UT 84070
(801) 255-3737

Diamond Racing Wheels
(800) 937-4407

EIP Tuning
1532 Liberty Rd.
Eldersburg, MD 21784
(800) 784-8100 (info)
(410) 549-1748 (tech)

Electromotive, Inc.
9131 Centreville Road
Manassas VA 20110
(703) 331-0100

Erebuni Corp.
158 Roebling Street
Brooklyn, NY 11211
(718) 387-0800

Eurospec Sport
6205 Engle Way
Gilroy, CA 95020
(408) 848-4203

Euro Sport Accessories
1464 N. Hundley St.
Anaheim, CA 92806
(714) 630-1555

Eurotech Racing
4013 W. Osborne Ave.
Tampa, FL 33614
(813) 879-9863

Extrude Hone
8075 Pennsylvania Ave
Irwin, PA 15642
(412) 864-9438

Falken Tire
(800) 723-2553

Ferodo America Inc.
1375 Heil Quaker Blvd.
LaVergne, TX 37086
(800) 251-3390

Fittipaldi Motoring Accessories, Inc.
1425 NW 82nd Ave.
Miami, FL 33126
(305) 592-8177

German Parts Restoration
202 Tank Farm Road, Bldg. 5
San Luis Obispo, CA 93401
(800) 321-5432
(805) 549-8945

Goodyear Race Tires
Authorized Distributors:
East (610) 375-6191
West (310) 538-2914
Midwest (517) 592-6681
South (904) 274-5332
Southwest (405) 789-8253

Haltech
2156 W. Northwest Hwy. #309
Dallas, TX 75220
(214) 831-9800

Havoc Motorsport
14021 Linder Ave.
Crestwood, IL 60445
(708) 371-4180

Hella, Inc.
201 Kelly Dr.
Peachtree City, GA 30269
(800) 247-5924

H&H Specialties, Inc.
20 Reid Road
Chelmsford, MA 01824
(508) 256-9465

Holley Performance Products
(800) 2-HOLLEY (sales)
(502) 843-8630 (customer relations)
(502) 781-9741 (tech)

**Hoosier Racing Tires
(Continental General Tire)**
1900 Continental Blvd.
Charlotte, NC 28273
(704) 588-1600

HPC (High Performance Coatings)
(800) 456-4721

H&R Springs North America
3300 Corte Malpaso
Camarillo, CA 93012

I/O Port Racing Supplies
14 Juniper Drive
Lafayette, CA 94549
(800) 949-5712

Jeg's
(800) 345-4545

Jet Performance Products
17491 Apex Circle
Huntington Beach, CA 92647
(714) 848-5515

JT Motorsport (Oettinger)
290 Easy Street
Simi Valley, CA 93 065
(805) 579-9123

K&N Engineering
P.O. Box 1329
Riverside, CA 92502
(909) 684-9762

Koni
8085 Production Ave.
Florence, KY 41042
(800) 994-KONI (sales)
(606) 727-5035 (tech)

Kraftswerk
11066 Mercantile
Stanton, CA 90680
(714) 901-5055

Kumho USA Inc.
(217) 583-3244

Metric Motorsport
1412 Descanso Ave. Suite D
San Marcos, CA 92069
(760) 471-2807

MotorSport Specialties Inc. (Wheels)
(800) 621-8408

New Dimensions Ltd.
2240 De La Cruz Blvd
Santa Clara, CA 95050
(408) 980-1691

Oettinger Technik Gmbh
Max-Planck-Str. 36
61281 Friedrichsdorf, GERMANY
49 (0) 6172-95330

OPM Motorsports
602 Old Buford Rd.
Cumming, GA 30130
(770) 886-8199

O.Z. Wheels (Motoring Accessories)
1425 N.W. 82nd Ave.
Miami, FL 33126
(305) 594-1882

Panasport Wheels
(310) 373-0071

Pegasus Auto Racing Supplies, Inc.
2475 South 179th Street
New Berlin, WI 53146-2150
(800) 688-6946 (orders)
(414) 780-2913 (tech)

Performance Friction
83 Carbon Metallic Highway
Clover, SC 29710
(800) 521-8874

PIAA
(503) 646-8389

R+A Applied Arts Inc.
555 Gutheil Place
Lyndhurst, NJ 07071
(201) 933-8833

Rapid Parts
178 Route 59
Monsey, NY 10952
(914) 352-1138

Red Line Synthetic Oil Corp.
6100 Egret Court
Benicia, CA 94510
(707) 745-6100

Revolution Wheels
Racing Wheel Services
140 Bordentown Road
Tullytown, PA 19007
(215) 945-3834

Robert Bentley, Publishers
1734 Massachusetts Avenue
Cambridge, MA 02138
(800) 423-4595

Robert Bosch Corp.
2800 S. 25th Ave.
Broadview, IL 60153
(708) 865-5200

Ronal USA
15692 Computer Lane
Huntington Beach, CA 92649
(714) 891-4853

Ron's Parts, Inc.
#6 & #7 1610 Langan Ave
Port Coquitlam, B.C. Canada V3C 1K6
(604) 944-0494

Sachs Automotive of America
2002 Stephenson Hwy.
Troy, MI 48083
(810) 528-2970

Sachs Boge of America
146 Liberty Ct.
Elyria, OH 44035
(216) 324-3765

Shine Racing Service
8 Production Road
Walpole, MA 02081
(508) 660-7974

Summit Racing Equipment
1200 Southeast Ave.
Tallmadge, OH 44278
(800) 230-3030
(330) 630-0250

SuperTrapp
4540 W. 160th St.
Cleveland, OH 44135
(216) 265-8400

Swain Technology Inc.
(Swain Tech Coatings)
35 Main St.
Scottsville, NY 14546
(716) 889-2786

Techtonics Tuning
P.O. Box 295
Sheridan, OR 97378
(503) 843-2700

Tokico America Inc.
1330 Storm Parkway
Torrance, CA 90501-5041
(310) 534-4934

Toyo Tires
(800) 678-3250

Transatlantic Racing Services, Ltd.
(800) 533-6057
(770) 889-0499

TSW Alloy Wheels
(800) 479-9332

Uniroyal Goodrich
(800) 521-9796

Velocity Sport Tuning
4613-B Manhattan Beach Blvd.
Lawndale, CA 90260
(310) 643-0005

Volkswagen of America
(800) 822-8987

VW Sport
6560 Backlick Rd., Ste. 225
Springfield, VA 22150
(703) 451-5134

Wolf Sport
1453 Fourth St.
Berkeley, CA 94710
(510) 525-0157

Yokohama Tire Corp.
601 S. Acacia Ave.
Fullerton, CA 92631
(714) 870-3800

**Zelenda Automotive
(VW Factory-Authorized Special Tools)**
66-02 Austin St.
Forest Hills, NY 11374
(718) 896-2288
(888) 892-8348

Zender
108 Otto Circle
Sacramento, CA 95822
(916) 422-4222

Index

W

> **WARNING** —
> • *Automotive service, repair, and modification is serious business. You must be alert, use common sense, and exercise good judgement to prevent personal injury.*
>
> • *Before using this book or beginning any work on your vehicle, thoroughly read the Warning on the copyright page, and any Warnings and Cautions listed on page 218.*
>
> • *Always read a complete procedure before you begin the work. Pay special attention to any Warnings and Cautions, or any other information, that accompanies that procedure.*

Please read these Warnings and Cautions before proceeding with modifications or maintenance and repair work.

WARNING—

• Do not reuse self-locking nuts or any other fasteners that are fatigued or deformed in normal use. They are designed to be used only once, and become unreliable and may fail when used a second time. This includes, but is not limited to, bolts, washers, self-locking nuts, circlips and cotter pins that secure the subframe, control arms, stabilizer bar, ball joints and other suspension, steering and brake components. Always replace these fasteners with new parts.

• Never work under a lifted vehicle unless it is solidly supported on stands designed for the purpose. Do not support a vehicle on cinder blocks, hollow tiles, or other props that may crumble under continuous load. Do not work under a vehicle supported solely by a jack.

• Make sure that the ground is level before beginning work on the vehicle. Block the wheels to keep the vehicle from rolling. Never work under the vehicle while the engine is running. Disconnect the battery ground strap to prevent others from starting the vehicle while you are under it.

• Never run the engine unless the work area is well ventilated. Carbon monoxide kills.

• Friction materials such as brake or clutch discs may contain asbestos fibers. Do not create dust by grinding, sanding, or by cleaning with compressed air. Avoid breathing asbestos fibers and asbestos dust. Breathing asbestos can cause serious diseases such as asbestosis or cancer, and may result in death.

• Tie long hair behind your head. Do not wear a necktie, a scarf, loose clothing, or a necklace when you work near machine tools or running engines. If your hair, clothing, or jewelry were to get caught in the machinery, severe injury could result.

• Disconnect the battery ground strap whenever you work on the fuel system or the electrical system. When you work around fuel, do not smoke or work near heaters or other fire hazards. Keep an approved fire extinguisher handy.

• Keep sparks, lighted matches, and open flames away from the top of the battery. If hydrogen gas escaping from the cap vents is ignited, it will ignite gas trapped in the cells and cause the battery to explode.

• Catch draining fuel, oil, or brake fluid in suitable containers. Do not use food or beverage containers that might mislead someone into drinking from them. Store flammable fluids away from fire hazards. Wipe up spills at once, but do not store the oily rags, which can ignite and burn spontaneously.

• Always observe good workshop practices. Wear goggles when you operate machine tools or work with battery acid. Gloves or other protective clothing should be worn whenever the job requires it.

• Some of the vehicles covered by this book may be equipped with a Supplemental Restraint System (SRS) that automatically deploys an airbag in the event of high impact. The airbag unit is an explosive device. Handled improperly or without adequate safeguards, the system can be very dangerous. The SRS system should be serviced only through an authorized dealer for your vehicle.

• Illuminate your work area adequately but safely. A fluorescent worklight is preferable to an incandescent worklight. Use a portable safety light for working inside or under the vehicle. Make sure the bulb is enclosed by a wire cage. The hot filament of an accidentally broken bulb can ignite spilled fuel or oil.

• Do not attempt to work on your vehicle if you do not feel well. You can increase the danger of injury to yourself and others if you are tired, upset or have taken medicine or any other substance that may impair you from being fully alert.

• Remove finger rings so that they cannot cause electrical shorts, get caught in running machinery, or be crushed by heavy parts.

CAUTION—

• If you lack the skills, tools and equipment, or a suitable workshop for any procedure described in this book, we suggest you leave such repairs to an authorized dealer for your vehicle or other qualified shop. We especially urge you to consult an authorized dealer before beginning repairs on any vehicle that may still be covered wholly or in part by any of the extensive warranties issued by the original manufacturer.

• Before starting a job, make certain that you have all the necessary tools and parts on hand. Read all the instructions thoroughly, consult the appropriate service manual for your vehicle, and do not attempt shortcuts. Use tools appropriate to the work and use only replacement parts meeting original equipment specifications. Makeshift tools, parts, and procedures will not make good repairs.

• Use pneumatic and electric tools only to loosen threaded parts and fasteners. Never use these tools to tighten fasteners, especially on light alloy parts.

• Be mindful of the environment and ecology. Before you drain the crankcase, find out the proper way to dispose of the oil. Do not pour oil onto the ground, down a drain, or into a stream, pond, or lake. Consult local ordinances that govern the handling and disposal of chemicals and wastes.

• Before doing any electrical welding on vehicles equipped with the Antilock Braking System (ABS), disconnect the ABS control unit connector.

• Do not quick-charge the battery (for boost starting) for longer than one minute, and do not exceed 15.0 volts at the battery with the boosting cables attached. Wait at least one minute before boosting the battery a second time.

• The original manufacturer of your vehicle offers extensive warranties, especially on components of the fuel delivery and emissions control systems. Therefore, before deciding to repair or modify a vehicle that may still be covered wholly or in part by any warranties issued by the original manufacturer, consult an authorized dealer.

Please read the Safety Notice and disclaimer on the Copyright page.

Art Credits

Art courtesy of Autotech: Fig. 2-5, 4-4, 5-28, 5-31, 5-32, 8-12, 8-14, 11-4, 11-5, 11-6, 11-18.

Art courtesy of Robert Bentley, Publishers, Inc.: Fig. 6-2.

Art courtesy of Les Bidrawn: Front Spring/Shock Installation How-To Fig. C, D, E, and F, 3-15, 5-13, 5-14, 5-16, 5-20, 5-21, 5-22, 5-26, 5-27, Camshaft Installation How-To Fig. F, G, I, 9-7, 10-5, 12-10, 13-1.

Art courtesy of Euro Sport: Fig. 3, 13, 1-4, Front Spring/Shock Installation How-To Fig. G, 2-25, 2-28, 2-37, 4-5, 5-1, 5-2, 5-12, Camshaft Installation How-To Fig. A, B, C, D, E, H, J, K, L, 6-4, 7-1, 7-2, 7-4, 7-5, 7-8, 7-9, 8-1, 8-2, 8-3, 8-4, 8-6, 8-7, 8-8, 8-10, 8-11, Exhaust System Installation How-To photos, 8-15, 9-3, 11-12, 11-14, 12-13, 13-3, 13-5, 13-10, 14-1, 14-2, 14-5, 14-7, 14-10, 14-11, 14-16, 14-18.

Art courtesy of Neuspeed (APS): Fig. 2, 2-6, 2-7, 2-13, 2-18, 2-35, 3-1, 4-7, 5-17, 5-18, 5-19, 11-15.

Art courtesy of New Dimensions: Fig. 9, 10, 11, Stress Bar Installation How-To photos, Brake Pad/Rotor Change How-To photos, 5-5, Computer Chip Installation How-To photos, 5-25, 7-13, 9-5, Steering Wheel Installation How-To photos, 14-8.

Art courtesy of OPM Motorsports: Fig. 1-22, 1-24.

Art courtesy of Per Schroeder: Preface photos, Fig. 1, 4, 5, 6, 7, 14, 15, 16, 17, 18, 19, 20, 1-2, 1-3, 1-5, 1-6, 1-7, 1-8, 1-9, 1-10, 1-11, 1-12, Salvage Yards How-To photos, 1-13, 1-14, 1-15, 1-16, 1-18, 1-19, 1-20, 1-23, 1-25, 1-27, 2-1, 2-8, 2-10, 2-11, 2-12, 2-14, 2-15, 2-17, 2-19, Front Spring/Shock Installation How-To Fig. A and B, 2-20, 2-21, 2-22, 2-23, 2-24, 2-26, 2-27, 2-29, 2-30, 2-31, 2-32, 2-33, 2-34, 2-36, 3-2, 3-3, 3-4, 3-5, 3-6, 3-7, 3-8, 3-9, 3-10, 3-11, 3-12, 3-13, 3-14, 3-16, 3-17, 3-18, 3-19, 3-20, 3-21, 3-22, 3-23, 4-1, 4-3, 4-8, 4-9, 4-10, 4-11, 5-3, 5-4, 5-6, 5-7, 5-8, 5-15, 6-1, 6-3, 6-5, 7-7, 7-12, 8-5, 8-9, 8-13, 9-1, 9-4, 9-6, 9-8, 10-1, 10-2, 10-3, 10-4, 11-3, 11-7, 11-13, 11-16, 11-17, 12-1, 12-2, 12-4, 12-5, 12-6, 12-7, 12-8, 12-9, 12-11, 12-12, 13-2, 13-6, 13-7, 13-8, 13-9, 13-12, 13-13, 14-3, 14-4, 14-6, 14-9, 14-12, 14-13, 14-14, 14-17.

Art courtesy of Kim Stewart: Fig. 1-26.

Art courtesy of Bob Tunnell: Fig. 1-1, 1-17, 1-21, 1-28, 2-4, 12-3.

Art courtesy of Velocity Sport Tuning: Fig.4-2, 4-6, 5-9, 5-10, 5-11, 5-23, 5-24, 5-29, 6-7, 7-3, 7-6, 7-10, 7-11, 7-14, 9-2, 11-1, 11-2, 11-8, 11-9, 11-10, 11-11, 14-15.

Art courtesy of Volkswagen of America, Inc.: Fig. 8.

Graphed data for Fig. 5-30, 5-33, and 6-6 courtesy of Techtonics.

Graphed data for Fig. 8-16 and 8-17 courtesy of Eurosport.

Graphed data for Introduction Fig. 12 courtesy of New Dimensions.

Original illustrations for Fig. 2-2, 2-3, 2-9, 13-4, 13-11 courtesy of Jason Plummer; stylized by Cathy Earl.

Selected Books and Repair Information From Bentley Publishers

Driving

The Unfair Advantage *Mark Donohue*
ISBN 0-8376-0073-1(hc); 0-8376-0069-3(pb)

Going Faster! Mastering the Art of Race Driving *The Skip Barber Racing School*
ISBN 0-8376-0227-0

A French Kiss With Death: Steve McQueen and the Making of *Le Mans*
Michael Keyser ISBN 0-8376-0234-3

Driving Forces: The Grand Prix Racing World Caught in the Maelstrom of the Third Reich *Peter Stevenson*
ISBN 0-8376-0217-3

Sports Car and Competition Driving
Paul Frère with foreword *by Phil Hill*
ISBN 0-8376-0202-5

Engineering

Supercharged! Design, Testing, and Installation of Supercharger Systems
Corky Bell ISBN 0-8376-0168-1

Maximum Boost: Designing, Testing, and Installing Turbocharger Systems
Corky Bell ISBN 0-8376-0160-6

Bosch Fuel Injection and Engine Management *Charles O. Probst, SAE*
ISBN 0-8376-0300-5

Race Car Aerodynamics *Joseph Katz*
ISBN 0-8376-0142-8

Scientific Design of Exhaust and Intake Systems *Phillip H. Smith and John C. Morrison* ISBN 0-8376-0309-9

Other Enthusiast Titles

Road & Track Illustrated Automotive Dictionary *John Dinkel* ISBN 0-8376-0143-6

Civic Duty: The Ultimate Guide to the Honda Civic *Alan Paradise*
ISBN 0-8376-0215-7

Harley-Davidson Evolution V-Twin Owner's Bible™ *Moses Ludel*
ISBN 0-8376-0146-0

Jeep Owner's Bible™ *Moses Ludel*
ISBN 0-8376-0154-1

Audi

Audi A4 Repair Manual: 1996–2001, 1.8L turbo, 2.8L, including Avant and quattro
Bentley Publishers ISBN 0-8376-0371-4

Audi A4 1996–2001, S4 2000–2001 Official Factory Repair Manual on CD-ROM
Bentley Publishers ISBN 0-8376-0833-3

Audi A6 Sedan 1998–2002, Avant 1999–2002, allroad quattro 2001–2002, S6 Avant 2002 Official Factory Repair Manual on CD-ROM *Bentley Publishers*
ISBN 0-8376-0836-8

Audi 80, 90, Coupe Quattro Official Factory Repair Manual: 1988–1992 including 80 Quattro, 90 Quattro and 20-valve models *Audi of America*
ISBN 0-8376-0367-6

BMW

BMW 3 Series Enthusiast's Companion™
Jeremy Walton ISBN 0-8376-0220-3

BMW 3 Series (E46) Service Manual: 1999–2001, 323i, 325i, 325xi, 328i, 330i, 330xi Sedan, Coupe, Convertible, Sport Wagon
Bentley Publishers ISBN 0-8376-0320-X

BMW 3 Series (E36) Service Manual: 1992–1998, 318i/is/iC, 323is/iC, 325i/is/iC, 328i/is/iC, M3 *Bentley Publishers*
ISBN 0-8376-0326-9

BMW 3 Series (E30) Service Manual: 1984–1990 318i, 325, 325e(es), 325i(is), and 325i Convertible *Bentley Publishers*
ISBN 0-8376-0325-0

BMW 5 Series Service Manual: 1989–1995 525i, 530i, 535i, 540i, including Touring
Bentley Publishers ISBN 0-8376-0319-6

BMW 7 Series Service Manual: 1988–1994, 735i, 735iL, 740i, 740iL, 750iL
Bentley Publishers ISBN 0-8376-0328-5

Chevrolet

Zora Arkus-Duntov: The Legend Behind Corvette *Jerry Burton* ISBN 0-8376-0858-9

Corvette from the Inside: The 50-Year Development History *Dave McLellan*
ISBN 0-8376-0859-7

Corvette by the Numbers: The Essential Corvette Parts Reference 1955–1982:
Alan Colvin ISBN 0-8376-0288-2

Chevrolet by the Numbers 1965–1969: The Essential Chevrolet Parts Reference
Alan Colvin ISBN 0-8376-0956-9

Camaro Exposed: 1967–1969, Designs, Decisions and the Inside View
Paul Zazarine ISBN 0-8376-0876-7

Corvette Fuel Injection & Electronic Engine Management 1982–2001:
Charles O. Probst, SAE ISBN 0-8376-0861-9

Corvette 427: Practical Restoration of a '67 Roadster *Don Sherman*
ISBN 0-8376-0218-1

Ford

The Official Ford Mustang 5.0 Technical Reference & Performance Handbook: 1979–1993 *Al Kirschenbaum*
ISBN 0-8376-0210-6

Ford F-Series Pickup Owner's Bible™
Moses Ludel ISBN 0-8376-0152-5

Ford Fuel Injection and Electronic Engine Control: 1988–1993 *Charles O. Probst, SAE*
ISBN 0-8376-0301-3

Porsche

Porsche 911 Carrera Service Manual: 1984–1989 *Bentley Publishers*
ISBN 0-8376-0291-2

Porsche 911 SC Coupe, Targa, and Cabriolet Service Manual: 1978–1983
Bentley Publishers ISBN 0-8376-0290-4

Volkswagen

Battle for the Beetle
Karl Ludvigsen
ISBN 08376-0071-5

Volkswagen Scan Tool Companion 1990–1995: Working with On-Board Diagnostics (OBD) Data for Engine Management Systems
Bentley Publishers ISBN 0-8376-0393-5

Volkswagen Model Documentation: Beetle to 412, including Transporter Model *Joachim Kuch* ISBN 0-8376-0078-2

Jetta, Golf, GTI Service Manual: 1999–2002 2.0L Gasoline, 1.9L TDI Diesel, 2.8L VR6, 1.8L Turbo *Bentley Publishers*
ISBN 0-8376-0388-9

Passat 1998–2002 Official Factory Repair Manual on CD-ROM
Bentley Publishers ISBN 0-8376-0837-6

New Beetle 1998–2002 Official Factory Repair Manual on CD-ROM
Bentley Publishers ISBN 0-8376-0838-4

New Beetle Service Manual: 1998–1999 2.0L Gasoline, 1.9L TDI Diesel, 1.8L Turbo
Bentley Publishers ISBN 0-8376-0385-4

Jetta, Golf, GTI, Cabrio Service Manual: 1993–1999, including Jetta$_{III}$ and Golf$_{III}$
Bentley Publishers ISBN 0-8376-0366-8

Eurovan Official Factory Repair Manual: 1992–1999 *Volkswagen of America*
ISBN 0-8376-0335-8

Eurovan 1992–2002 Official Factory Repair Manual on CD-ROM
Bentley Publishers ISBN 0-8376-0835-X

Jetta, Golf, GTI 1993–1999, Cabrio 1995–2002 Official Factory Repair Manual on CD-ROM *Bentley Publishers*
ISBN 0-8376-0834-1

Jetta, Golf, GTI Service Manual: 1985–1992 Gasoline, Diesel, and Turbo Diesel, including 16V *Bentley Publishers*
ISBN 0-8376-0342-0

Super Beetle, Beetle and Karmann Ghia Official Service Manual: Type 1, 1970–1979 *Volkswagen of America*
ISBN 0-8376-0096-0

Corrado Official Factory Repair Manual: 1990–1994 *Volkswagen of America*
ISBN 0-8376-0387-0

About the Author

Per Schroeder lives in northern Illinois with his wife, Chris, and two Siamese cats. He can be found most weekends running over pylons and changing tires at regional and national SCCA Solo II events. He was the SCCA Southeast Division Champion (Solo II H-Stock) in 1996, has won several SCCA National Tours, and was a 1997 Solo II Nationals trophy winner. When not racing, Per, a graduate of Rensselaer Polytechnic Institute, is a Clinical Data Analyst with Abbott Laboratories, north of Chicago.